Introductory Ethics

Introductory Ethics

FRED FELDMAN

University of Massachusetts, Amherst

Prentice-Hall, Inc., Englewood Cliffs, N. J. 07632

Library of Congress Cataloging in Publication Data

FELDMAN, FRED, (date).
    Introductory ethics.

    Includes bibliographical references and index.
    1. Ethics—History.   I. Title.
BJ71.F44   170   77-4836
ISBN   0-13-501783-1

Printed in the United States of America

10   9   8   7   6

Prentice-Hall International, Inc., *London*

Prentice-Hall of Australia Pty. Limited, *Sydney*

Prentice-Hall of Canada, Ltd., *Toronto*

Prentice-Hall of India Private Limited, *New Delhi*

Prentice-Hall of Japan, Inc., *Tokyo*

Prentice-Hall of Southeast Asia Pte. Ltd., *Singapore*

Whitehall Books Limited, *Wellington, New Zealand*

Contents

v

Preface

In this book, I have attempted to present clear and accurate statements of some of the most important theories in Western moral philosophy. I have also attempted to present the most persuasive and historically important arguments for and against each of these views.

Since I hope that this book will be accessible to readers with no previous philosophical training, I have tried to keep things as simple as possible. Whenever a technical term is introduced, its meaning is explained. The arguments are presented in such a way that readers with no knowledge of formal logic will be able to understand them without trouble.

Quite a few individuals have helped in the writing of this book. David Blumenfeld, Peter Markie, Lynn Stephens, Steve Skerry, Rick Wiley, and many of the students who took Introduction to Ethics with me were especially helpful. Although their contributions were of a different sort, I am also deeply indebted to Roderick Chisholm, Edmund Gettier, and Herbert Heidelberger.

FRED FELDMAN

1

Morality and Ethics

This book is about ethics. You probably already have a fairly clear idea of what ethics is. Nevertheless, it may prove interesting to attempt to draw out this fairly clear idea and try to make it much clearer. We can do this by asking ourselves what the word "ethics" means.

Some philosophers say that ethics is the philosophical study of morality. If we hope to clarify in this way what ethics is, then we must already have a clear idea of what morality is, and we must also have a clear idea of what is meant by "philosophical study." Otherwise, we will just have explained the meaning of one fairly obscure term ("ethics") by appeal to two other fairly obscure terms ("morality" and "philosophical study"). Such a procedure would hardly be enlightening. So let us consider the question "What is morality?" as well as the question "What is a philosophical study?" If we can answer these questions satisfactorily, then we may be able to give a satisfactory answer to our original question, "What is ethics?" We will be able to say that ethics is the philosophical study of morality.

What Is Morality?

When faced with a question such as "What is morality?" one may be stumped. Is morality an idea? Or is it an institution? Perhaps it is a set of rules. Some may say that morality is a feeling, or a kind of behavior. Of course, morality can't be all of these things. Thus, it is hard to begin to answer the question when it is put in such abstract terms.

In this sort of case, we often find that we can achieve more useful results if we consider a somewhat less abstract version of the question.

The word "morality" is a noun. It is intimately related to the adjective "moral." We use this adjective often, in phrases such as "moral judgment," "moral act," "moral choice," and "moral principle." Perhaps we can shed some light on the meaning of the noun "morality" by considering the adjective "moral." Proceeding in this way will enable us to deal with a less abstract concept, and we may thereby be more successful. So instead of asking "What is morality?" let us pick one of the most interesting of these uses of the adjective "moral" and ask instead, "What is a moral judgment?" This should be a far more manageable question. It may help us understand the meaning of "moral," which in turn may shed some light on the meaning of "morality," which in turn may shed some light on the meaning of "ethics."

There seems to be an obvious intuitive difference between moral judgments and judgments of other sorts. In ordinary cases, most of us can make this distinction with little trouble. If someone says that abortion is wrong, we know that he's made a moral judgment. If someone says that Marblehead is north of Boston, we know he's made a nonmoral judgment. So the difference is, in a way, pretty obvious. But what, in general, is the basis of this distinction? What is it about moral judgments that makes them recognizable as moral? What interesting features do moral judgments have that nonmoral ones lack?

A very simple answer to these questions might be based on some features of the sentences that are used to express moral judgments. When an English-speaking person expresses a moral judgment, she usually makes use of words such as "right," "wrong," "obligatory," "good," "bad," "evil," "ought," and "should." Although this list is obviously incomplete, it is probably long enough to enable any competent speaker of English to make her point. All the words in this list may be called "value terms." Surely, most of us can tell an English value term when we see one. So we could probably add quite a few more value terms to the list, if we had to. And we undoubtedly could tell that an enormous number of words do not belong in the list of value terms.

Making use of this concept of "value term," we can introduce a proposal concerning moral judgments. The proposal is based on the idea that whenever someone makes a moral judgment, he must use a value term. For the sake of convenience, let us restrict our attention to sentences in English. Now we can say:

M_1:   An English sentence expresses a moral judgment if and only if it contains a value term.

According to this proposal, the following sentences express moral judgments:

(1) Abortion is always wrong.

(2) Everyone ought to love his neighbor.

(3) Under certain circumstances, suicide is right.

(4) Torturing babies is bad.

Most people would agree that each of these sentences does express a moral judgment—although, of course, not everyone would agree that each of them expresses a *true* moral judgment. For the present, however, our interest is not so much in distinguishing the true from the false moral judgments. Our interest here is primarily in distinguishing the moral from the nonmoral judgments. We are just trying to isolate the sphere of the moral.

None of the following sentences contains any value term. Hence, according to M_1, none of them expresses a moral judgment:

(5) My telephone is black.

(6) Marblehead is north of Boston.

(7) Everybody loves somebody sometime.

(8) Torturing babies is boring.

Most people would agree that each of these sentences does not express a moral judgment. Thus, we seem to have eight positive instances of M_1. That is, we seem to have eight cases in which the result yielded by the application of M_1 is correct.

But it should be obvious that M_1 is not, in general, correct. There are plenty of cases in which the application of M_1 will yield incorrect results. Here are some:

(9) When rebuilding my engine, I put in the timing gears all wrong.

(10) If you want larger yields, you ought to use more fertilizer.

(11) He turned right at the corner.

(12) The acting was good, but the lighting was bad.

M_1 implies that each of these sentences expresses a moral judgment. For each of them contains a word from our list of value terms. It is clear, however, that none of the sentences has a thing to do with morality. Surely, no one would say that there is a specifically moral obligation to put timing gears into engines correctly. The word "wrong" in (9) is not used in a moral sense. Similarly, the word "ought" in (10) is used in a nonmoral sense; it has more to do with prudence than with morality. The "right" in (11) is not used to express any sort of value. And finally, the "good" and "bad" in (12) might be used to express aesthetic rather than moral values. Thus, none of (9)–(12) in fact expresses a moral judgment, although M_1 incorrectly implies that each of them does.

It should be clear that this approach will not work. Moral judgments cannot be distinguished from nonmoral judgments simply on the basis of the words used to express them. A more fruitful approach might be to consider the subject matter of the sentences. Perhaps moral judgments all have to do with the same set of issues.

We can formulate a short list of "moral issues." The list might include such topics as abortion, suicide, euthanasia, civil rights, sexual behavior, honesty, fairness, keeping promises, and showing respect. Now we can propose that moral judgments are judgments about these moral issues:

M_2:   An English sentence expresses a moral judgment if and only if it is about some moral issue.

The application of theory M_2 yields correct results in many cases. For example, it implies that (1) and (3) express moral judgments, and in fact they do. M_2 also implies that (5) and (6) do not express moral judgments, and in fact they don't. Thus, the application of M_2 yields correct results in these cases.

But it isn't hard to see that M_2 is utterly misguided. Although we often do make moral judgments about these moral issues, we just as often make nonmoral judgments about them. Thus, every one of the following sentences is about a moral issue, but none of them expresses a moral judgment:

(13) Abortion is illegal in some places.

(14) Suicide occurs more frequently during economic depressions.

(15) People sometimes request euthanasia for themselves.

(16) Vigorous sexual activity can be good exercise.

In light of examples such as these, it appears that we cannot distinguish moral judgments from nonmoral ones simply on the basis of their subject matter.

Perhaps some of you will feel that the most promising way of dealing with this puzzle would be to combine the ideas behind M_1 with those behind M_2. That is, you may feel, first, that moral judgments are expressed by sentences that contain value terms, and, second, that moral judgments are about moral issues. This idea deserves consideration.

One of the most interesting developments of this approach is that of John Hartland-Swann.[1] His version is based on the fact that every society has a variety of customs. Among these customs, some are considered by the members of the society to be of very great "social importance." To violate a custom of very great social importance is to threaten the very existence of the society. For example, in our society we have the custom of, in general, not stabbing our neighbors when they annoy us. If we began to violate this custom, the whole fabric of our society might begin to unravel. Other customs are viewed as being of intermediate social importance—for example, the custom of keeping our promises. Finally, some customs are viewed as being of very slight social importance. In our society, a custom of this sort would be that of shaking hands with another person when we are introduced.

According to this view, each sort of custom is associated with a sort of punishment. If you violate a custom, your punishment should be of the appropriate degree of severity. Thus, if you violate a custom of very great social importance, you may be fined, sent to prison, or even executed. If you violate a custom of intermediate social importance, your fellow citizens may reproach you or give you the cold shoulder—they will let you know that they think you have behaved poorly. Finally, if you violate a custom of slight social importance, you will be held up to slight condemnation. People may kid you about your gracelessness, or laugh at you.

Hartland-Swann maintains that in any society, the rules governing the most important customs turn out to be the *laws* of that society. This set of rules expresses the legal obligations of the citizens of that society. The rules governing the customs of intermediate social importance turn out to be the rules of *morality* for that society. This set of rules expresses the moral code of those people. Finally, the rules governing the least socially important customs are the rules of *etiquette* for that society.

Although Hartland-Swann does not put it in this way, we can develop his idea as follows. First, we can introduce the notion of a "moral custom." Let us propose that a custom is a moral custom in a society if it is believed by the members of that society to be of intermediate social importance. So, for example, it might be said that the custom of keeping promises is a moral custom in our society. On the basis of our proposal, we can identify the sphere of the moral without drawing up some static list of "moral issues." That is, what counts as a moral issue will vary from society to society, but it will always be something that the people of that society believe to be of intermediate social importance.

Now we can combine our two earlier proposals. We can say, first, that sentences used to express moral judgments contain words from our list of value terms, and, second, that they have as their subject matter customs that are moral customs for their societies. According to this proposal, then, a sentence must pass two tests to count as expressing a moral judgment. It must have the right sort of subject matter, and it must say the right sort of thing about it. Thus, our third proposal is:

M_3: An English sentence expresses a moral judgment for a society if and only if (i) it is about a moral custom of that society, and (ii) it contains a value term.

Proposal M_3 is designed to capture a number of important insights.

First, like M₁, it captures the insight that moral judgments are expressed in English with such terms as "right," "wrong," and "obligatory." Second, like M₂, it captures the insight that there is a special subject matter for moral judgments. But unlike M₂, M₃ allows this subject matter to vary from society to society. Finally, M₃ is based on the idea that moral issues are more socially important than matters of mere etiquette, but less socially important than matters of law. All in all, M₃ seems to be a very interesting suggestion.

However, if we reflect on it for a minute, we will soon realize that M₃ is not acceptable. There are plenty of sentences that express moral judgments in fact, but that do not express moral judgments according to M₃. Consider, for example, these sentences:

(17) Killing people is always wrong.
(18) Torturing babies is evil.

It should be obvious that each of these might be used to express a moral judgment for our society. (Of course, there might be some debate as to whether (17) expresses a *true* moral judgment for our society.) Yet M₃ implies that neither of these sentences expresses a moral judgment for our society. For in each case, the sentence is about a custom that is *not* of *intermediate* social importance in our society. But in each case, the custom *is* of *great* social importance. Surely, there are few customs of greater social importance in our society than that of refraining from killing other people, and that of refraining from inflicting pointless pain on innocent babies.

In the other direction, there are plenty of moral judgments that are not moral according to M₃. For example, suppose a man is living alone on a desert island. Suppose that there are many beautiful butterflies on the island, and that the man enjoys seeing them. Perhaps he would like to collect one butterfly of each species, but out of a respect for life and an appreciation for their beauty he decides to let them all live freely. He might say to himself:

(19) It would be wrong to kill any of these butterflies.

It seems reasonable to maintain that when the man says (19), he is making a moral judgment. Yet M₃ apparently implies that (19) does not express a moral judgment for any society. For according to M₃, a judgment is moral for a society only if it is about a custom considered by the members of that society to be of intermediate social importance. In our example, however, there doesn't seem to be any society—the man is living alone on a desert island. Thus, there may be no society in which the custom of refraining from killing the butterflies is considered to be of intermediate social importance. In this case, the judgment is not a moral judgment for any society.

The result is the same even if we assume that the lonely man constitutes a society all by himself. For although the man might consider the matter of the butterflies to be of some importance, it is doubtful that he would consider it to be a *custom*, or that he would consider it to be of *social* importance. The matter of the butterflies, if it is important at all, is not important from the point of view of society. It has little to do with one person's relations with others. Rather, it has to do with a person's relations with a part of nature. Many people feel that there are moral obligations to avoid needless injury to nature. Such moral obligations, if there are any, provide counter-instances to any attempt to define morality in terms of purely social concerns.

It appears, then, that we have not as yet been able to distinguish moral judgments from nonmoral ones, either on the basis of the words used to express them, or on the basis of their subject matter, or even on the basis of a combination of their words, their subject matter, and their degree of social importance.

A final approach to the problem of distinguishing the moral from the nonmoral is based upon some insights of the great German philosopher Immanuel Kant.[2] We will consider Kant's views in much greater detail in Chapters 7 and 8, but it may be worthwhile to see, in a rather rough way, how Kant might deal with our present question.

Kant draws a distinction between what he calls "the imperative of morality" and the nonmoral imperatives. Thus, Kant's comments are directed not to our question about moral *judgments*, but rather to a corresponding question about moral *imperatives*. For our purposes, we may think of imperatives as sentences containing the word "ought," or some equivalent. Thus, each of these is an imperative:

(20) If you want to blow up the bank, you ought to use dynamite.

(21) You ought to be more considerate.

(22) You ought to save your money for a rainy day.

The first of these imperatives is explicitly hypothetical in form. That is, it is of the "if you want———, then you ought to———" form. It says that if you want to achieve a certain end, then you ought to use certain means. In this particular case, the end is blowing up the bank, and the recommended means is the use of dynamite. By itself, (20) does not imply that you ought to use dynamite. It only implies that you should do this if you want to blow up the bank. Of course, most of us don't want to blow up banks.

Some imperatives, though not explicitly hypothetical in form, may be said to be implicitly hypothetical. That is, although they are not actually of the "if you want———, then you ought to———" form, the person who uses them has some hypothetical thought in mind. If you were to ask this person to explain her meaning, she would quickly produce an explicitly hypothetical imperative. This can be seen in the case of (22). If someone asserts that you ought to save money for a rainy day, and you ask her to expand upon her view, she is likely to reply like this:

(23) If you want to be happy in your old age, you ought to save money for a rainy day.

or

(24) If you want to avoid needless pain later, you should save money for a rainy day.

Such imperatives, then, though not explicitly hypothetical, are implicitly hypothetical.

There are some imperatives, finally, that are neither implicitly nor explicitly hypothetical. (21) is an example. Suppose a person utters (21) and, when asked to expand upon his meaning, says that he simply means that you ought to be more considerate. He says that he does *not* mean that *if* you want people to like you, then you ought to be more considerate. Similarly, he does *not* mean that *if* you want to be happy, then you ought to be considerate. He insists that he means that regardless of what you want, you ought to be more considerate simply because it is the right thing to do. Kant would say that the imperative this person uttered, (21), is a *categorical* imperative. It is an ought-statement that is neither explicitly nor implicitly hypothetical in form. Kant's extremely interesting thesis is that the categorical imperative is the imperative of morality. In other words:

M_4: An English sentence is a moral imperative if and only if it is a categorical imperative.

Although this version of Kant's view is of considerable interest, and although its application yields correct results in many cases, it is fairly clear that, as stated, it is incorrect. To see why, consider this case. A young woman is thinking of going to the Merchant Marine Academy. Since women have traditionally not gone to the Academy, she wonders if it would be morally right for her to go. She expresses her concern to her mother, who says:

(25) If you want to go, then you ought to go.

Perhaps her mother's view is that the only morally relevant issue here is whether her daughter wants to go. Perhaps the mother thinks that the traditional barrier against women is morally irrelevant. Thus, when she asserts (25), she means to be uttering a moral imperative. This all seems quite plausible. Yet M_4 would incorrectly imply that her imperative is not moral, since it is explicitly hypothetical in form.

It is by no means clear that this example would refute more sophisticated versions of the Kantian position. But it does refute M₄. Perhaps we should draw the modest conclusion that although it is provocative and initially quite plausible, in its simplest form the Kantian proposal seems to be incorrect. It would be interesting to see if some modern-day Kantian can develop this view so as to make it both clear and correct. I, for one, do not know how to do it.

So we have to admit, right at the outset, that it is not easy to say just what it is that makes a judgment a moral judgment, or what it is that makes an imperative a moral one. Hence, we have not succeeded in answering the questions we set out to answer. We have not said what the adjective "moral" means. In light of this, it seems unlikely that we will be able to give a fully satisfactory answer to the more abstract question, "What is morality?"

It may be fair to assume, in spite of this, that most of us have some intuitive grasp of the distinction between the moral and the nonmoral. It is by appeal to this intuitive grasp of the distinction that we evaluate proposals such as M_1–M_4. So even though we haven't said just what it is that makes a moral judgment or imperative moral, we may still be able to recognize a moral judgment or imperative when we see one. Perhaps this will be enough for our present purposes. Assuming, then, that we have some rough idea of what the adjective "moral" means, let us consider what morality might be.

The morality of a society, it seems, is the set of moral principles that are accepted in that society. The morality of a person, similarly, may be taken to be the set of moral principles he or she accepts. Morality in general, if there is such a thing, may be thought of as the set of all the true or correct moral principles. Although this is obviously rather rough, and makes use of the undefined concept of "moral principle," it may be sufficient. So let us turn to our second question, "What are the main forms of philosophical enquiry into morality?"

The Philosophical Study of Morality

Moral beliefs vary from society to society. In one place, people are morally outraged at the sight of nude sunbathers on a public beach. In another community, such behavior is considered quite acceptable. The study of varying moral beliefs is an interesting and worthwhile pursuit. Those who engage in it often discover curious and important facts about human attitudes and behavior. Furthermore, they may develop a sort of enlightened tolerance for moral diversity. This sort of study, which may be called *descriptive morals*, is therefore quite legitimate.

However, descriptive morals is not in itself a particularly philosophical enterprise, though it is not easy to say exactly why. Anthropologists, sociologists, social historians, and others may be better suited to the task of describing and comparing the moral codes of different groups. Philosophers, though, may be quite good at what they do even though they have very little expertise in the social sciences. It is interesting to note, however, that some philosophers have had remarkable success in combining descriptive morals with more specifically philosophical studies in ethics.[3]

Another form of moral enquiry might be called *nontheoretic morals*. We can say that people engage in nontheoretic morals when they attempt, without making any explicit appeal to fully general moral principles, to develop and defend positions on important moral issues. For example, if we were to discuss the morality of war, euthanasia, sexism, or vegetarianism without first agreeing on general moral principles, we would be engaged in nontheoretic morals. An informal version of this sort of enquiry goes on in dormitories, bars, coffee shops, and wherever intelligent people have a chance to engage in serious discussion of moral issues. A more formal version of nontheoretic morals is undertaken in many ethics courses and in many books on moral problems.

A third sort of moral enquiry is generally called *normative ethics*. Understood in one way, normative ethics is the attempt to discover, formulate, and defend the most fundamental principles about morally right action. In order to obtain a clearer idea of what this involves, let us consider some examples of what people do when they engage in normative ethics.

Some philosophers have maintained that the most fundamental principle about morally right action is something like this:

U_8:   An act is morally right if and only if it produces the greatest happiness of the greatest number.

This principle is a rather garbled version of *act utilitarianism*. According to this view, what makes an act right, if it is right, is a certain fact about its results, or consequences. The fact in question is that the act produces more happiness for more people than anything else the agent could have done. You will probably discover, if you think about it for a minute, that deep down inside you believe in something like this.

Many philosophers have attacked the utilitarian position. They have insisted that it cannot be the case that in all our action we should aim only at maximizing happiness. To do so, they have claimed, would be utterly immoral. We should aim, in addition, at increasing knowledge, virtue, and justice. Indeed, some philosophers have said that justice is far more important than happiness. In some cases, they have argued, it would be better to insure that justice be done even if it would be possible to make more people happy by allowing injustice to reign. When philosophers criticize a normative view in this way, they are also engaging in normative ethics.

A fourth kind of moral enquiry is usually called *metaethics*. In metaethics we attempt, among other things, to discover and explain the meanings of the crucial terms of moral appraisal. Thus, we raise the question "What does the word 'good' mean?"

Often, philosophers who engage in metaethics attempt to explain the meaning of "good," "bad," "right," and other terms of moral appraisal by giving formal definitions. For example, a philosopher who adopted this approach might claim that the real meaning of "good" is explained by this definition:

D_1: x is good = df.[4] I approve of x.

Other philosophers have claimed that the most fundamental terms of moral appraisal cannot be defined. Some have said that these terms cannot be defined because they express simple, unanalyzable properties, and no term expressing a property of this sort can be defined. Others have said that these terms cannot be defined because, strictly speaking, they don't have any meaning at all! The study of such views, and the arguments pro and con, fall under the heading of metaethics.

Other sorts of moral philosophy also fall into the category of metaethics. One of these has to do with the logical features of moral concepts. It is sometimes said that the concept of moral obligation has a number of interesting logical characteristics. For example, we might want to consider whether the following principle is valid:

> If a person morally ought to do an act a, and it is impossible for him to do a without also doing b, then he morally ought to do b.

Another interesting possible principle is this one:

> If a person morally ought to do an act a, and he also morally ought to do another act b, then he morally ought to do both a and b.

A final sort of philosophical activity may be called *moralizing*. The authors of books on ethics often attempt to make their readers become morally better people. Authors may exhort their readers to pay more attention to the needs of others, or to reflect more carefully on the possible consequences of their actions. This sort of enterprise surely has its place. Since there are so many bad people, it is clear that someone ought to try to do something to make them better. Traditionally, philosophers have tried to do this.

What's in This Book

However interesting and useful descriptive morals may be as a form of enquiry, it is not the topic of this book. What we consider here is more abstract and more general. Nor is this book a study of nontheoretic morals. Of course, every general moral theory that we consider has its consequences for pressing moral concerns. And so, in the course of our discussions of various abstract moral theories, we often consider their impact on the morality of abortion, murder, civil rights, euthanasia, and other important moral issues. Thus, although these forms of enquiry are not the central focus of this book, they are not entirely ignored here either.

Chapters 2 through 10 of this book concern theories in normative ethics. One of these theories, the act-utilitarian doctrine, has been formulated, and mis-formulated, in a variety of ways. If we are to understand the doctrine well enough to come to a reasoned decision about its truth, we must first formulate it adequately. In Chapter 2, we devote our attention to this task.

Chapters 3 and 4 are devoted to a discussion of arguments for and against act utilitarianism. In Chapter 5, we discuss some rather interesting attempts to avoid certain pitfalls of act utilitarianism. According to these reformulations of the utilitarian view, what makes an act morally right is not so much *its* consequences as the consequences of the moral rule that requires the act. Such theories are forms of *rule utilitarianism*.

Some people have insisted that the most fundamental principle about morally right action is that each person ought to look out for his own self-interest. Such views are often criticized as utterly selfish and immoral, but when properly understood, this doctrine of *egoism* may seem fairly plausible. At any rate, some people claim to believe in it, and many people act as if they believe in it. Hence, it is a position in normative ethics that is worth considering, and it is a position we take up in Chapter 6. The discussion of egoism is delayed until this point because certain conceptual machinery needed for its correct formulation is not introduced until then.

Utilitarianism is one of the two great traditions in normative ethics. *Formalism* is the other. According to formalists, what makes an act morally right is not its consequences. Rather, it is some formal feature of the rule under which the act is performed. The most influential defender of this sort of position is Kant. In Chapters 7 and 8, we discuss some of his most important views on normative ethics. In a recent book, *A Theory of*

Justice, John Rawls has proposed the original and interesting thesis that Kant can be interpreted as a "social-contract theorist" in normative ethics. In Chapter 9, this proposal is explained and considered. In Chapter 10, we discuss the rather different views of another formalist, W. D. Ross.

Chapter 11 is devoted to a discussion of various interpretations of the view that "what's right in one society may be wrong in another." This view may be taken as the motto of those who believe in *relativism* in normative ethics.

In Chapters 12–15, we turn our attention away from normative ethics and toward metaethics. In these chapters, we consider four of the main recent views in metaethics: naturalism, nonnaturalism, emotivism, and prescriptivism. In the final chapter, we consider some possible complaints and try to explain some of the ways in which moral philosophy may be useful.

This book does not contain much moralizing. If you feel that you are in need of moral uplift, you will have to look elsewhere for it.

The Value of Moral Philosophy

Now that we have briefly considered the varieties of moral philosophy and outlined the contents of this book, we should stop for a minute to think about the purpose of it all. Why should we study moral philosophy? What good will it do? Will it make us better persons? Will it help us to learn "the true moral theory"?

Different individuals will answer these questions in different ways. Some thoughtful individuals sincerely believe that in order to be a fully moral person, one must study moral philosophy. Others, equally thoughtful, feel that the study of moral philosophy does not in any way help one to become a morally better person.

An intermediate position seems to me to be the closest to the truth. Most of us hold at least a fairly ragged assortment of moral views. We believe that certain kinds of action are morally right. We believe that certain kinds are morally wrong. And we just don't know what to think about several other kinds. Yet when we are asked to give reasons, we are often somewhat confused at the outset. When we think about one issue, we tend to support our view by appeal to one principle. When we think about another issue, we defend our position by appeal to a different principle. Unfortunately, it often happens that the principles to which we have appealed are inconsistent. In this sort of case, the study of moral philosophy may be extremely useful. For when we study moral principles, we come to understand that some are incompatible with others, and we develop the ability to determine when this is the case. Hence, one great value of moral philosophy is that it may be able to help us sort out our principles, and thereby enable us to avoid maintaining inconsistent sets of principles.

On a more fundamental level, the study of moral philosophy may help us discover what our moral principles actually are. Many of us, prior to our first exposure to moral philosophy, have never thought very deeply about such questions as "What makes morally right actions morally right?" Thus, it is hardly surprising that we don't already have a well-formulated version of a satisfactory answer. Furthermore, if we did reflect deeply on this question and then tried to state our prephilosophical view precisely, it is likely that our thoughts would follow one or another of the classic patterns of normative ethics. The study of moral philosophy may help us, therefore, to understand better the moral theory we already (in a rough form) hold. If it can do this, clearly moral philosophy can be of considerable value.

Moral philosophy may be useful in a third way. When we reflect upon general moral principles and attempt to formulate them precisely, we may come to see that some of these general principles do not have some of the consequences we originally thought them to have. Equally, we may come to see that such principles do have certain consequences we originally thought them not to have. This sort of thing happens quite readily in the case of the hedonistic form of act utilitarianism discussed in Chapters 2, 3, and 4. Many people feel, before they study it carefully, that this doctrine entails some sort of gross sensualism. Similarly, they may feel that it has no direct bearing on the problem of justice. Each of these views seems to be mistaken. Surely, if one holds a moral theory at all, it is better to hold that theory with some understanding of what it implies and what it does not imply in particular cases.

A final use of moral philosophy should be mentioned. For some reason, many of us seem to be willing, even eager, to adopt some well-defined moral stance. We feel uneasy if we haven't aligned ourselves with some doctrine. This demand for moral doctrines generates a supply. Plenty of popular moralists appear on the scene, offering novel and exciting moral views for our consumption. Once we have studied moral philosophy for a while, we may begin to see the enormous difficulty of the subject, and we may recognize how absurd most popular moral slogans really are. We may begin to sense the complexity and subtlety of our moral concepts. Once we have done this, we will less likely be carried away with faddish moral doctrines. We will know how to evaluate such doctrines, and we will be able to recognize their defects, if they are defective.

If it is better for us to avoid holding inconsistent moral principles and to understand the principles we hold; and if it is better for us to be clear about the consequences of our moral principles and to be skeptical about faddish moral doctrines, then the careful study of moral philosophy can help us to be better persons.

Some people believe that the study of moral philosophy can also lead us to a recognition of true moral principles. If this were so, it would surely show this subject to be a useful one. In my view, however, the most we can expect from moral philosophy is that it may show us that some principles are false. For after we have done our best as moral philosophers, we may be left with two fully general moral principles. Each may be self-consistent and independently quite plausible. Yet we may also recognize that not both of them can be true; they may be incompatible with each other. At this stage, should it arise, moral philosophy may have nothing further to offer. Each of us, using his or her own insight, will then have to try to come to a reasonable and responsible decision concerning the two principles.

But let's not spend any more time now on these speculations. Let's turn to a consideration of one of the most plausible and popular views in normative ethics—act utilitarianism.

NOTES

1. John Hartland-Swann, *An Analysis of Morals* (London: Allen & Unwin, 1960).

2. Immanuel Kant, *Groundwork of the Metaphysic of Morals*, translated and analyzed by H. J. Paton (New York: Harper & Row, 1964).

3. See, for example, Richard Brandt, *Hopi Ethics* (Chicago: University of Chicago Press, 1954); and John Ladd, *The Structure of a Moral Code: A Philosophical Analysis of Ethical Discourse Applied to the Ethics of the Navaho Indians* (Cambridge, Mass.: Harvard University Press, 1957).

4. = df: This symbol may be read "means, by definition" or "is definitionally equivalent to."

2

What Is Act Utilitarianism?

Even if you have never previously heard of utilitarianism, it is likely that a substantial part of your moral thinking is basically utilitarian in character. To see how natural and intuitive utilitarianism can be, consider the following case. A young man, Bob, has been seriously injured in a motorcycle accident, and is lying comatose in an intensive care unit. The doctors have determined that Bob will never regain consciousness, but will linger indefinitely in a purely vegetative state. All his vital functions have been taken over by sophisticated machines. If any of these were removed, Bob would die. Two of his friends are discussing the poor youth's condition. One says that it would be utterly immoral to "pull the plug" and thus let Bob die peacefully. The other disagrees. He reasons as follows: "If the doctors pull the plug, Bob will die peacefully. He will feel no pain—after all, he's completely unconscious. Nor will Bob be deprived of any future happiness, for at best he will never regain consciousness even if he lives a long time. Bob's parents will be better off if he dies, since it will cost them a lot of money to keep him alive, and they surely will gain no happiness from spending their money in that way. They won't be any sadder knowing him to be dead than knowing him to be reduced to this miserable vegetative state. As for us, his friends, we have nothing to gain from keeping him alive. I know I'd be happier to see him dead than to see him existing in this way. Thus, in my view the right thing to do in this case is clear. Since the consequences of letting him die peacefully are better than the consequences of keeping him alive in this vegetative state, Bob should be allowed to die."

There are two essential points to notice about this line of reasoning. First, the argument is based upon the view that the morality of pulling the plug depends, at least in part, on what would happen if the plug were pulled. In other words, the question about the morality of pulling the plug is at least in part a question about the consequences this act would have if it were performed. Second, we should note that the argument is based upon the idea that the morally relevant feature of the consequences has something to do with pleasure and pain, or happiness. Thus, the fact that Bob would feel no pain and the fact that Bob's parents and friends would not feel any less pleasure are considered relevant to the determination of the morality of the act.

If you feel that such considerations as these are in fact morally relevant, then you may be well on the road toward becoming a utilitarian. If you would argue in the manner illustrated, or if you would be moved by such an argument if you agreed about the amounts of pleasure and pain that would result, then you already accept the basic premise of the utilitarian doctrine. Even if you would disagree about the correctness of pulling the plug in this particular case, you may still be a utilitarian. The basic question is this: Do you think that the moral status of an action is determined by the amount of happiness for all concerned that would result if it were performed? If so, you are probably a utilitarian.

With this as background, let us turn to a more careful consideration of the fundamental principle of act utilitarianism. The classic statement of this normative theory can be found in John Stuart Mill's *Utilitarianism*. In that work, Mill says:

> ... actions are right in proportion as they tend to promote happiness, wrong as they tend to produce the reverse of happiness. By "happiness" is intended pleasure, and the absence of pain; by "unhappiness" pain, and the privation of pleasure.[1]

This is perhaps the most famous formulation of the utilitarian view. Yet it is in many ways not as clear as it should be if we are to understand it fully. In order to clarify this principle, let us backtrack a bit and reflect for a while on the nature of it. What sort of principle is it intended to be? Just what is it supposed to tell us?

A general principle of morality, such as Mill's utilitarian principle, has as its subject matter actions—things people do. The point of the principle is to provide an account of the normative status of these actions. That is, it is supposed to state the conditions under which an act is morally right, morally wrong, or morally obligatory. Let us first consider actions; then we can think about moral evaluation.

Actions

We can draw a broad distinction between generic actions and concrete actions. A *generic action* is a general kind of behavior—something that can be done over and over again by different persons on different occasions. For example, each of the following is a generic action: walking, talking, driving a car, reading, twiddling one's thumbs, and tickling babies. Each is a thing that different persons can do on different occasions. The generic actions mentioned here are not often the subject of moral evaluation. We hardly ever discuss the morality of walking, for example. But other generic actions are often subject to moral scrutiny. For example, people often debate the moral status of such generic actions as telling lies, aborting babies, breaking promises, and inflicting needless pain on innocent persons.

Unlike a generic action, a *concrete action* occurs on exactly one occasion and has exactly one agent. It cannot be done over and over again, nor can anyone else ever perform it. The first walk on the moon, for example, is a concrete action. It was performed by Neil Armstrong, and he performed it on July 23, 1969. The act of reading that you are performing now is also a concrete act. It has only one agent—you—and only one time of performance—now. Although you can perform other acts like it, you cannot perform this very act of reading on any other occasion. Although others can perform acts like it, no one else can perform the very same act of reading that you are performing now. It is a unique, unrepeatable act.

Every concrete act is an instance of some generic act. Thus, the first walk on the moon is a concrete act, and it is an instance of the generic act, walking. But, at least according to one view on the matter, it is also an instance of all of the following generic acts: walking in a funny suit, walking while carrying a flag, and walking on the moon. In general, we can say that each concrete act is an instance of many different generic acts.

Mill's principle is best construed as a principle about the normative status of concrete acts. The reasons for this may emerge shortly. But first, we have to explain what is meant by "normative status."

Evaluations of Normative Status

Concrete actions are open to evaluation from many points of view. For example, we can evaluate someone's act aesthetically. We do this when we say of an act that it was graceful, or beautiful, or grotesque. We can evaluate an act from the point of view of etiquette. If someone sneezes in your face, you may feel that this action was in poor taste. If you express your opinion, you will be evaluating the act from the point of view of etiquette. We can evaluate acts from the point of view of the law, too. We do this when we say that an act was legal, or felonious, or conspiratorial. But when we evaluate acts from the point of view of morals, we say such things as these: "What Sam did was morally wrong." "Under the circumstances, Jane's act was morally wrong." "You have no choice; it's the only right thing to do."

Moral evaluations of actions generally fall into one of three categories. Either we say that the act is *obligatory*, or we say that it is *permissible*, or we say that it is *forbidden*. Of course, most of the time we don't use such pretentious terminology. We can say that an act is obligatory by saying, "It is something you must do," or, "It is your duty," or "It is what you ought to do." Any of these expressions, and many others as well, can be used to express the view that a certain concrete act is obligatory. Every one of them means, when used in this way, that the act is morally required. It is what should be done. Of course, these expressions can be used in nonmoral ways too.

We express the idea that an act is permissible by saying such things as: "It would be all right to do it." "It would be right." "It is okay to do." "It is acceptable." These expressions also have nonmoral uses, and so they express moral permissibility only some of the time. But if, when making a moral judgment, we say that some concrete act is right, okay, acceptable, all right, or permissible, we are assigning that act to the category of the morally permissible.

Forbidden acts are acts that are wrong, that we should not do, and that are unacceptable from a moral point of view.

There are some interesting logical connections among these concepts. In fact, it could even be argued that we need only one basic concept of normative evaluation. Suppose, for example, that some individual knows what it means to say that an act is morally permissible, but he does not know what "obligatory" and "forbidden" mean. We can easily define these other terms of normative evaluation by reference to the concept of permissibility. An act is obligatory, we might say, if and only if it is not permissible to fail to do it. In other words, to say that you have to perform a certain act is the same as to say that you are not permitted to fail to do it. What you *must* do is what you cannot fail to do. We can state this in terms of a formal definition:

D_1: a is obligatory =df. it is not permissible to fail to do a.

Equally, we can explain, purely in terms of the permissible, what it means to say that an act is forbidden. An act is forbidden only when it is not permissible to do it. In other words, it is wrong to do an act if and only if it would not be right to do it:

D_2: a is forbidden =df. it is not permissible to do a.

Thus, we can define "obligatory" and "forbidden" in terms of "permitted." But we could equally well have defined "permitted" in terms of either "obligatory" or "forbidden." These terms of normative evaluation are, therefore, interdefinable. They constitute an important, logically interrelated set of terms.

It may seem, in fact, that this logically interrelated set is a kind of closed circle. For if someone doesn't know what any of them means, we may find that we have no way of explaining any of them to her. Another way to put this would be to say that the fundamental term of normative evaluation, the one in terms of which the others are defined, must itself be indefinable. This thesis, which many philosophers find quite plausible, may be called *the doctrine of the autonomy of morals*.

A *criterion of morality,* or *fundamental principle of morality,* is a statement of necessary and sufficient conditions for obligatoriness, permittedness, and forbiddenness. Since we have seen that these concepts of normative appraisal are logically related, we don't have to present three separate moral principles. We need state only one such principle; that is, we need give necessary and sufficient conditions for the correct application of only one of the terms of moral appraisal. That principle, together with D_1 and D_2, will yield corresponding doctrines about the other two terms.

If we find a condition, A, that every right act must satisfy, then we can state a *necessary condition* of rightness. That is, we can state a condition that it is necessary for an act to satisfy, if it is right. Then we can truly assert something of this form:

   N: An act is right only if it satisfies A.

If we find some condition, B, such that every act that satisfies it must therefore be right, then we will have found a *sufficient condition* of rightness. If we know that some act satisfies B, that will be enough—we will then know that it must be right, too. For satisfying B is sufficient for rightness. Then we can truly assert something of this form:

   S: An act is right if it satisfies B.

But if we find a condition, C, that is both necessary and sufficient for rightness, then we will have found a *criterion of right action*. We will have found a condition, C, such that all right acts satisfy C, and all acts that satisfy C are right. In other words, the class of right acts coincides exactly with the class of acts that satisfy C. Then we can say something of this form:

   NS: An act is right if and only if it satisfies C.

The fundamental principle of morality is some statement of this form. The main difference is that it contains reference to some genuine condition that all and only right acts satisfy, instead of our meaningless "C."

Mill's Theory

Now let us return to Mill and recall what he proposed to be the fundamental principle of morality. In a passage already quoted, Mill said:

> . . . actions are right in proportion as they tend to promote happiness, wrong as they tend to produce the reverse of happiness. By "happiness" is intended pleasure, and the absence of pain; by "unhappiness" pain, and the privation of pleasure.

There are a number of odd features in Mill's statement. For one, he speaks of an act being right "in proportion as." This suggests that he believes that there are "degrees of rightness." But does it make sense to say of two morally permissible acts that one is "more permissible than" the other? Do we normally think that of two right acts, one can be "righter" than the other? Many people find these terms to be of doubtful significance. They think that either the act is right or it is not right—it can not be righter than some but less right than others. Thus, there is some reason to suspect that it does not make much sense to speak of acts being "right in proportion as" they do something or other.

A second odd feature of Mill's statement is this. He says that acts are right in proportion as they "tend to promote happiness." This suggests that a given concrete act may *tend* to promote, or cause, happiness. It clearly does make sense to speak of the tendencies of generic acts—"Telling lies tends to make people trust you less," "Stabbing people tends to make them bleed," and so on. When we say that a generic act tends to have a certain effect, we mean that many or most of its instances do in fact have that effect. To say that the generic act, stabbing, tends to make people bleed is seemingly to say that most concrete acts of stabbing do make people bleed. But what would it mean to say of a concrete act that it *tends* to have a certain effect? Surely not that its instances do in fact have that effect—for a concrete act does not have any instances. Nor can it mean that it usually has that effect—for a concrete act occurs only once. Either it has that effect on that occasion, or it does not.

Some philosophers have decided to deal with these oddities in Mill's statement by assuming that what he meant may just as easily be expressed in some way such as this:

U_1:   An act is right if and only if it promotes happiness.

Since Mill explicitly defines "happiness" as "pleasure and the absence of pain," and since "promotes" undoubtedly means "causes," we can fill out this version of utilitarianism as follows:

U_2:   An act is right if and only if it causes pleasure and the absence of pain.

Although U_2 may seem at first glance to capture what Mill meant, it is still not a good formulation of the utilitarian doctrine. For it seems to imply that an act is morally right only if it "causes the absence of pain." But what could this mean? Perhaps an act causes the absence of pain if it causes there to be no more pain. But if so, no one has ever performed a right act. Surely, even after the best act you ever performed, someone, somewhere, was still feeling some pain. Maybe a man in New Zealand was having a tooth filled, or a woman in Mexico just hit her thumb with a hammer. It is unlikely that anyone has ever performed an act that caused there to be no more pain.

Perhaps the real intent of U_2 is expressed more adequately by this principle:

U_3:   { An act is right if and only if it causes pleasure and does not cause pain.

Principle U_3 seems fairly plausible. Its application apparently does generate acceptable results in at least a few cases. For example, suppose a mother gives a carrot to her son. Her act, let us suppose, causes some pleasure to the son and causes no pain at all. Most of us would agree that unless there is something odd about the circumstances, what the mother does is permissible from a moral point of view. Her act of giving a carrot to her son seems to be a right act. And U_3 agrees. Since the act causes pleasure and does not cause pain, U_3 implies that it is right. So far, then, U_3 seems reasonable.

Consider another case. Suppose a man bites his neighbor's leg for no good reason at all. Such an act seems wrong. It is just the sort of thing we should try to avoid. And U_3 says it is not right. The act does cause some pain; hence, it is not right, according to U_3. In order to be right, an act must cause some pleasure and must not cause any pain.

But some other examples show some serious defects in U_3. For one thing, sometimes the right act *does* cause some pain. Often, when we must make the best of a bad situation our best choice is the lesser of two evils, and causes some pain. For example, suppose you see a man standing next to a rattlesnake. The snake is about to strike, and the man is wearing bermuda shorts. Just before the snake strikes, you leap into action, knocking the man down and putting him out of range of the snake. By performing this heroic deed, you prevent the man from suffering a serious injury. But let us suppose that when you knock the man down, he scrapes his knee. In this case, then, what you did caused a little pain. Thus, it would clearly be incorrect to say that your act caused pleasure and did not cause pain. Hence, according to U₃, what you did was not right. But, as should be evident, if you did the best you could under the circumstances, your behavior was right. In those circumstances, anything you could have done would have resulted in at least a little pain. Hence, the application of U₃ seems to generate the wrong result in this case.

Indeed, it should be evident that U₃ sets an impossibly high standard for many situations. We cannot require that right acts cause no pain at all, for in most morally interesting cases the right act will cause some pain. The question is, perhaps, whether right acts cause unnecessary pain, or more pain than pleasure.

Strangely enough, U₃ may also set too low a standard for some cases. That is, there may be cases of wrong actions that nevertheless cause pleasure and do not cause pain. Such actions are right, according to U₃. Suppose a young student is on an archaeological expedition with a great professor. The professor has always treated the student generously, and has helped him obtain a fellowship. The professor's whole life has been devoted to a search for the missing ancestral link between the pigeon and the dove. All his life, he's been looking for evidence that would show that such a bird once existed. While digging, the student finds a fossil bone from the missing bird. He recognizes it at once. It is the very bone the professor has always wanted to find. But instead of handing the bone over to the professor, the student uses it for a toothpick and then throws it in the incinerator.

Surely, the student's act was wrong. However, it may have caused pleasure and no pain. For if the student felt pleasure as a result of picking his teeth, and if the professor never found out about the destruction of the bone, then the act seems to satisfy both conditions for rightness stated in U₃. Thus, U₃ seems to imply that the act is right. But we can all see that it was not right.

These examples point out two features that U₃ lacks. First, we want to take into consideration not only how much pleasure and pain the act causes, but also how much pleasure and pain would have been produced by the other acts the agent could have done instead. This is clear from the cases described above. In the rattlesnake case, we want to say that even though the act caused some pain, the other acts the agent could have done instead (such as letting the snake bite) would have caused even more pain. In the fossil case, another act (giving the bone to the professor) would have caused more pleasure than using the bone as a toothpick. These facts about the amounts of pleasure and pain that the other acts would have produced are obviously of moral significance.

A second feature that U₃ lacks is some effective way of ranking acts in terms of how much pleasure and how much pain they cause. We want to combine the amounts of pleasure and pain in such a way that the result may easily be compared with the results of all the other acts an agent has in his power at a given time.

Our next project is to attempt to incorporate these two features into our formulation of utilitarianism.

Utility

First, we have to make some assumptions. Let us suppose that pleasure can be quantified. That is, let us suppose that every episode of pleasure can be given a score, or rating. We can pretend that there is a standard unit of pleasure, which we can call the "hedon." The pleasure resulting from eating a tasty meal might be rated as being worth 10 hedons. The pleasure of a quick cup of coffee might be worth only half a hedon. Some people who enjoy walking in the woods on a fall day might think that the pleasure produced by that activity is worth 15 hedons.

Our second assumption is that episodes of pain can be evaluated in a similar fashion. We can call our standard unit of pain a "dolor." One dolor might be the amount of pain caused by a slight headache. A migraine headache might cause 5 or 10 dolors worth of pain. The emotional pain felt at the loss of a loved one might be 100 or 150 dolors—depending upon how close you were, how sensitive you are, and other factors.

The third assumption is the most difficult. We must assume that hedons and dolors are *commensurate*. This means, roughly, that you can add and subtract hedons and dolors. The "pleasure-pain value" of a state of affairs in which you feel 10 hedons and I feel 2 dolors is exactly the same as the pleasure-pain value of a state of affairs in which I feel 12 hedons and you feel 4 dolors. In each case, we have a final pleasure-pain value of +8. So the idea is that hedons and dolors are *not* like apples and oranges. Rather they are like "inches westbound" and "inches eastbound." The negative effect of one dolor exactly counterbalances the positive effect of one hedon.

The fourth assumption is that we can make sense of the notion of *consequences*. That is, we must assume that there is some clear meaning that can be attached to the phrase, "This episode of pleasure is a consequence of that action."

Having made these four assumptions, we can define the central concept of the utilitarian theory—that is, the concept of *utility*:

> D_3:   The utility of an act is the result of subtracting the sum of the doloric value of all the episodes of pain that would occur as consequences of that act from the sum of the hedonic values of all the episodes of pleasure that would occur as consequences of that act.

how hedons + dolors work.

Let's consider some examples. Suppose a bully insults someone in front of a small audience. Some of the people who observe this act feel hurt and saddened to see someone insulted. The bully feels pleasure. The one who is insulted feels embarrassed and sad. The relevant consequences are as follows: pleasure felt by bully—5 hedons; pain felt by insulted person—5 dolors; pain felt by first bystander—1 dolor; pain felt by second bystander—1 dolor; pain felt by third bystander—½ dolor. The total utility of the bully's act therefore, is −2½.

Suppose someone assassinates a popular political figure. One million people are saddened by this act, and each of them feels 10 dolors of emotional pain. The act thus causes a total of 10 million dolors. Suppose the assassin and a few other fanatics are delighted. Each feels 100 hedons. If there are five of these fanatics, the total is 500 hedons. The utility of the act of assassination is the result of subtracting the dolors from the hedons. In other words, it is −9,999,500.

It would be wrong to formulate utilitarianism in either of these ways:

U_4:   An act is right if and only if its utility is greater than zero.
U_5:   An act is right if and only if its utility is very high.

For in the fossil case already discussed, the act was wrong but had a positive, perhaps even high, utility. In the snakebite case, the act was right but did not have a very high utility. What we want to say, roughly, is that a person acts rightly when he produces as much utility as he can. In other words:

U_6:   An act is right if and only if its utility is higher than the utility of any other act the agent could have done instead.

U_6 is close to our final formulation, but even it is not quite correct. Its problem is that it does not deal adequately with cases in which a person has two equally good choices open to him and no other choice better than these two. In such (admittedly rare) cases, U_6 yields a bizarre result. To see why, consider this example. A man has one piece of unbreakable candy. He can give it to either of his twin daughters, Jean and Joan. If he gives it to Jean, she will feel 5 hedons of pleasure, and if he gives it to Joan, she will feel 5 hedons of pleasure. In neither case will anyone feel any pain. A third alternative would be to give the candy to neither twin, but that would produce no pleasure at all. So the man's choices seem to be:

act	*utility*
1. Give candy to Jean.	+5
2. Give candy to Joan.	+5
3. Give candy to no one.	0

In this case, most people would say that either giving the candy to Jean or giving it to Joan would be permissible. The man would act rightly in either case. Yet U6 yields the bizarre result that nothing he can do in this case would be right. For none of the acts mentioned has higher utility than all the others. Giving the candy to Jean does not have higher utility than all the others, since giving it to Joan has equally high utility. Giving it to Joan does not have higher utility than all the others, since giving it to Jean has equally high utility. Giving it to no one comes in a poor third.

This sort of case calls for a trivial modification of our principle. We must not require that right acts have a higher utility than their alternatives have. We must require only that right act be such that none of their alternatives has a higher utility than we have. This is our final formulation of Mill's doctrine:

> U7:   An act is right if and only if there is no other act the agent *act utilitarianism* could have done instead that has higher utility than it has.

If we use U7, we see that either giving the candy to Jean or giving it to Joan would be right. Giving it to no one would be wrong, since that act has alternatives with higher utility.

Principle U7 is a formulation of *act utilitarianism.* It is the doctrine that many philosophers feel Mill meant to defend. It is hard to say whether or not Mill actually had something like U7 in mind. But in any case, U7 is perhaps the most plausible and widely considered form of utilitarianism known. It almost invariably provides the basis for discussions of more exotic forms of utilitarianism.

U7 is a *consequentialist* moral principle. It makes the normative status of acts depend entirely upon their consequences and the consequences that would have been produced by their alternatives. Under U7, there can be no appeal to such features as "being a murder," or "being a lie," or "being in accord with nature." The only morally relevant feature of *teleological* actions is to be found among their consequences and the consequences of their alternatives. Another way of putting this point is to say that U7 is a *teleological* moral principle.

U7 is also a *hedonistic* doctrine. It makes the normative status of an *hedonistic* act depend entirely upon how much pleasure and pain it would cause, as compared with the pleasure and pain that would be produced by its alternatives. Act utilitarianism has been attacked on this point, and in the next chapter we will consider this objection in some detail.[2]

Before closing this chapter, however, let us compare U7 with some principles that are easy to confuse with it, but that are in fact quite different from it.

Defective Formulations of Act Utilitarianism

Some people speak as if act utilitarianism were the doctrine of "the greatest happiness of the greatest number." This apparently means that they think utilitarianism is the view expressed by this principle:

U_8:   An act is right if and only if it produces the greatest happiness of the greatest number.

This principle is different from U_7. With U_7, it does not matter how many people enjoy the pleasure caused by an act. If 10 people feel 10 hedons each as a result of some act, and if no other pleasures or pains result, then that act has a utility of $+100$. If 100 people feel 1 hedon each as a result of some act, and if no other pleasures or pains result, then that act also has a utility of $+100$. According to U_7, neither of these acts is morally preferable to the other. The wider distribution of pleasure in the second case does not add to the value of the act. If some alternative to these acts makes one person feel pleasure worth 101 hedons, and produces no pain, then it is to be preferred to either of the others. With U_8, however, the wider distribution of pleasure would apparently make a difference.

[handwritten margin note: the mac people happy is made important then the level of happiness]

Thus, U_8 is clearly different from U_7. However, it was said earlier that U_8 is "garbled." Let us consider why this is so. The main trouble with U_8 is that it requires us to maximize two independent variables. On the one hand, it suggests that right acts must produce "the greatest happiness." This may be understood to mean that right acts have higher utility than their alternatives. But U_8 also suggests that right acts must distribute this happiness to "the greatest number." This apparently means that when a person performs a morally right act, he makes more people happy than he would have if he had performed any of its alternatives.

In some cases, the act with the highest utility will also result in the widest distribution of happiness. That is, of all the alternatives open to the agent at the time, there will be one that both has the highest utility and makes the most people happy. But, obviously, this need not be the case. It may turn out that the act that has the highest utility does not have the widest distribution of happiness. To see how this can happen, let us consider the following example. An agent has two alternatives open to her. She can do act a_1 or act a_2. Act a_1 would affect only 2 persons, but it would make each of them feel 50 hedons of pleasure, and no pain. So the utility of a_1 is $+100$. Act a_2 would affect 20 persons and would make each of them feel 4 hedons of pleasure, and no pain. Thus, the utility of

a_2 is +80. It does not matter what the acts actually are. The only thing that matters here is that the act that has the higher utility is not the act that makes more people happy.

In a case such as this, U_8 blows a fuse. It requires that the agent do the act that both produces the highest utility and makes the largest number of people happy. But in this case, a_1 has the higher utility but affects fewer people. Act a_2 makes "the greatest number" happy, but it doesn't produce "the greatest happiness" of that number. Thus, according to U_8, nothing the agent can do here would be morally right. And this is absurd. The trouble with U_8, then, is that it requires the agent to maximize two independent variables—utility and total number of people made happy. U_7, on the other hand, requires only that utility be maximized. In this case, it implies that the agent should do a_1, even though a_2 would make more people happy.

Another defective formulation of act utilitarianism is this:

U_9:   An act is right if and only if it causes more pleasure and less pain than any other act the agent could have done instead.

This principle is quite different from U_7, and it is also unacceptable. Here's why. Suppose an agent has three choices open to him on a certain occasion. We can call them a_1, a_2, and a_3. Once again, it doesn't matter what the acts actually are. Suppose these three acts would cause pleasure and pain in the following amounts:

a_1	100 hedons	99 dolors	+1	utility
a_2	90 hedons	10 dolors	+80	utility
a_3	10 hedons	9 dolors	+1	utility

According to U_7, the only right act in this case is a_2, since it has a much higher utility than either of its alternatives. But we must notice that a_2 does not cause more pleasure than a_1. In fact, a_1 causes 10 hedons more than a_2. Nor does a_2 produce less pain than a_3: a_3 produces only 9 dolors, whereas a_2 produces 10. Thus, a_2 satisfies neither condition stated in U_9. It does not produce more pleasure than each of its alternatives, and it does not produce less pain than each of its alternatives. Hence, on the basis of U_9, a_2 would not be right. Indeed, on the basis of U_9, nothing would be right in the case described. Once again, the trouble is that we are required to maximize two independent variables. In this case, we have to produce both the most pleasure and the least pain. In some cases, as we have seen, this is impossible.

One final point should be emphasized. With U_7, it does not matter who feels the pleasure and pain produced by an act. No preference is given to acts that cause pleasure to their agents, or to their family and friends. The only criterion of morally right action, according to U_7, is the total amount of utility that would be produced by an act, as compared with the amounts of utility that would be produced by its alternatives.

So much, then, for the formulation of act utilitarianism. Let us turn now to some arguments that are designed to show that it is false.

NOTES

1. John Stuart Mill, *Utilitarianism*, ed. Oskar Piest, (New York: Bobbs-Merrill, 1957), p. 10.

2. U_7 is sometimes called *hedonistic utilitarianism*. It is possible to formulate nonhedonistic versions of *utilitarianism* that are otherwise very much like U_7. For example, some philosophers, believing that happiness is different from pleasure, have claimed that right acts are acts that maximize the amount by which happiness exceeds unhappiness. This view has been called *eudaimonistic utilitarianism*. Other nonhedonistic versions may be formulated, but for our purposes it will be best to stick with the more classic hedonistic form of the theory.

3

Act Utilitarianism: Arguments Pro and Con

In Chapter II of *Utilitarianism*, Mill discusses several objections that have been directed against the utilitarian doctrine. In each case, he tries to show that the objection fails to refute this theory. Some of these objections and replies are important, not only because they show how utilitarianism can be defended against certain kinds of attack, but also because they help to make clear just what the utilitarian principle says.

The "Doctrine of Swine" Objection

Mill introduces the first objection by admitting that some of his opponents feel "inveterate dislike" for the utilitarian doctrine:

> To suppose that life has (as they express it) no higher end than pleasure—no better and nobler object of desire and pursuit—they designate as utterly mean and grovelling; as a doctrine worthy only of swine.[1]

Before considering Mill's reply to this objection, we should try to develop a clear account of the problem these objectors see. Just what are they trying to say? What, according to them, is wrong with utilitarianism? One way to interpret the "doctrine of swine" objection would be to take it as an assertion that utilitarianism must be false, since it entails that pleasure is "the end of life" when in fact pleasure is not the "end of life." But to put the objection in this way would be rather unhelpful. What does it mean to say that pleasure is "the end of life"? Did Mill ever commit himself one way or the other on this question? It isn't clear.

Interpreting the objection in another way may be more promising. As we have seen, according to principle U7, the only considerations relevant to the determination of the normative status of an act are the amounts of pleasure and pain it would produce, and the amounts of pleasure and pain its alternatives would produce. According to U7, nothing else makes any moral difference. Many philosophers have felt that this is a serious defect in utilitarianism. In their view, things other than the amounts of pleasure and pain an act would produce do make a difference in the normative status of that act. For example, some of these philosophers have claimed that "being in accord with virtue," or "being natural," or "being harmonious," may serve to elevate the normative status of an act, whether or not the act causes any pleasure. Considerations such as these, it has been claimed, also play a role in the determination of the rightness or wrongness of an act. Hence, it is not the case that the *only* considerations relevant to a determination of an act's normative status are the amounts of pleasure and pain it and its alternatives would produce.

An example may help put the issue into sharper focus. Suppose an old woman finds herself near death. She has a large fortune, and her only living relatives are two distant nephews she has never met before. She calls the two men to her bedside, and asks each what he would do with the money if he were to receive the inheritance. The first nephew says he would use the money to support his research into the origins of the universe. The second nephew says he would use the money to buy food, alcohol, and party hats. Then he would celebrate wildly until all the money was spent.

The objectors claim that if we apply U7 to this case, it implies that the only right act for the old woman is to finance the debauchery of the second nephew. This follows from the fact that more pleasure would be produced by using the money for this purpose than would be produced by giving it to the first nephew. But, according to the objectors, the result generated by the application of U7 is morally wrong. Financing the second nephew's party is not the right thing for the old woman to do. Rather, it would be better for her to give the money to the first nephew, even though doing so would produce much less pleasure. Hence, the objectors conclude, U7 is false.

This objection is based on the idea that, in some cases at least, considerations other than how much pleasure and pain an act would produce are relevant to the determination of the normative status of that act. In the example, the objectors would say that the fact that the first nephew would gain knowledge and would act virtuously make it preferable to give him the money instead of giving it to the other nephew. The other nephew might obtain a lot of pleasure as a result of having the money; nevertheless, he would be acting in an undesirable way. Hence, giving him the money would be wrong, contrary to what U7 seems to imply.

We can put this objection into the form of an argument:

"Doctrine of swine" objection

(1) If U_7 were true, the only morally relevant considerations would be how much pleasure and pain an act and its alternatives would produce.

(2) It is not the case that the only morally relevant considerations are how much pleasure and pain an act and its alternatives would produce.

(3) Therefore, U_7 is not true.

This objection is logically *valid*. That is, the conclusion follows from the premises: if both (1) and (2) are true, then (3) must be true as well. But are the premises true? In other words, is the argument *sound*? Now, perhaps, we are in a better position to consider how Mill replies to the "doctrine of swine" objection.

Mill responds by drawing a distinction between the "quality" of a pleasure and the "quantity" of a pleasure:

> It is quite compatible with the principle of utility to recognize the fact, that some *kinds* of pleasure are more desirable and more valuable than others. It would be absurd that while, in estimating all other things, quality is considered as well as quantity, the estimation of pleasures should be supposed to depend upon quantity alone.[2]

Mill seems to be suggesting that each episode of pleasure can be evaluated from at least two distinct points of view. On the one hand, we can enquire into the amount of pleasure that the episode contains. Presumably, we would determine this amount by considering the intensity of the pleasure and its duration. If we look at pleasure in this way, we are considering only its *quantity*.

On the other hand, we can enquire into the kind of pleasure the episode contains. Is it a sensual pleasure? An intellectual pleasure? An aesthetic pleasure? What sort of thing is the object of the pleasure? If we look at pleasure in this way, we are considering the *quality* of the pleasure.

We can refine and develop Mill's point by making some assumptions. Let us suppose that each episode of pleasure can be measured on three scales. The first scale is *duration*. We can say of any episode of pleasure that it lasts a certain amount of time. Perhaps the pleasure of a good meal will last for one hour; the pleasure that one derives from hearing a beautiful piece of music may last for several hours; some sensual pleasures may last for no more than a minute or two. We can assign a number to each episode of pleasure on the basis of its duration.

Perhaps that number will be the total number of minutes that the episode lasts.

Second, we can measure each episode of pleasure on a scale of *intensity*. This presents some rather serious technical and even conceptual problems, but perhaps it can be done. Perhaps someone will develop a polygraph-like machine with electrodes on it that can be connected to various parts of the body of the person whose pleasure is to be measured. Then this person could drink the wine, read the poem, or do whatever is to cause the pleasure we want to evaluate. Then we would look at the dials or the graph line and read the intensity rating of the pleasure being experienced. On this basis, we could assign to the episode a number representing its intensity as measured on our second scale.

If we multiply the number representing the duration by the number representing the intensity, we obtain a figure that represents the total quantity of pleasure in the episode. We multiply these figures for the following reason: We want to say that if two pleasures are equally intense, but one lasts twice as long as the other, the longer one contains twice as much pleasure. Equally, if two pleasures last equally long, but one is twice as intense as the other, we want to say that the more intense one contains twice as much pleasure as the less intense one. If an episode of pleasure is three times as long and twice as intense as another, we say it contains six times as much pleasure. Multiplying intensity by duration allows us to say these things.

When we measure pleasure in this way, we are only measuring quantity. But Mill also wants us to take quality into account. How can this be done? We must assume that for each episode of pleasure there is a number that represents its quality. Perhaps a "low" pleasure, such as one of the pleasures allegedly enjoyed by those who engage in lascivious behavior, would rate a 1 or a 2. A "higher" pleasure, such as the pleasure one receives from exercising his intellect, would be scored a 20 or a 25. An even "higher" pleasure, such as the pleasure we experience when we behave nobly, would rate a 50 or a 60. In each case, the numbers represent the quality of the pleasure being felt.

There are profound problems with this proposal. Some of these problems are of a rather practical nature; others are more conceptual. The basic practical problem is that there is no clear method by which the quality rating of a given kind of pleasure can be determined. Furthermore, different persons would undoubtedly come to different conclusions, even about the relative quality ranking of different sorts of pleasure. Mill suggests a way of dealing with this problem. He proposes that one kind of pleasure is of higher quality than another kind of pleasure if and only if most people who have experienced both kinds of pleasure prefer the one to the other. Mill goes on to assert that if this test were applied, we would find that the pleasures that "employ the higher faculties" are of higher quality than the pleasures that "employ the lower faculties."

However, Mill's assertion is open to serious doubts. For one thing, in order to make use of his test, we would have to be able to determine, with respect to the different pleasures to be tested, that they are equal in intensity and duration. Otherwise, the preference might be based on considerations other than quality alone. Yet it is not clear that such a determination can be made. Furthermore, it is not clear that people would always, or even most of the time, prefer higher-quality to lower-quality pleasure. For example, suppose you have been enjoying a high-quality pleasure all day, and have become bored with it. You might like to enjoy a lower-quality pleasure for a little while, just for a change of pace. It would be extremely difficult in practice to insure that no such factors influence the results of the test. In general, therefore, Mill's test would be very hard to apply.

The basic conceptual problem with the quality-measurement proposal is that it is not clear that it makes any sense to say that one pleasure is "twice as high in quality" as another. When measuring amounts of quality, it might make sense to say that a certain pleasure ranks above some other pleasures and below still others. But some philosophers have said that it would not make sense to assign numerical values to these ratings. Yet according to our proposal, assigning such values would have to make sense.

Assuming that the concept of quality can be made clear, we can go on to describe how Mill might want to use it. If we want to find out how many hedons a given episode of pleasure contains, we must first determine its intensity, duration, and quality. Then we multiply the figures representing each value. Their product represents the total number of hedons in that episode of pleasure. Similar calculations would be employed to determine the number of dolors in each episode of pain.

The utility of an act, as we have already seen, is the result of subtracting the total number of dolors it would produce from the total number of hedons it would produce. In other words, you consider all the episodes of pleasure the act would cause. For each such episode, you calculate the number of hedons in it as described above. Then you add the resulting hedonic values. The result is the total number of hedons caused by the act. Then you consider all the episodes of pain the act would cause, and perform similar calculations to determine the total number of dolors the act would produce. Then you subtract the dolors from the hedons. The result is the utility of the act. Thus, an act's utility is not just a measure of *how much* pleasure it would produce. It is also, indirectly, a measure of the *quality* of the pleasure it would produce. Acts that produce higher-quality pleasure, other things being equal, have higher utility than acts that produce lower-quality pleasure.

Perhaps it is already clear how this maneuver, if it could be defended, would help Mill's defense against the "doctrine of swine" objection. Mill could say that the first premise of this argument is false. U_7 does not imply that the only morally relevant consideration is *how much* pleasure and pain an act and its alternatives would cause. Rather, according to utilitarianism, the only morally relevant considerations are how much and *what kind* of pleasure and pain an act and its alternatives would cause. Quantity alone is not the final arbiter of normative status. Quality counts too.

To see how this would work in a concrete case, let us return to the rich old woman and her two nephews. Mill could admit that if we consider only the amounts of pleasure that would be produced by the woman's actions, perhaps U_7 would imply that she should finance the second nephew's celebration. But now we can see that Mill could deny that his version of utilitarianism has this consequence. He could say that we should consider not only the quantity of pleasure that would be produced by the act, we should also consider the quality of that pleasure. When we do this, we discover that the woman should not finance the party. She should support the research of the first nephew.

The old woman has, let us suppose, three main alternatives. She can will that her money be used for the first nephew's research; she can will that it be used for the second nephew's party; or she can "take it with her." If she performs the second act, the second nephew will hold his party. In doing so, he will experience a moderately long-lasting, very intense, low-quality pleasure. Perhaps its duration would have a rating of 75, its intensity 50, and its quality 2. The utility of the act that causes all this pleasure, assuming it does not cause any pain or any other pleasure, would be $75 \times 50 \times 2$, or 7,500.

The act of giving the money to the first nephew would not cause as intense a pleasure, Mill would admit. Perhaps the pleasure the nephew would derive from doing his research would be worth only a 25 on the intensity scale. But this pleasure would be of very high quality, since it would be pleasure taken in the exercise of the intellect. So we can say that the first nephew's pleasure might receive a quality rating of 25. Let us also say that the first nephew's pleasure would last as long as the second nephew's pleasure. Assuming that no other pleasure or pain would be produced by the woman's act of giving the first nephew the money, the resulting utility would be 46,875. Clearly, this figure is much higher than the utility of the woman's giving the money to the second nephew, as well as the utility of her taking it with her. Thus, U_7 implies that the old woman should use the money to support the research, not the celebration.

If we consider not only quantity, but quality as well, then utilitarianism does not tell us to try to obtain as much pleasure as possible. Rather, it tells us to try to bring into the world the best combination of quality and quantity of pleasure. We can follow utilitarianism without living like pigs.

The "Too High for Humanity" Objection

Let us turn next to another objection discussed by Mill. He describes another class of objectors as claiming that "it is exacting too much to require that people shall always act from the inducement of promoting the general interests of society."[3] Mill says that these critics charge that the standard set by utilitarianism is "too high for humanity." What, then, is their objection?

These objectors seem to be claiming that utilitarianism requires that we always act from a certain kind of motive. Apparently, they think that utilitarianism implies that we act rightly only if our actions are motivated by a desire to "promote the general interests of society." What they mean, surely, is that our motive must be to perform that act that, of all the alternatives open to us, will produce the greatest utility. In other words, our actions must be motivated by a desire to perform that act that, of all those open to us on the occasion, would bring about the greatest balance of pleasure over pain in society at large.

But it appears that it is only rarely that anyone acts with such a lofty motive. Most of the time, we give little thought to such matters. I treat my neighbors with respect, but not to "promote the general interests of society." Rather, I do it because I like them, and because I prefer to get along well with my neighbors. You give to the United Fund, but your motive is, perhaps, to avoid feeling guilty. Do these instances mean that we have done wrong, according to utilitarianism? If so, utilitarianism seems to be mistaken.

The objection can be reformulated as follows:

"Too high for humanity" objection

(1) If U_7 is true, then an act is morally right only if it is motivated by a desire to promote the general interests of society.

(2) Some acts are morally right even though they are not motivated by a desire to promote the general interests of society.

(3) Therefore, U_7 is not true.

This argument is valid too. But Mill replies, in effect, by rejecting the first premise and thereby showing the argument to be unsound. He says that the "too high for humanity" objection is based upon a confusion. Those who object in this way confuse

the rule of action with the motive of it. It is the business of ethics to tell us what are our duties, or by what test we may know them; but no system of ethics requires that the sole motive of all we do shall be a feeling of duty.[4]

Mill's point seems to be straightforward and simple. There is a difference between requiring, on the one hand, that our actions be in accord with, or consistent with, a certain rule of action, and requiring, on the other hand, that our actions be motivated by a desire to be in accord with that principle. He claims that utilitarianism requires only that our actions be consistent with U7 It requires only that we perform, on each occasion, an action whose utility is at least as high as the utility of any other action we could have performed instead. Utilitarianism says nothing about what sort of motives we should have when we perform an act.

This seems to be an adequate reply to the objection, but it also points out some rather odd features of the utilitarian position. Suppose an assassin is trying to murder a beloved religious leader. The shot misses, it hits a rock, and out flows some oil. Those watching check more closely, and they discover a previously unknown oil reserve containing enough oil to make them all rich and happy. Everyone then shares in the wealth and lives happily ever after. In this case, the act had a terrible motive, but it nevertheless produced a tremendous amount of utility, far more than would have been produced by anything else the assassin could have done instead. According to U7, what he did was morally right!

On the other hand, suppose a doctor goes to the jungle to heal the villagers. Unknowingly, she carries some disease to them. As a result of her visit, the villagers catch the disease and suffer. In this case the doctor's motive may have been excellent, but U7 says she did the wrong thing. She should have stayed home.

Thus, Mill's response to the "too high for humanity" objection is this: Premise (1) is false. U7 does not imply that right acts must be motivated by a desire to promote the general interests of society. U7 implies only that right acts in fact do promote the general interests of society more than their alternatives would have. The motives underlying these acts have very little to do with their normative status.

Some readers may feel that Mill's response to this objection is unsatisfactory. They may think his answer leaves him open to a further objection. Shall we then praise the would-be assassin? Shall we blame the doctor? The assassin does not deserve to be praised for trying to kill the religious leader, even if his act happened to have some good results. The doctor does not deserve to be blamed for trying to help the natives, even if her act happened to have some bad results. Surely, their motives do make a moral difference.

This objection is also based on a misunderstanding. U7 does not say that we should praise people for performing right acts, and it does not say that we should blame them for performing wrong ones. In fact, U_7 gives clear directions about when we should praise and when we should blame. Praising someone is an act. U_7 implies, therefore, that we should praise someone if and only if doing so would produce at least as much utility as anything else we could do instead. Similarly, we should blame someone if and only if doing that would produce at least as much utility as anything else we could do instead. Thus, it may be right for us to blame or even punish the would-be assassin, even though his act was right. And it may be right to praise or even reward the doctor, even though her act was wrong. We cannot conclude from utilitarianism that right acts all deserve praise, and wrong ones blame.

The "Lack of Time" Objection

Toward the end of Chapter II of *Utilitarianism*, Mill discusses a third interesting objection. This one can be called the "lack of time" objection. Those who offer this objection hold "that there is not time, previous to action, for calculating and weighing the effects of any line of conduct on the general happiness."[5]

It certainly does seem that in many cases it would be impractical to attempt to determine what all your alternatives are, and what the utility of each is. For example, suppose a man is standing by the side of a road. He notices an occupied baby carriage roll off the sidewalk and into the path of an oncoming cement mixer. He realizes that no one else will be able to save the baby. His dilemma is to decide what to do. Surely, it would be pointless of him to take out a pad and pencil and attempt to draw up a list of all his alternatives and their utilities! For it would take a long time to list even a few of the alternatives, and it would be almost impossible for him to determine the utility of any of them. Who can say how much pleasure and pain would result from his calling for an ambulance, or his shouting at the truck driver? By the time he's calculated the utility of just two or three of his alternatives, the baby will have been seriously injured.

If utilitarianism implies that before we set out to act, we should always list all of our alternatives and calculate the utility of each, then utilitarianism is morally wrong. For in some cases, such as the one just described, that would not be the right thing to do. Indeed, whenever quick action is called for, the calculation of utilities would be wrong. Thus, utilitarianism seems to require us to act in a way that will often yield bad results.

We can formulate this objection as follows:

"Lack of time" objection

(1) If U_7 were true, then it would always be right for us to calculate the utilities of all our alternatives before acting.

(2) Sometimes it is not right to calculate the utilities of all our alternatives before acting.

(3) Therefore, U_7 is not true.

Mill's response to this objection is rather spirited:

> It is truly a whimsical supposition that, if mankind were agreed in considering utility to be the test of morality, they would remain without any agreement as to what *is* useful, and would take no measures for having their notions on the subject taught to the young and enforced by law and opinion. There is no difficulty in proving any ethical standard whatever to work ill if we suppose universal idiocy to be conjoined with it; but on any hypothesis short of that, mankind must by this time have acquired positive beliefs as to the effects of some actions on their happiness.[6]

What Mill seems to be saying is that premise (1) is false. Utilitarianism does not imply that we are obligated to calculate the utilities of our actions before we decide what to do. Indeed, it can be argued, in some cases at least, that utilitarianism implies that we are obligated to avoid calculating utilities. For example, in the cement-mixer case, the man's alternatives and the utility of each, might be as follows:

remove baby carriage from road	+50
shout at truck driver	−10
cover eyes to avoid seeing crash	−8
call ambulance	−9
calculate utilities of alternatives	−10

Here we can see that principle U_7 implies that it would be wrong to calculate the utilities of the alternatives. This follows from the fact that the utility of performing that action is lower than the utility of removing the baby carriage from the road. The only right act, according to U_7, is the act of saving the baby.

Mill suggests that any reasonable, reflective, properly trained adult would know what to do in a case such as this one. He would use the moral principles he learned as a child. There is no need to use U_7 to figure out what to do in such a case. U_7 is not designed to be used in this fashion.

This way of dealing with the "lack of time" objection seems to raise an even more serious problem for Mill. If U_7 is not intended to serve as a guide to action, or as a principle upon which we make our moral decisions, then what good is it? What is the point of formulating a theory of moral rightness if we don't use it to determine what actions would be morally right?

In order to answer these questions, we must distinguish between two easily confused sorts of enquiry. On the one hand, there is what we can call *practical normative ethics*. This is the attempt to formulate a *morally useful* principle about the normative status of actions. A morally useful principle would be one that could be learned easily, that would be relatively easy to use, and that would generally lead people to make morally correct decisions.

On the other hand, there is what we can call *theoretical normative ethics*. This is the attempt to formulate a *true* principle about the normative status of actions. If our goal is to state a true principle, then we have no reason to be concerned about such issues as whether it is overly complicated, or hard to learn, or difficult to apply. We will be concerned only about whether or not it states what are in fact the necessary and sufficient conditions for the moral rightness of concrete acts.

The distinction between theoretical and practical normative ethics may perhaps be elucidated by analogy to a distinction we can draw among scientific principles. In medicine, doctors may seek a generally useful diagnostic principle about a certain disease. Such a principle might look like this:

M_1:   A patient has measles if and only if he has spotty skin, elevated temperature, and runny nose.

Principle M_1 does not purport to explain *why* a patient has measles. It does not give an account of the cause of measles, nor does it provide a completely accurate account of who has measles. But M_1 may be very useful. It may be close enough to the truth to provide a good guide to action. Doctors may use it as a quick guide when diagnosing measles.

On the other hand, those who do research in medicine may want to discover a more profound principle about measles. Perhaps they seek a principle that looks more like this:

M_2:   A patient has measles if and only if her blood contains more than 1,500 healthy measles germs per ounce.

Clearly, M_2 could not be used on a wide scale for the quick diagnosis of suspected cases of measles. It might take days to perform the blood tests that would be necessary in determining whether or not there are indeed more than 1,500 healthy measles germs per ounce. But this is no defect in M_2; it may still be a true principle about measles, and it may be useful for purposes other than quick diagnosis.

Similarly the philosopher who tries to discover a true principle about the normative status of actions may not be concerned with whether or not his principle is easy to learn or apply. He may be concerned only with finding the truth. Perhaps he just wants to know what the connection is, if any, between rightness, on the one hand, and the production of pleasure and pain, on the other. If the resulting principle is complex, inapplicable, hard to remember, or unlearnable, then he should not advocate its use as a practical guide. But he may still be convinced that it is true.

So we can see that there is some merit in the "lack of time" objection. If Mill intended his principle to be a guide to action—that is, a principle of practical normative ethics—then this objection points out a defect in Mill's proposal. This defect is that U_7 is too hard to apply; it is not well suited to the task of helping us make quick moral decisions. For this purpose, it might be better to use the golden rule, or the maxim of moderation in all things, or the Ten Commandments.

On the other hand, if Mill had been engaged in theoretical normative ethics, then the "lack of time" objection could be rebutted easily. For the inapplicability of the principle in no way detracts from its truth (assuming that it is true).

Unfortunately, it is not clear whether Mill was engaged in practical normative ethics or in theoretical normative ethics. Some passages of *Utilitarianism* suggest one, and other passages suggest the other. So we simply cannot tell whether the "lack of time" objection has any bearing on the problem Mill was attempting to solve. For our purposes, however, we can assume that U_7 was intended to be a principle of theoretical normative ethics. If we take it in this way, we must conclude that none of the objections discussed in this chapter refutes it.

Mill's Proof

From the absence thus far of a satisfactory refutation of Mill's theory, we should not, of course, infer that the theory is true. For all we know, it may still be false. We have not yet seen an argument in favor of U_7.

In Chapter IV of *Utilitarianism*, Mill presents some considerations that he apparently hopes will be sufficient to convince his readers of the truth of the utilitarian doctrine. Some commentators have treated this passage as if it were a straightforward argument for Mill's theory. Most of these commentators have claimed that the argument, so understood, is extremely weak. Others have insisted that Mill never intended to present an argument for his view. These commentators have interpreted the passage in question in a variety of different ways. Let us look more closely at this controversial part of Mill's book.

Mill's aim in this passage *seems* to be to establish, or at least make plausible, the conclusion that "the general happiness is the sole criterion of morality." This claim can be interpreted to mean that the only mark of morally right action is the degree to which it promotes the general happiness. In other words, U7 is true.

Mill starts out by drawing an analogy between visibility and desirability:

> The only proof capable of being given that an object is visible is that people actually see it. The only proof that a sound is audible is that people hear it; and so of the other sources of our experience. In like manner, I apprehend, the sole evidence it is possible to produce that anything is desirable is that people do actually desire it.[7]

Mill's point here, according to one interpretation, is this: From the fact that people see something, we can validly infer that it is visible. By analogy, from the fact that people desire something, we can validly infer that it is desirable. But, of course, Mill goes on to point out that people do in fact desire happiness. Hence, he infers that happiness is desirable. Saying that happiness is desirable, of course, is equivalent to saying that happiness is good. And this is what Mill concludes: "Each person's happiness is a good to that person. . . ."[8]

In order to make this part of the argument fit with later parts, it is necessary to make a few minor modifications in Mill's terminology. When these alterations are made and some suppressed premises are added, the result is as follows:

Mill's Proof: The Analogical Argument

(1) Each person desires his own happiness.

(2) If each person desires his own happiness, then each person can desire his own happiness.

(3) If each person can desire his own happiness, then each person's happiness is desirable for that person.

(4) If each person's happiness is desirable for that person, then each person's happiness is a good for that person.

(5) Therefore, each person's happiness is a good for that person.

When formulated in this way, this part of the argument seems to be logically valid. If all the premises are true, then apparently the conclusion must be true as well. It may seem that all the premises are true. Let us take a closer look at them.

The first premise is at least close to being true. Almost everyone does desire his own happiness. This can be understood to mean that everyone wants to be happy. Let us grant this premise, even though there may be a few masochists who don't want to be happy.

The second premise is an instance of the general principle that if something in fact does happen, then it can happen. In other words, whatever is true is possible. Surely we must admit that if people in fact do desire their own happiness, then this is something they can do. Thus, we must grant (2).

The third premise is an instance of what may be called the "can-able principle." From the fact that some paint can be scrubbed, it follows that it is scrubbable. From the fact that a mountain can be climbed, it follows that it is climbable. From the fact that some paper can be erased, it follows that it is erasable. In general, for many English verbs this schema seems to be true: "If *x* can be——ed, then *x* is——able." Sometimes, of course, we use "ible" instead of "able" as the suffix. The third premise of the argument is the application of this general principle to the case of "desire." From the fact that something can be desired, we infer that it is desirable. Barring certain complications we will discuss in a moment, this seems to be true.

The fourth premise is based on the idea that "desirable" means pretty much the same as "good." What's desirable for a person is what's good for him. Thus, if his own happiness is desirable for each person, then his own happiness is good for each person. So, (4) seems fairly plausible.

The fifth line is a conclusion that is derived from the preceding four premises. Assuming that there is nothing amiss in these earlier premises, it would seem that (5) follows validly from them. Each person's happiness is a good to that person.

The next part of the argument builds upon the conclusion of the part just discussed. Having established that each person's happiness is a good to that person, Mill proceeds to attempt to prove that "happiness is one of the criteria of morality." By this, Mill seems to mean that the production of happiness is one of the things that makes actions morally right. Mill argues that

> each person, so far as he believes it to be attainable, desires his own happiness. This, however, being a fact, we have not only all the proof which the case admits of, but all which it is possible to require, that happiness is a good, that each person's happiness is a good to that person, and the general happiness, therefore, a good to the aggregate of all persons. Happiness has made out its title as *one* of the ends of conduct and, consequently, one of the criteria of morality.[9]

Put in very simple terms, the argument seems to be as follows:

Mill's Proof: The Aggregation Argument

(5) Each person's happiness is a good to that person.

(6) If each person's happiness is a good to that person, then the general happiness is a good to the aggregate of people.

(7) If the general happiness is a good to the aggregate of people, then the general happiness is a criterion of morality.

(8) Therefore, the general happiness is a criterion of morality.

In the final part of his argument, Mill claims that everything we desire is desired either as a part of or as a means to happiness. Mill then seems to claim that since this is the case, nothing other than happiness is a criterion of morality. Combining this conclusion with (8), he arrives at his ultimate conclusion: happiness is the sole criterion of morality. By this, he seems to mean that an act is morally right if and only if it maximizes happiness. In other words, U_7 is true. So the last stage of the argument is as follows:

Mill's Proof: The Parts and Means Argument

(9) People can desire nothing other than parts of or means to happiness.

(10) If people can desire nothing other than parts of or means to happiness, then nothing other than happiness is a criterion of morality.

(11) Therefore, nothing other than happiness is a criterion of morality.

(12) Therefore, happiness is the sole criterion of morality. (from (8) and (11))

This part of the argument is extremely obscure. Mill does not make clear what he means when he says that something is desired "as a part of happiness." Nor is it clear why he thinks (if indeed he does) that (10) is true.

Mill has been accused of committing some pretty serious blunders in this argument. The main charge directed against the analogical part of the argument is the charge of equivocation. Many commentators have claimed that Mill fails to distinguish between two different senses of the word "desirable." The two senses in question are easily distinguished. In one sense, to say that something is desirable is just to say that it can be desired:

D_1: x is desirable$_1$ =df. x can be desired.

Obviously, just about everything is desirable$_1$. In the second sense, desirability is a value property. Not everything is desirable$_2$:

D_2: x is desirable$_2$ =df. x is worthy of being desired.

The objection to the analogical part of the argument now goes as follows: If "desirable" in lines (3) and (4) of the argument is understood as "desirable$_1$," then (3) is true, but (4) is false. For according to this interpretation, (4) would mean the same as:

(4') If each person's happiness can be desired by that person, then each person's happiness is a good for that person.

Surely, however, it does not follow from the fact that people *can* desire their own happiness that their happiness is a good for them. In general, we should say that people can desire plenty of things that are not good for them at all.

On the other hand, if "desirable" in (3) and (4) means "desirable₂," then (4) is true but (3) is false. For according to this interpretation, (3) would mean the same as:

(3') If each person can desire his own happiness, then each person's happiness is worthy of being desired by that person.

It should be obvious that it does not follow from the fact that people can desire happiness that happiness is worthy of being desired. So, (3') is false.

Finally, if "desirable₁" is meant in line (3) and "desirable₂" is meant in line (4), then both lines are true. But the argument is then no longer valid; it then suffers from equivocation. Thus, no matter how we interpret this part of the argument, it does not succeed in showing that each person's happiness is a good for that person.

The problems with the aggregation part of the argument are almost as serious. Let us assume, for the moment, that Mill has established that each person's happiness is a good for that person. In other words, let us assume that (5) has been proved. Still, (6) strikes many readers as being rather odd. Some have claimed that (6) is an example of the *fallacy of composition*. This fallacy is the error of inferring from the fact that all the members of a group have a certain property, that the group as a whole has that property. These statements are clear examples of the fallacy of composition:

(13) If every part of the car is in good working order, then the car is in good working order.

(14) If every player on the team is ready for the big game, then the team is ready for the big game.

(15) If every brick in the chimney weighs less than ten pounds, then the chimney weighs less than ten pounds.

It is easy to see that (13) may be false—perhaps the parts of the car are not assembled. Similarly, (14) may be false—perhaps the team has no pitcher. There should be no need to point out why (15) might be false.

If Mill's argument involved a pure instance of the fallacy of composition, (6) might look like this:

(6') If each person's happiness is a good, then the general happiness is a good.

But, as we have seen, (6) is slightly different from this. It contains references to "each person" and "the aggregate of people." Whether (6) involves the fallacy of composition or not is unclear. Nevertheless, it seems to embody some sort of fallacy.

But the main puzzle with (6) is not that it is fallacious. The real problem is that (6) is so obscure. What does Mill mean when he speaks of "the general happiness"? Is it reasonable to suppose that each person's happiness is a part of it? And what does he mean when he says that the general happiness is a good *to* the aggregate of people? None of this is clear enough to be evaluated.

So it seems that a serious question can be raised concerning each main part of Mill's proof. The first part, the analogical argument, seems to involve the fallacy of equivocation. "Desirable" has to be used in two different senses in order for the premises to be true. The second part, the aggregation argument, seems to involve something similar to the fallacy of composition, though it is hard to tell for sure. Finally, the third part, the parts and means argument, is so obscure as to make evaluation difficult. If we interpret Mill's proof in this way, we must conclude that it is an extremely weak argument.

In defense of Mill, it has been pointed out that he states, "Questions of ultimate ends do not admit of proof, in the ordinary acceptation of the term."[10] In other passages he seems to express the view that a basic moral principle, such as U_7, simply cannot be proved. If this is indeed Mill's view, then the passages we have been discussing should not be interpreted as a proof of the utilitarian doctrine. But in this case, one wonders what they are supposed to be.

In conclusion, let us reflect upon what we have found in this chapter. We have seen that several standard objections to act utilitarianism can be answered. In some cases, the objections admittedly do raise some puzzling questions. However, a thoroughgoing, consistent utilitarian need not feel too embarrassed by these questions. We have also seen that Mill's main argument in favor of utilitarianism (if it is an argument) is seriously defective. So far, then, the utilitarian doctrine has not been proved false and has not been proved true. In the next chapter, we'll consider some further arguments against it.

NOTES

1. John Stuart Mill, *Utilitarianism*, ed. Oskar Piest, (New York: Bobbs-Merrill, 1957), p. 11.

2. *Ibid.*, p. 12.

3. *Ibid.*, p. 23.

4. *Ibid.*

5. *Ibid.*, p. 30.
6. *Ibid.*, pp. 30–31.
7. *Ibid.*, p. 44.
8. *Ibid.*, p. 45.
9. *Ibid.*, pp. 44–45.
10. *Ibid.*, p. 44.

4

Problems for Act Utilitarianism

In the previous chapter we saw that several standard objections to act utilitarianism do not succeed in showing that doctrine to be false. Now let us turn to some other objections, which may prove to be more decisive.

Supererogatory Actions

Suppose that in the course of his daily rounds a mailman comes upon a burning house. The firemen believe that there is a baby in one of the upstairs rooms, but they cannot get close enough to save it. The flames are simply too intense. The mailman puts down his mailbag, dashes into the burning house, and saves the baby from a terrible fate. We may want to describe this action as being "beyond the call of duty," or "heroic." We say that such action is beyond the call of duty apparently because we feel that the mailman does not have any duty, or moral obligation, to behave in this way. The action is so difficult, and so dangerous, that we would not feel that he had shirked his duty if he had refrained from going in after the baby.

On the other hand, the act of saving the baby is certainly not wrong. We admire and praise the mailman for his heroism. We think he deserves a medal, or some special commendation, or a reward of some sort. His action is considered to be especially meritorious from the moral point of view.

Actions such as this are said to be *supererogatory*. To say that an action is supererogatory, then, is to say two main things about it. First, the agent is not morally obligated to perform it, in other words, he is permitted to refrain from performing it. Second, the action is morally praiseworthy; it would be a very good thing for it to be performed.

Any number of actions fit into this category. In wartime, a soldier may save the lives of his comrades by sacrificing his own. A businessman may make large investments in order to prevent a panic, knowing that his own fortune may be lost as a result. A person may undergo dangerous and painful surgery in order to provide a kidney to a sick child. In these cases, and in many others like them, we may want to say that the agent has performed a supererogatory action. He has done something we could not demand of him, yet something for which we are grateful. His action was beyond the call of duty.

The existence of supererogatory actions poses a serious problem for act utilitarianism. For act utilitarianism seems to imply that there cannot be any such actions. In a nutshell, the puzzle is this: If the allegedly supererogatory action really is so meritorious, then it must produce a lot of utility. But if it produces more utility than any other act the agent could have performed instead, then act utilitarianism implies that the agent is morally obligated to perform it. In this case, far from being "beyond the call of duty," the action is exactly what duty requires. On the other hand, if the allegedly supererogatory action does not produce more utility than each of its alternatives would have, then act utilitarianism implies that it is not morally right; the agent should not perform it at all. In this case, instead of being "beyond the call of duty," the act is simply inconsistent with the call of duty.

In order to make the problem clearer, let us reconsider the example of the mailman and the baby. Suppose the mailman has the following alternatives: first, he can attempt to enter the burning house and save the baby; second, he can try hard to put out the fire, and resolve to search for the baby as soon as it is safe to enter the house; third, he can get a rope ladder, throw it up to the window of the room containing the baby, and hope the baby will be able to figure out how to use it. The last alternative, of course, will not work. In addition to these alternatives, the mailman has innumerable trivial and irrelevant alternatives—such as going back to the post office—that have lower utility than any of the first three alternatives mentioned here.

For the purpose of this example, let us assume that the utilities of the mailman's alternatives are roughly as follows:

enter house and save baby	$+500$
help fight fire, save baby later	$+25$
throw rope ladder, hope for miracle	-10
go back to post office	-10

Given principle U_7, and our definitions D_1 and D_2 (see Chapter 2), we can prove that it is morally right, or permissible, for the mailman to save the baby in this case. It is morally wrong, or forbidden, for him to do any of the other acts listed. Finally, it is morally obligatory, or required, for him to save the baby. Hence, in this case act utilitarianism implies that the heroic act is not beyond the call of duty. Rather, it is just what duty requires. This seems wrong.

We can formulate one version of this objection as an argument:

Supererogation Objection

(1) If U_7 is true, the mailman in the example is morally obligated to save the baby.

(2) Since saving the baby is supererogatory, the mailman is not morally obligated to save the baby.

(3) Therefore, U_7 is not true.

There are several different ways in which act utilitarians might attempt to reply to this objection. For one, they might insist that our common-sense notion of supererogatory actions, or actions beyond the call of duty, is confused. Really, they might say, if the act will in fact maximize utility, it *is* obligatory. Our feeling that it is not obligatory, and our unwillingness to demand that people perform such acts, may stem from our knowledge that most people are simply unable to perform them. If an agent is genuinely unable to perform the act, then it is not one of his alternatives. Thus, U_7 would not imply that the act is obligatory. Since supererogatory actions are generally so difficult, and often impossible, we adopt the general policy of not blaming people who fail to perform them. Perhaps we feel that although a supererogatory act is morally required in any case in which the agent is able to perform it, there is simply no point in requiring it to be performed, since it is very likely that the agent won't be able to perform it, even if he wants to.

It is not clear that this sort of response is ultimately acceptable. Thus, the existence of supererogatory acts remains a problem for the act utilitarian.

Trivial Actions

Another class of actions provides a sort of mirror image of the last problem. As we have seen, U_7 passes moral judgment on *every* act. It implies, with respect to every action, that it is obligatory, permitted, or forbidden. Nothing escapes its notice. This feature of U_7 has some rather surprising consequences.

Suppose a girl comes into the kitchen early one morning. Sleepily, she opens the cupboard and looks for some breakfast cereal. She sees three boxes—Wheat Toasties, Rice Toasties, and Oat Toasties. She's never paid much attention to breakfast cereals, and she really doesn't care very much which cereal she eats, although she will get slightly more pleasure from eating the Oat Toasties than she will from eating either of the other cereals. Neither she nor anyone else will suffer any pain from any of the three possible cereal choices, although she will have a hunger pang if she eats nothing at all. Her main alternatives, then, and the utility of each, seem to be as follows:

eat Rice Toasties	$+\frac{1}{2}$
eat Wheat Toasties	$+\frac{1}{2}$
eat Oat Toasties	$+\frac{3}{4}$
skip breakfast	$-\frac{1}{2}$

Principle U_7 and our definitions entail that the girl is morally obligated to eat Oat Toasties for breakfast, and that she is morally forbidden to eat either of the other cereals or nothing at all. But many people find this result absurd. They feel that there is no moral obligation to eat Oat Toasties in a case such as this. That the girl might get slightly more pleasure from eating the Oat Toasties strikes many people as being morally irrelevant. The objection of such people to U_7 might be presented like this:

Triviality Objection

   (1) If U_7 is true, the girl is morally obligated to eat Oat Toasties.

   (2) The girl is not morally obligated to eat Oat Toasties.

   (3) Therefore, U_7 is not true.

One possible line of response to this argument involves the rejection of (2). Act utilitarians could insist that the girl in the example really is obligated to eat Oat Toasties. They could then try to explain away our contrary intuition by drawing a distinction between two kinds of actions. On the one hand, there are actions that are morally obligatory. On the other hand, there are actions that we are willing to demand of people. They could go on to say that we surely would not be willing to demand that the girl eat the Oat Toasties. Nor would we be willing to blame her if she failed to eat them. That's because the action is so trivial, has so few effects on others, and really isn't any of our business. In spite of this, act utilitarians could say, the girl is still morally obligated to eat the Oat Toasties. Although we are led to accept (2) as a result of confusing "demand-worthiness" with moral obligation, (2) is in fact false.

It is left to the reader to determine whether this is a satisfactory way of dealing with the triviality objection.

Promises

It is widely agreed that the practice of making and keeping promises
provides a number of serious problems for act utilitarianism. Before we
consider a rather general and abstract line of attack, let us consider a
somewhat bizarre but nevertheless quite instructive example.

Suppose a young man has been generously supported throughout
his college career by his kindly grandfather. As a graduation present, the
grandfather has taken the youth on a round-the-world sailboat trip. The
grandson is delighted to go on the trip, since he loves fishing. However,
a storm wrecks their boat, and they are washed ashore on a deserted
tropical island. The youth feels fit and healthy, but the ordeal is hard on
the grandfather. The old man weakens, and at last is on the verge of
death. He calls the youth to his side, and asks one last favor. "Before I
die," he says, "promise me that once I am gone you will bury my body in
a suitable grave, and say a prayer over it." "Certainly, Grandfather," says
the youth. "I promise that your remains will be treated with respect."
Then the grandfather dies.

The grandson reflects on his alternatives. He could treat the body as
he has promised. This would be somewhat painful, since it would require him to dig a grave, carry the grandfather's body to it, and then fill
it up again. That would entail a lot of hard work, and would produce no
pleasure at all. For the grandson, being a cold-hearted ingrate, would get
no pleasure from seeing the promise kept, and the grandfather, being
dead, is in no position to benefit from a proper burial. Since the island is
otherwise deserted, no one else will be affected in any way by the
grandson's action.

Another alternative would be to cut up the grandfather's body and
use it for bait. The grandson loves fishing, and would really like to do
some surf casting. Of course, he doesn't *need* to go fishing, since the
island is well stocked with bananas, pineapples, and mangoes. Nevertheless, he would enjoy using the body for this purpose. Furthermore, he is
so callous that he would feel no shame, horror, or disgust at thus misus-
ing the body of his deceased benefactor.

Of course, the grandson really has a very large supply of alternatives. We will consider only the main ones, and the utility of each:

use body for bait	+25
bury body, according to promise	−10
let body rot where it is	−2
throw body in sea	−1

Many decent people, if confronted with this example, would conclude that the grandson ought to treat the grandfather's body with respect, regardless of the amount of utility that would be produced. Since he has promised to bury it properly, he should fulfill his promise. Admittedly, we might allow that the obligation to keep the promise could be overridden by imminent danger of starvation or terrible pain involved in burying the body. But in this case, as it has been described, there simply aren't any such mitigating circumstances. The grandson has no excuse. He is morally obligated to bury the body as he promised, even though doing so will not maximize utility. So the objection is as follows:

Promise-to-the-Dead-Man Objection

(1) If U_7 is true, the grandson is not morally obligated to bury the body.

(2) The grandson is morally obligated to bury the body.

(3) Therefore, U_7 is not true.

Utilitarians may respond to this objection in any of several different ways. One line of response involves the denial of the first premise. It might be suggested, for example, that we have calculated the utilities incorrectly. We neglected to include such factors as the pain the grandson will feel when his conscience begins to bother him; the pain that will be caused when other people find out how horribly the youth has acted; the resulting disutility to the general practice of promising—for others will now be less likely to keep their promises as a result of the youth's example. Thus, we should have said that the utility of using the grandfather's body as bait is really -25, not $+25$.

This line of reply is not satisfactory. In the first place, the youth in our example will not be conscience-stricken. This follows from the fact that he is a cold and callous individual. Furthermore, if he is a utilitarian, he will come to the conclusion that he has done the right thing. So there is no reason to expect him to feel guilty. Second, if the island really is deserted, we may imagine that no one will ever find out that the youth has used his grandfather's body in this unusual way. So, in this particular case no disutility arises on that basis. Finally, there seems to be no reason to suppose that the youth's behavior will have any bad consequences for the practice of promising. Since no one else will know about his "evil" deed, no one else will be motivated by his example to break promises.

Another way in which utilitarians might respond to the promise-to-the-dead-man objection would be to deny (2). They might claim that in a case as odd as this one, there simply isn't any moral obligation to keep the promise. It is hard to pass judgment on this reply. We must simply reflect on the case and try to determine for ourselves whether the youth ought to keep the promise.

Before we leave this discussion of the promise-to-the-dead-man objection, a general point ought to be made. As stated, this objection involves a "desert island case." That is, we are asked to imagine a case in which the promiser and the promisee are the lone inhabitants of an otherwise deserted island. The function of this supposition is straightforward. We want to isolate our promise in such a way as to avoid certain complicating considerations. For example, we want a case in which the breaking of the promise will have negligible impact on the admittedly useful practice of promising. For another, we want to rule out the occurrence of emotional pain in bystanders who would hate to see a promise broken. Putting the grandson and the grandfather on a deserted island serves these purposes. But it should be clear that similar circumstances might occur in the heart of a crowded city. The central point of the promise-to-the-dead-man example remains the same as long as the utility of breaking the promise exceeds the utility of keeping it, and as long as the promise is one we intuitively feel to be binding.

Let us now consider a more general sort of problem about the utilitarian account of promising. It has been said that act utilitarianism misconstrues the source of the obligation to keep promises. Or, to put it more simply, it can be said that utilitarianism provides the wrong answer to the question "Why should I keep my promise?"

According to U_7, the only morally relevant feature of an act is its utility, as compared with the utilities of its alternatives. From this it seems to follow that if keeping some promise is morally right, then it is morally right simply because keeping that promise will produce more utility than breaking it would. So we can say that according to act utilitarianism, what makes it right to keep a promise, when it is right to do so, is simply the fact that doing so has higher utility than doing otherwise has. The source of the obligatoriness of promise keeping is to be found in its utility. You should keep your promise because doing so will be more useful than doing otherwise.

Many moralists find this unacceptable. They feel that we are bound to keep our promises, not because of the utility of doing so, but because of the fact that we have promised. To promise is to bind ourselves, or commit ourselves, to some course of action. We should keep our promises because we are thus bound, or committed, and not because of the utility that will be produced.

Of course, these moralists would admit, there are exceptional cases in which the utility of keeping the promise does seem to matter. For example, if a doctor promises to play tennis at noon, but is called upon to perform emergency surgery at 11:45, he may break his promise. And we may say that his excuse is based upon utilitarian considerations. Much more good would be produced by performing the surgery than by playing tennis. Equally, sometimes more utility is produced by keeping the promise. But in such cases, it seems that the fact that the promise has been made is more important, from the moral point of view, than the fact that keeping it would produce a lot of utility.

The objection may be put in this way:

Morality-of-Promises Objection

(1) If U_7 is true, then the only moral reason for keeping a promise is that doing so would maximize utility.

(2) It is not the case that the only moral reason for keeping a promise is that doing so would maximize utility; the fact that it would be a case of promise keeping is also a moral reason for keeping it.

(3) Therefore, U_7 is not true.

Objections such as this have traditionally been thought to constitute one of the most serious problems for act utilitarianism.

Before we conclude this discussion of promising, a general point may be in order. This has to do with the importance of promising. Our examples may be somewhat trivial, even frivolous, but it cannot be denied that promising plays a very significant role in our moral life. In business, law, education, and family life, we make, keep, and break promises all the time. In an extended sense, virtually every transaction involving trust can be seen as sort of an implicit promise. Thus, any moral theory that fails to give a reasonable account of the rightness of promise keeping is seriously defective. And so it appears that some facts about promising provide us with a major objection to act utilitarianism, as ordinarily understood.

Punishment

Reflection on the question of how punishment is to be justified is a rich source of moral perplexity. Doesn't it seem odd that we should feel obligated to bring pain into the world? And isn't it odder that we should feel that doing so is a suitable way of dealing with those whose only crime is that they brought some pain into the world? How can additional suffering help to make things better? The problem is especially acute for those who think that pain is bad in itself. How can we be justified in producing something intrinsically bad as a response to those whose main fault is that they produced something intrinsically bad? Can two evils make a good? These are puzzles indeed.

The utilitarian position on punishment is clear. We should punish when and only when nothing else we can do instead would produce more utility than punishing would. In other words, the act of punishing someone is judged entirely on its consequences. If it would produce more utility than anything else we can do, it is morally right. If something else would produce more utility than it would, then it is morally wrong.

Utilitarians have developed a general position on punishment. They point out three main ways in which punishment seems to be useful. In the first place, when we punish wrongdoers, we may help to *rehabilitate* them. That is, we may do something that tends to make them better persons. Rehabilitation surely has high utility. If we rehabilitate wrongdoers, they are less likely to produce pain in those with whom they subsequently deal. If we don't rehabilitate them, but simply allow them to proceed as before, they will go on mugging, robbing, or committing whatever crimes they like to commit. In this case, they will cause a lot of pain in other people. Thus, failing to rehabilitate has low utility. So utilitarians can claim that punishment is sometimes justified on the grounds that it will tend to rehabilitate wrongdoers, and that rehabilitation has higher utility than nonrehabilitation.

In the second place, punishment may produce utility because it serves to deter others from committing similar crimes. If we punish a kidnaper, some potential kidnapers may be motivated to take up other lines of work. Thus, fewer people will be kidnaped, and in turn people will in general be happier. In some cases, then, the *deterrent effect* of punishment helps to make the utility of punishment higher.

A third way in which punishment may produce high utility is somewhat less attractive. When a person has committed an ugly crime, we may want to see him suffer. We may enjoy knowing that he will be made to feel pain. In this way, we feel the pleasure of *vengeance*. If enough people enjoy seeing the wrongdoer suffer, the act of punishment may have very high utility. (It has been suggested, however, that the pleasure of vengeance is of very low quality. If this is correct, then such pleasure must be fairly intense and fairly widespread if it is to make a very significant contribution to the utility of the act of punishment.)

As with all forms of utilitarian justification, this justification of punishment is totally forward-looking. That is, the justification of punishment in any given case depends entirely upon what will happen as a result of the act of punishment, as compared with what would happen as a result of not punishing. The utilitarian justification of punishment pays attention only to the consequences of punishment and the consequences of nonpunishment. However, it often seems that facts about the past have an important bearing on whether or not some particular act of punishment would be justified. Most obviously, justification seems to depend upon whether or not the person to be punished actually committed the crime or not! If the utilitarian justification of punishment is required to look only into the *consequences* of punishing, isn't it possible under this theory to justify punishment in a case in which the person to be punished didn't commit the crime for which he is to be punished? To see the answer to this question, consider the following case.

Suppose a deranged killer has committed a series of horrible crimes. Finally, he commits suicide. The police suspect that the man who committed suicide is in fact the man who committed the crimes, but they have no proof. At this point, some otherwise law-abiding individuals unaware of the suicide of the suspect, decide that they have an especially good opportunity to commit similar crimes. By following the pattern set by the deranged killer, they make it seem that he's still on the scene and doing his thing. They assume that the police will never suspect that anyone other than the original killer is involved.

In this sort of situation, we can suppose, the populace might go into a panic. People would live in fear. The police would appear helpless to deal with the crime wave. Some sort of decisive action would be required—but what?

Now let us imagine that a high-ranking police official makes the following proposal to the police chief: "Let us arbitrarily select some innocent citizen, proclaim him to be the killer, produce a large body of manufactured evidence against him, and then, when he has been found guilty, hang him in public. Doing this will stop the crime wave, since the imitators will have no cover under which to hide; it will relieve the fear and panic of the populace; and it will result in promotions for all of us. Only, let us be certain to keep it secret!"

Although it is unlikely that such a situation would ever arise, it is surely *possible*. And equally, it is surely *possible* that the police official's suggestion might be correct. Let us suppose that in this particular case, punishing an innocent person would in fact have a much higher utility than anything else the police chief could do instead. For surely the hanging might have as much deterrence value as any justified execution could have, and it might have a great vengeance value too. As long as the populace at large never knows that conviction was a frame-up, their pleasure will be undiminished. Admittedly, the hanging won't have any rehabilitation value, but that seems to be a feature of all instances of capital punishment. Under the circumstances we have imagined, then, the main alternatives open to the police chief, and the utility of each, seem to be the following:

authorize the frame-up	+1000
try to catch all imitators	−500
try to calm public by explaining facts	−600
call FBI	−250
retire	−800

In this imaginary case, act utilitarianism implies that it is morally obligatory for the chief to authorize the frame-up. An innocent man must be hanged. This follows from the fact that nothing else the chief can do will produce as much utility. Yet we can all see that this result is utterly incorrect. We all know that the chief has no such moral obligation, even if he knows that the utilities of the alternatives open to him are as listed. Even if punishing an innocent person would produce a lot of utility, it would still be morally wrong. So the objection is as follows:

Punish-the-Innocent Objection

(1) If U_7 is true, the chief is morally obligated to authorize the frame-up.

(2) The chief is not morally obligated to authorize the frame-up.

(3) Therefore, U_7 is not true.

This objection is based on the idea that there can be cases in which punishment is *not* justified in fact, but in which it would maximize utility. Other examples can be developed that seem to show the reverse—that there can be cases in which punishment is justified, but in which it would not maximize utility. Either sort of example, if it really works, serves to refute act utilitarianism.

Those who accept the retributive theory of punishment may be moved to accept objections such as these. The retributive theory of punishment is the view that punishment is justified when and only when it is proportional to the crime. If someone has committed some terrible crime, she deserves very severe punishment. If she has committed a rather trivial crime, she deserves gentle punishment. If she has committed no crime at all, she deserves no punishment at all. This idea is expressed in the biblical maxim "An eye for an eye, and a tooth for a tooth."

The retributive theory of punishment is essentially backward-looking. It bids us to look to the past in order to see what crime has been committed. It implies that we should not be concerned about the consequences of punishing a wrongdoer. Our act of punishing may be morally obligatory even if it has no good consequences. We should be concerned only with insuring that the punishment "fits" the crime. In this respect, the retributive theory of punishment is utterly incompatible with the utilitarian theory of punishment.

Perhaps the retributive theory of punishment is too one-sided. With its utter lack of concern about consequences it may require us to be too merciless in our decisions about punishment. But it must be admitted nevertheless that the utilitarian theory of punishment is also unacceptable. Who can adopt a view according to which the question of guilt or innocence has no bearing at all upon the moral justification of punishment?

This last consideration leads us to another objection to act utilitarianism. This objection is based on the idea that act utilitarianism is too narrow-minded. It can be formulated as follows:

Morality-of-Punishment Objection

(1) If U_7 is true, the only moral reason for punishing someone is that doing so would maximize utility.

(2) It is not the case that the only moral reason for punishing someone is that doing so would maximize utility; the fact that this person has committed a crime and deserves punishment is also a moral reason for punishing him.

(3) Therefore, U_7 is not true.

It is left to the reader to consider whether there is any way in which a utilitarian might rebut this objection. For our purposes, it may be sufficient to note that objections such as this one have been held to be decisive by many philosophers.

Problems about Justice

A final category of objections to act utilitarianism is based on the contention that this theory is unable to account for some facts about justice and injustice. The problems of act utilitarianism in regard to punishment may be seen as instances of this more general problem. Surely it is unjust to punish an innocent person. Let us consider another example, which may serve to illustrate the more general problem.

Suppose a dictator has it in his power to enact either of two laws governing taxation. Under one law, each citizen pays exactly ten percent of his income in taxes. Under the other law, all members of the dictator's political party pay no taxes at all, and each member of the opposition party pays twenty percent of his income in taxes. Assume that the revenue collected would be the same in either case, and that each citizen has the same income as every other citizen. It might happen that the total amount of utility that would be produced by the uniform taxation scheme would be exactly equal to the total amount of utility that would be produced by the discriminatory taxation scheme. This could happen, for example, if the pain caused by paying twenty percent is just twice as great as the pain caused by paying ten percent and if paying no taxes produces no pain at all.

Principle U_7 seems to imply that in this case, either taxation scheme would be morally right. For neither is preferable to the other. After all, they produce the same amount of utility, and utility is allegedly the only thing that matters from the moral point of view. In opposition to this, many moralists would insist that unless there are some extraordinary circumstances, it would be very unjust to exact high taxes from half the people and none from the rest. So it would appear that the injustice of the discriminatory taxation scheme makes it morally worse than the uniform scheme. Thus, it would be contended, the application of act utilitarianism in this case generates the wrong result.

In general, we might put this objection as follows:

Justice Objection

(1) If U_7 is true, then the only moral reason for preferring one distribution of goods over another is that the one would produce more utility than the other.

(2) But it is not the case that the only moral reason for preferring one distribution of goods over another is that it would produce more utility than the other; another reason is that one might be more just than the other.

(3) Therefore, U_7 is not true.

We have now considered several different objections to act utilitarianism. In each case, it was alleged that some action, or kind of action, receives an incorrect evaluation under U_7. Objections such as these must be weighed carefully. Each reader must reflect, in regard to each objection, whether the results of the application of U_7 are correct, or whether the intuitions of the objectors are correct. Aside from this appeal to the intuitions of impartial, reflective, and careful individuals, there seems to be no way to determine whether act utilitarianism has been refuted.

For our purposes, however, it will be more convenient to assume that act utilitarianism *has* been refuted. The views to be considered in the next chapter may be seen as attempts to deal more adequately with the cases that prove so difficult for the simplest utilitarian doctrine, act utilitarianism.

5

Rule Utilitarianism

Some utilitarians, moved perhaps by objections similar to those discussed in the preceding chapter, have attempted to reformulate the utilitarian principle. They have seen that some of the results generated by the application of a thoroughgoing act utilitarianism are morally unacceptable. They may also have seen that there appears to be a pattern in the objections. For each objection seems to show, in its own way, that act utilitarianism is too *atomistic*. That is, act utilitarianism requires that each act be judged entirely on its own consequences. Wouldn't it be better, some have urged, to consider whole classes of action rather than isolated individual acts? It seems that we can show in some such way that promising in general is useful, and that there is thus moral justification for keeping each promise, even those unusual ones that fail to maximize utility. Thus, we may be able to deal with the promise-to-the-dead-man objection. Similarly, it may seem that the general practice of punishing the guilty has a utilitarian justification. Perhaps it could be shown that under some revised form of utilitarianism, punishing the innocent is wrong, even when it happens to produce more utility than its alternatives. Similarly, it might be proposed that injustice in general is less useful than justice. Hence, individual acts of injustice are wrong, even if useful.

So the motivation behind the attempt to formulate a coherent *rule utilitarianism* seems to be something like this: Utility is clearly of moral significance. But if we consider only the utility of individual acts, we derive unacceptable results. Thus, we must consider the utility of general patterns of behavior rather than of "atoms" of behavior. Particular acts will be shown to be right by showing them to fit into generally useful patterns. The amount of utility produced by individual acts will thus become less significant from the moral point of view.

Rules are relevant to the development of this idea for the following reason. When we wish to consider a general pattern of behavior, we may find it difficult to isolate the pattern in question. What is it that all the acts have in common? One answer is that what the acts have in common is some rule, which each of the acts is in accord with or is permitted by. For example, each act of promise keeping may be seen as an instance of the general rule "If you have made a promise, then keep it."

So the general pattern of rule utilitarianism is this: An individual act is morally right if and only if it is required by a correct moral rule. A moral rule is correct if and only if it would produce at least as much utility as any of its alternatives.

No sooner is rule utilitarianism's general pattern stated than a series of further questions immediately arises. What does it mean to say that an action is "required by" a rule? What, for that matter, *is* a rule? Since rules are not actions, it is not obvious that rules produce any consequences. Then how shall we make sense of the idea that rules can be evaluated in terms of their utility? Finally, what does it mean to say that a rule is an "alternative" to another rule?

Primitive Rule Utilitarianism

These are important questions. Without clear answers to them, rule utilitarianism is quite empty. Perhaps the easiest way to answer them would be to describe a rather simple form of rule utilitarianism. It is not clear that any philosopher ever believed in just this version of rule utilitarianism. But since the primary purpose here is clarification of some central notions that appear in some actually adopted forms of rule utilitarianism, we may find that there is some value in reflecting on this rather implausible version of the doctrine. The view in question has been called *primitive rule utilitarianism*.[1] Later in this chapter we will consider some more sophisticated versions of rule utilitarianism.

Let us assume that a rule is a sentence of a certain form. The form in question is exemplified by the following sample rules:

R_1:   If you have made a promise, then keep it.
R_2 If you have made a promise, then break it.
R_3:   If you have made a promise, then do whatever you feel like doing.

Each of these rules has an *antecedent*, or "if-clause," and a *consequent*, or "then-clause." The antecedent picks out a certain sort of situation. In our three rules, the situation is that a promise has been made. The consequent prescribes a certain kind of action. In R_1, the prescribed action is the keeping of the promise. In R_2, it is the breaking of the promise. Let us say that each of these rules "governs" the same situation. That is, each of them prescribes an action for the same situation. Because these two rules govern the same situation, we may say that they are alternatives to each other. It is important to note that when we say that rules are alternatives, we use the word "alternatives" in a sense different from that in which we use it when we say that acts are alternatives.

We already have a few technical terms. In order to keep them clearly in view, let us define them more formally as follows:

> D_1: R is a rule =df. R is an "if-then" sentence that prescribes some action for some situation.
>
> D_2: Rule R governs situation S = df. R prescribes some action for situation S.
>
> D_3: Rule R is an alternative to Rule R' =df. R governs the same situation as R'.

Now let us attempt to develop a coherent concept of utility that will be applicable to rules. Since rules are not actions, or events of any kind, they do not occur, or happen. Thus, they do not have any casual consequences. For this reason, it would not make much sense to say that the utility of a rule is the amount of pleasure it would produce minus the amount of pain it would produce. Rules don't "produce" anything. When we speak of the utility of a rule, we may have in mind the total amount of utility that would be produced by all the actions that the rule prescribes. To say that a rule has high utility, then, would be to say that if everyone followed the rule, their actions would collectively produce a lot of utility. This intuition about the utility of rules is the basic idea behind the concept of *conformance utility*. Roughly, the conformance utility of a rule is the amount of utility that would be produced by everyone's acting in accord with, or conforming to, the rule. This is not the only way of assigning utilities to rules, but it may be one of the simplest.

There are two points to notice about conformance utility. First, we do not want the conformance utility of a rule to be the utility that would be produced by everyone's *believing in* the rule. For belief in a rule may not result in action in accordance with the rule. There may be rules that have the following odd feature: it would be good for people to perform the acts the rules require, but it would be bad for them to believe in the rules. Such rules would have high conformance utility, but low "belief-in" utility. So we must be careful to formulate our definition of conformance utility in such a way that it measures only the utilities of the acts prescribed by the rule, not such other acts as, for example, believing in the rule or teaching the rule.

Second, conformance utility is not a measure of the utility that would be produced by *all* the acts people would perform if they were to conform to the rule. For in conforming to the rule, people would also perform several acts that are utterly irrelevant to conforming with the rule. For example, people would go on eating and drinking even if they also conformed to rule R_1. Surely we do not want to assign the utility of eating and drinking to rule R_1. We want to consider only the utilities of the acts that would be done *in accordance with* R_1—that is, acts of promise keeping.

Perhaps we are now in a position to state what the conformance utility of a rule is:

> D_4:   The conformance utility of a rule, R, is the sum of the utilities of all the acts prescribed by R that would be performed, if everyone in the situation governed by R who could do the act prescribed by R were to do that act.

A simple way to think of conformance utility is this: it is the amount of utility that would be produced by everyone's conforming to the rule when in the situation it governs. This way of putting it is rough, but perhaps serviceable.

Now we can give one account of what it means to say that a rule is *correct*. The intuition behind this account is rather simple. A rule is correct provided that more utility would be produced by people following it in the situation it governs than would be produced by people following any other rule that governs that situation. So a correct moral rule is one that has maximal conformance utility. None of its alternative rules has higher conformance utility than it has:

> D_5:   Rule R is correct =df. no alternative to R has higher conformance utility than R has.

We can think of correctness simply as the property a rule has if and only if more good would be produced by people's conforming to it than would be produced by their conforming to any other rule for the same sort of situation.

Primitive rule utilitarianism is the doctrine that an act is right if and only if it is prescribed by a correct rule for the situation in which it occurs. If we call the situation in which an act occurs "its situation," then we can state this doctrine quite simply:

> *PRU*:   An act is morally right if and only if it is prescribed by a correct moral rule for its situation.

Perhaps now we can see how this version of rule utilitarianism attempts to make the rightness of an act depend not upon its individual utility, but upon the utility of the rule that requires it. Thus, we may also be able to see why it might be thought that in primitive rule utilitarianism we have a theory that will not run afoul of the promise-to-the-dead-man objection or the punish-the-innocent objection. For it appears that each of these objections turns on the fact that under unusual circumstances more utility is produced by an act of a kind whose general performance would be bad. If we considered the utilities of the rules in question, the particular acts may be assigned their correct normative status. Reconsideration of the promise-to-the-dead-man example may help to make this somewhat clearer.

In this example, the grandson was in an unusual situation. He had made a promise, but more utility would be produced by breaking that promise than would be produced by keeping it. Perhaps this was insured by the fact that no one other than the callous youth himself would ever be affected by his behavior in that situation. This situation is clearly unlike the typical case in which a promise has been made. Normally, it may seem, more utility is produced by keeping promises. Thus, of all the rules that govern the situation on that deserted island, it may appear that none has higher conformance utility than rule R_1: "If you have made a promise, then keep it."

If this is so, then primitive rule utilitarianism implies that it is right for the grandson to keep the promise and give his grandfather a suitable burial. For no other rule that governs the grandson's situation has higher conformance utility than R_1. Thus, R_1 is the only correct rule for the situation. Primitive rule utilitarianism thus implies that the boy acts rightly if and only if he performs the action prescribed by R_1. That action is the action of keeping the promise. Since the grandson promised to bury the body appropriately, it seems that the right action is the action of giving the grandfather an appropriate burial. Or so it seems.

By now, one of the main defects of primitive rule utilitarianism may be emerging. The problem is a serious one, and it infects many forms of rule utilitarianism. It has been called the problem of *extensional equivalence*. To say that two normative theories are extensionally equivalent is to say that they generate exactly the same normative judgments. Any act judged to be right according to one theory is judged to be right according to the other. In itself, extensional equivalence is neither good nor bad. But if it can be shown that a given theory is extensionally equivalent to another theory that is known to be unacceptable, then we have a refutation of the given theory. For in any case in which the unacceptable theory implies an incorrect normative judgment, the new theory must have the same unacceptable implication.

Primitive rule utilitarianism is extensionally equivalent to act utilitarianism. Since the application of act utilitarianism generates the wrong results in certain cases, the application of primitive rule utilitarianism must generate the same wrong results in those cases.

Hence, in those cases primitive rule utilitarianism is just as unacceptable as act utilitarianism. To see why this is so, let us reconsider the promise-to-the-dead-man example.

We assumed that R_1 must be the correct rule for the situation in which a promise has been made. This accords with the intuition that in general, more good comes from keeping promises than from breaking them. But it should be obvious that for this situation, another rule must have even higher conformance utility than R_1 has. That rule is as follows:

R_4:   If you have made a promise, then do whatever will maximize utility.

Clearly, if everyone who has made a promise were to conform to R_4, more utility would be produced than if they all were to follow R_1. This is because, as we noted above, R_1 requires promise keeping even when such action does not produce more utility than promise breaking. R_4, on the other hand, requires promise keeping in every case in which promise keeping produces maximal utility. In all the unusual cases in which promise breaking produces more utility, R_1 still requires promise keeping; R_4, however, "switches" and requires whatever will produce the most utility. Hence, if everyone conformed to R_4, we would get all the utility of promise keeping, plus the utility of promise breaking in just those cases in which promise breaking is more useful than promise keeping. Hence, the conformance utility of R_4 must be higher than that of R_1.

Since the conformance utility of R_4 is higher than that of R_1, R_1 is not the correct moral rule for the situation in which a promise has been made. Thus, R_1 is not the correct rule for the grandson's situation on the desert island. Rather, it seems that R_4 must be the correct rule for that situation. No rule that governs that situation can have higher conformance utility than R_4 has. So primitive rule utilitarianism implies that the grandson acts rightly if and only if he acts in accord with R_4. But in order to act in accord with R_4, he must do whatever maximizes utility. We have already seen that he maximizes utility only if he uses the grandfather's body for bait. Hence, the application of primitive rule utilitarianism generates the same absurd result that the application of act utilitarianism generates. The theories are extensionally equivalent, and they both generate the wrong result in this sort of case. Hence, both must be rejected.

Similar reasoning will show that in every situation, the correct rule will be something of the form, "If———, then do whatever maximizes utility." Thus, if we conform to correct rules, we must always do whatever maximizes utility. But to do this is to do exactly what act utilitarianism requires. Hence, an act is right according to primitive rule utilitarianism if and only if it is right according to act utilitarianism. Since the application of act utilitarianism yields the wrong results in several cases, the application of primitive rule utilitarianism must yield the same wrong results in every one of these cases. Thus, there is no advantage to this form of rule utilitarianism. We must try another.

Brandt's Ideal-Moral-Code Theory

One of the clearest and most persuasive forms of rule utilitarianism has been developed by Richard Brandt.[2] Brandt recognizes that theories like our primitive rule utilitarianism are extensionally equivalent to act utilitarianism. Since Brandt feels that act utilitarianism generates morally unacceptable results, he wants his form of rule utilitarianism to be different from primitive rule utilitarianism.

Two main features of Brandt's theory distinguish it from primitive rule utilitarianism. First, with Brandt's theory we do not compare the utilities of alternative *rules*. Rather, we compare the utilities of whole moral codes. A moral code is a complete set of rules. It covers every sort of situation that is likely to arise.

The second main difference between Brandt's theory and primitive rule utilitarianism is the utility measure. Instead of saying that a code is correct if it has maximal *conformance* utility, as we might expect, Brandt alludes to the notion of *currency utility*. This is a measure of the amount of utility that would be produced by the code's being current, or widely accepted, in the society.

The basic intuition behind Brandt's theory is simple and plausible. There are many different moral codes, any of which could be adopted by our society. Of these, one is superior on utilitarian grounds. That is, more good would be produced by the currency of that code here than would be produced by the currency of any of the other codes here. This superior code is called the "ideal" code for our society. We should endeavor to make our behavior conform to the requirements of this code. In other words, an act is morally right if and only if it is permitted by the ideal moral code for its society.

In order to come to a more adequate understanding of Brandt's theory, we must first understand some of the technical terms Brandt employs. Of these, it is most natural to start with the concept of *subscription*. Brandt gives a thoughtful and interesting account of what it means to say that a person subscribes to a moral rule.[3] Roughly, a person subscribes to a moral rule if and only if she sincerely accepts it as a correct moral rule. This does not entail that she in fact will abide by the rule. But it does suggest that she will try to abide by it should the occasion arise, will feel guilty if she believes herself to have failed to do so, and will think less of those who don't abide by it.

A moral code is a set of moral rules. Of course, not just any set will do. Let us assume that a set of rules must satisfy at least two conditions if it is to count as a moral code. First, it must be complete. That is, it must provide a prescription for every morally important situation. Second, it must be consistent. That is, it must not provide incompatible prescriptions for any situation. Obviously, to be a worthwhile moral code, a set of rules must satisfy many other conditions as well, but for our purposes these two may provide a starting point.

Making use of his concept of subscription, Brandt introduces the notion of *currency*.[4] To be current in a society, a moral code must satisfy two main requirements. First, each rule in the code must be such that at least ninety percent of the adult members of the society subscribe to it. Second, it must be that "a large proportion of the adults in the society would respond correctly if asked, with respect to [rules in the code] whether most members of the society subscribe to them."[5] In light of this account, we may define currency as follows:

D_6:   Moral code C is current in society S =df. (i) each rule in C is such that at least ninety percent of the adults in S subscribe to it; and (ii) each rule in C is such that most adult members of S believe that most members of S subscribe to it.

Brandt gives the following account of what is meant by saying that a moral code is "ideal" for a society: "A moral code is taken to be ideal if and only if its currency would produce at least as much good per person as the currency of any other moral code."[6] Perhaps it would be more convenient for our purpose to introduce a concept that is used, but not explicitly discussed, by Brandt. This is the concept of currency utility. We can say that the currency utility of a moral code is the amount of "good per person" the currency of the code would produce in the society. In other words, to determine the currency utility of a moral code for a society, ask yourself how much good would be produced by the code's being current there—that is, the total amount of pleasure minus the total amount of pain, if we are hedonists. Then divide the result by the number of people in the society. The result is the currency utility of the code for the society. We can define this concept as follows:

D_7:   The currency utility of moral code C for society S is the net good per person that would be produced by C's currency in S.

Notice that a code does not have to be current in a society in order to have a currency utility for that society. Its currency utility is the amount of good per person it *would* produce if it *were* current there.

Now we can provide a concise account of the notion of *ideality*. For we can say that an ideal code is one that has maximal currency utility. Or, more exactly:

D_8:   Moral code C is ideal for society S =df. there is no moral code that has higher currency utility for S than C does.

It is extremely important to recognize that Brandt's view does *not* imply that every ideal code is in fact current. A code may be ideal for a society even if no one in that society ever thought of it, and even if they would reject it if they did think of it. The moral code that is actually current in the society may be very different from the one that is ideal for it. Perhaps this will be clearer if we think of the ideal code for a society as the one that *would* produce the most utility if it *were* current. This clearly does not imply that the ideal code *is* current.

Brandt states his main thesis in these words: "An act is right if and only if it would not be prohibited by the moral code ideal for the society; . . ."[7] This statement of the ideal-moral-code theory is open to two minor objections. First, as Brandt recognizes, there is nothing in the theory to insure that there will always be exactly one ideal moral code for each society. Perhaps there will be two codes that have the same currency utility, and no other code has higher currency utility than each of them has. In such a case, it would be inappropriate to speak of "*the* moral code ideal for the society." The other objection has to do with Brandt's reference to "the society." To which society is Brandt referring? Perhaps he is assuming that for every act, there is exactly one society that is, in some sense, "the one in which it would be performed." We will make this assumption here and reflect further upon it later.

With these modifications, then, we may state a provisional version of the ideal-moral-code theory:

IMCT: An act, *a*, is morally right if and only if there is a society, S, and a moral code, C, such that (i) S is the society in which *a* would be performed; (ii) C is ideal for S; and (iii) C does not prohibit *a*.

Let us consider the workings of Brandt's theory. Suppose a government official is offered a bribe. Should he accept it or not? Perhaps it could be argued that bribe taking is permitted by the moral code that is in fact current in our society. Under the ideal-moral-code theory, this fact, assuming it is a fact, is morally irrelevant. The rightness of the act does not depend upon the judgment of the current moral code. The relevant question is whether bribe taking is permitted by a code that is *ideal* for the society in question, in the sense of "ideal" defined above. To simplify matters, we can imagine two good moral codes, alike in many respects but differing on the morality of bribe taking. One contains a rule prohibiting bribe taking; the other does not. It is reasonable to suppose that more good would be produced by the currency of the code that prohibits the taking of bribes than would be produced by the currency of the code that permits it. In fact, it is reasonable to suppose that no code with maximal currency utility for our society would permit the taking of bribes. For where public servants take bribes, the public is often poorly served. Hence, it is not the case that an ideal code for our society permits the taking of bribes. Under IMCT, it follows that it is not right for the government official to take the bribe.

Perhaps similar reasoning would show that promises ought to be kept, only the guilty should be punished, and justice should be done. If so, Brandt's ideal-moral-code theory will generate more plausible moral judgments than primitive rule utilitarianism and act utilitarianism in the cases we have discussed.

Perhaps the main objection to IMCT is that it is extensionally equivalent to the discredited act-utilitarian theory. Perhaps it appears that for every society the ideal code will contain just one rule—"Maximize utility." If so, the theory is no improvement over those we have already studied.

However, there is no good reason to suppose that the ideal-moral-code theory is open to this sort of objection. For such an objection to stick, it would have to be shown that no moral code can have higher currency utility than the code that contains just the rule, "Maximize utility." But how can this be shown? Our one-rule code (which we can call CU) undoubtedly has maximal *conformance* utility—that is because it is impossible for there to be a rule requiring action that would produce more utility than the action required by CU. But does CU have maximal *currency* utility? Would a great amount of utility be produced by a ninety-percent subscription to the single rule in CU? It appears not. For the rule is so general, and it is so hard to determine the actual features of the acts it requires, that the currency of CU would probably lead to moral chaos and confusion. No one would know what to do! Hence, the currency of CU would probably not lead to a maximization of utility. Thus, CU is probably not the ideal code for every society, and so IMCT cannot be shown to be extensionally equivalent to act utilitarianism.

Shall we conclude, then, that the ideal-moral-code theory is the correct theory in theoretical normative ethics? Probably not, for it still has some very important defects.

One difficulty with the ideal-moral-code theory is that it relies so heavily on the concept of "society." For example, IMCT assumes that for every act, there is exactly one society that is *the* society in which the act is performed. The problem is that in some cases an act seems to be performed in many different societies at the same time, and in other cases an act seems to be performed in no society at all.

Suppose a drug pusher sells some drugs to an addict, and the addict promises to pay for the drugs later in the day. How does IMCT assess the morality of the keeping of that promise? To answer this question, we must determine what moral code is ideal for the society in which the promise was made. But in what society did that act occur? Was it in the "drug culture"? Perhaps it was in "street society." Perhaps some will insist that it was performed in the American society of 1975. It might even be suggested that the pusher and the addict constitute a two-person "mini-society." The problem is that (a) there seems to be no way to determine the society of the act, and (b) different codes might be ideal for these different possible societies. Hence, depending upon which is "*the* society," we may get different moral evaluations of the act in question.

More serious problems for the ideal-moral-code theory arise from the fact that under it, we are required to follow rules that *would be* useful if they *were* current. The rules in question need not in fact *be* current. This leads to a variety of problems, one of which has to do with what we may call "de facto institutions." Consider marriage, for example. It may be the case that the institution of marriage would be banned by an ideal code for our society. Many commentators have argued that there is no utilitarian justification for marriage; communal living, they claim, is far more productive of pleasure. This line of thought may be correct. If it is correct, then the ideal-moral-code theory implies that everyone who marries acts immorally! We, who marry in a society in which marriage is a very widely accepted form of behavior, may be doing wrong! And our moral error, according to the ideal-moral-code theory, is that there is some moral code—unknown to us and thus not accepted by any of us, but whose currency would be useful—that prohibits marriage! Doesn't that seem like a preposterous reason to think that those who marry are doing wrong?

So it appears that Brandt's theory, at least in the form discussed here, is open to some fairly serious objections. Nevertheless, it must be admitted that Brandt has presented a clear and useful form of rule utilitarianism. He has shown one direction in which rule utilitarianism can be developed. Perhaps Brandt or someone else will refine this view in such a way as to overcome the difficulties that seem to beset it in its present form.

Rawls's Two Concepts of Rules

John Rawls has attempted to show how a more plausible form of rule utilitarianism can be formulated.[8] This new form of rule utilitarianism is designed to generate the correct results in some of the cases that cause so much trouble for act utilitarianism and primitive rule utilitarianism. The main innovation in Rawls's theory is based on a distinction between two

different views of the role of rules. Rawls suggests that many critics of
utilitarianism have thought of rules according to the "summary" conception. If we think of rules according to the "practice" conception, Rawls
proposes we may have a way of answering the objections.

In order to understand Rawls's rule-utilitarian theory, we must first
gain a clear understanding of these two ways of viewing rules. The first
and more typical way of viewing rules is the summary conception. According to this conception, rules develop something like this: First, people confront a lot of similar moral situations. In each case, they apply
their fundamental moral principle to the situation. Eventually, they
begin to notice a pattern in the results generated by the fundamental
principle: whenever the principle is applied to a situation of a given sort,
S, it yields a moral judgment of the same kind. Let's suppose the principle says to do an act of kind K. People then formulate a moral rule for
that sort of case. The rule says that when in situation S, one ought to do
an act of kind K.

The point of having this rule is simple: it is easier to use a relatively
convenient, easy-to-remember, generally reliable rule than it is to use the
basic moral principle itself. But the derived rule has no moral force of its
own—it gets its force from the fundamental principle. One should follow the rule only because the act the rule requires is generally the same
as the act that the fundamental principle would be found to require. If in
some unusual circumstances the derived rule yields a result incompatible
with that yielded by the fundamental principle, then one's real obligation
is to do the act required by the fundamental principle. At most, we can
say that the derived rule is a rule of thumb. It is a generally reliable guide
to action, but with no moral authority of its own.

According to Rawls, the summary conception of rules has four main
features:

1. One formulates summary rules only after a fair number of similar cases have arisen, and have been found to have a similar sort of
solution. In a way, a summary rule is like a scientific generalization. In
each case, one' may decide to adopt the principle after observing
similarities in a number of cases.

2. Individual cases are "logically prior" to the rules that govern
them. By this, Rawls seems to mean that we can identify and recognize
the acts governed by a rule even if we are unaware of the rule. The
important features of the acts are independent of the fact that the acts
are governed by just those rules. The acts would have had those important features even if the rules had never been formulated.

3. Rules are only guides, or rules of thumb. Hence, there is no
special moral reason why we ought to make use of these rules. Our main
reason for following them is simply that it is more convenient to follow

them than it is to use the fundamental moral principle afresh each time we need to make a decision.

4. We can now see how a rule may be thought of as being "generally correct." In order to keep the rule simple and easy to remember, we may have to frame it in such a way that it is not completely accurate. The rule is not, therefore, based on what is *always* right, but on what has, *for the most part*, been right in the past. Thus, we may sacrifice accuracy in order to achieve greater simplicity.

The other conception of rules is the practice conception. In order to explain this conception, we must first explain what Rawls means by "practice." Rawls says that a practice is "any form of activity specified by a system of rules which defines offices, roles, moves, penalties, defenses, and so on, and which gives the activity its structure. As examples one may think of games and rituals, trials and parliaments."[9]

This account of practices is not very clear or helpful. Perhaps it would be better to try to develop a similar concept on our own. First, let us introduce the notion of a "delicate situation." We can say that a delicate situation is a sort of situation that arises fairly frequently, that often has relatively large amounts of utility at stake, and that may be subjected to some kind of human control. For example, the situation in which a wealthy person has died, leaving an estate to be divided among his heirs, is a delicate situation.

We can say that a practice is a set of rules designed to deal with a delicate situation. In this set will be rules that assign roles to the individuals involved. In the inheritance example, for instance, the practice might contain rules defining the role of the executor, the role of the deceased, and so on. Such rules would determine what a person must do in order to qualify, for example, as an executor. Other rules in the practice will describe the required "moves." They will explain what each role player must do, and when he must do it. Other rules will describe penalties, still others will describe defenses, and so forth.

Rawls emphasizes that if a person wants to engage in a certain practice, he simply has to abide by the rules that constitute that practice. To violate those rules is simply to fail to engage in that practice. This seems to follow from the view that a practice is nothing more than a suitable set of rules. Rawls suggests that someone who is engaged in playing baseball, for example, does not have any authority to choose to abide by "better" rules than those currently in force. If he wants to play baseball, he must abide by the rules as they are at the time. During the off-season, he can endeavor to have them changed if he likes. Once the game has started, he has no such prerogative. The rules of practices are analogous to the rules of games.

We can now compare the practice conception of rules with the summary conception on the four points already mentioned.

1. According to the practice conception, rules are not like generalizations derived from lots of experience with similar cases. Rather, rules are decided upon and formulated before we have any of the relevant sort of experience. This is so because, for example, no one could have played the game of baseball before some sort of "baseball practice" was invented.

2. Contrary to what we find under the summary conception, under the practice conception the rules are prior to the acts falling under them. Perhaps this means that the most important features of the acts are features they have in virtue of the rules. The rules, we have seen, may define some moves. A certain sort of behavior, for example, is said to constitute the making of a promise. If there were no "promising practice," then that sort of behavior would not constitute promising. It would just be an odd sort of talking about the future. Thus, an important feature of the action is dependent upon the rules of the practice.

3. If we think of rules according to the practice conception, we will see that they are not merely convenient rules of thumb. We follow them not because it is more convenient to do so, but because there is simply no other way to engage in the practice. One's reason for pitching from the pitcher's mound is certainly not that it has been found convenient in the past to do so. Rather, one pitches in that way because the rules of baseball require it. Failure to do so would be failure to engage in the game of baseball as currently formulated.

4. Practice rules are not generalizations. They are not just "generally reliable." They are definitive of practices. Hence, if you want to engage in the practice, you may conceive of the rules as being completely accurate.

Although many aspects of the summary-practice distinction will undoubtedly remain obscure, perhaps we can now proceed to consider Rawls's use of the distinction. Rawls seems to hold that earlier utilitarians failed to recognize the summary-practice distinction. They treated moral rules according to the summary conception. That is, they treated the rules as if the rules had no moral authority of their own. Thus, such utilitarians failed to notice that sometimes an act is morally right primarily because it is required by a rule of practice. Utilitarian considerations, Rawls insists, apply in the first instance to the practices. Practices are judged to be good or bad on the basis of the utility they would produce. Actions are judged on whether or not they are in accord with the rules of their practices. As Rawls puts it, "Utilitarian considerations should be understood as applying to practices in the first instance and not to particular actions falling under them except insofar as the practices admit of it."[10]

It must be admitted that Rawls did not attempt to present a complete and precise statement of his version of rule utilitarianism. What he did present, however, is open to a variety of interpretations. Before we can evaluate his view, therefore, we must attempt to make it somewhat clearer and more precise. To do this is to depart from what Rawls actually said. Hence, what follows is somewhat speculative.

Let us say that a "de facto practice" is a practice that is actually in force, or current, in a given society. Thus, our present practice concerning the disposition of estates is now a de facto practice in our society. In contrast, the 1908 baseball rule book describes a practice that was de facto in 1908, but which is no longer de facto. So we can define this term as follows:

> D_9: A practice, P, is de facto in a society, S, at a time, t =df. the members of S believe in and generally adhere to the rules in P at t.

A given delicate situation may be handled in any of several different ways. Each such way of handling it will be codified in a set of rules that constitutes a practice. Each of these practices will be said to "govern" that delicate situation. We can thus say that practices are alternatives if they govern the same situation:

> D_{10}: Practice P is an alternative to practice P' =df. there is some delicate situation, D, such that P governs D and P' governs D.

Let us next attempt to sketch a concept of utility that will be applicable to practices. Since this is a topic that Rawls did not discuss, we are free to develop it in any way that seems reasonable. Perhaps this would not be too far afield: We can say that the utility of a practice for a society is the number of hedons, minus the number of dolors, that would result from its being de facto there. Now we can easily define "optimific":

> D_{11}: Practice P is optimific for society S =df. the utility of P for S is at least as great as the utility of any alternative practice for S.

It is important to recognize that a practice may be de facto in some society without being optimific for that society. Similarly, a practice may be optimific for a society without being de facto there. That is, the way in which we actually handle some delicate situation may be less productive of utility than some other way would be if we were to use it instead. In fact, it is pretty likely that few, if any, de facto practices are optimific. After all, how many delicate situations are handled in the very best way possible?

Interpretation A

Now we can state the first interpretation of Rawls's view. Rawls said that "utilitarian considerations apply in the first instance to practices." Perhaps he meant this:

A_1:   A practice is morally correct if and only if it is optimific.

Second, Rawls emphasizes that we often evaluate particular actions by reflecting on the rules of the practice within which they occur. This suggests the following:

A_2:   An act, a, is morally right if and only if there is some practice, P, such that P governs the situation in which a would occur; P permits a; and P is de facto in the society in which a would be performed.

It might be thought that interpretation A neatly solves some of the problems we have discussed. For example, in the punish-the-innocent case (see Chapter 4) A_2 seems to imply that the police chief ought to abide by the rules currently in force rather than taking the law into his own hands. Thus, he ought to keep on looking for the real killers, and he ought not to punish any innocent person, regardless of the utility that would result from doing so. This follows from the fact that the de facto practice concerning punishment does not allow punishment of the innocent, no matter how much utility would be produced.

Similarly, in the promise-to-the-dead-man case, A_2 would imply that the grandson ought to keep his promise. The low utility of doing so is irrelevant under A_2. What matters is that promise breaking is not permitted by the de facto practice of the society in which the young man was raised (and of which he may still be considered a member).

In spite of these apparent successes, interpretation A is quite seriously defective. Its main flaw emerges upon reflection on the fact that there are some societies that have utterly miserable de facto practices. For example, in some societies people believe in and accept such practices as slavery, torture, human sacrifice, and cannibalism. Surely, we do not want to say that a man who owns and mistreats slaves acts rightly simply because his fellow citizens accept the practice of slavery! Their belief in slavery surely does not serve to raise the normative status of his act. His ownership of slaves is wrong, regardless of what the other citizens think. But according to A_2, it would have to be judged to be morally right.

In general, we must conclude that interpretation A is not a utilitarian theory at all. It is merely a form of *conventionalism*, the view that acts are judged to be right merely by appeal to the de facto practices that govern them. This means, roughly, that an act is right if and only if most members of the society believe it to be right. The most cursory reflection on some of the darker pages of history should make clear that this view is not acceptable.[11]

Interpretation B

Perhaps we should state Rawls's view in a different way. Perhaps we should say that what makes a right act right is not the fact that it is permitted by a de facto practice, but rather the fact that it is permitted by a morally correct practice, whether de facto or not. Thus, our theory would be as follows:

B_1:   A Practice is morally correct if and only if it is optimific.

B_2:   An act, a, is morally right if and only if there is some practice, P, such that P governs the situation in which a would occur; P permits a; and P is optimific for the society in which a would be performed.

The main problems with interpretation B arise from the fact that it so often happens that the optimific practice is not de facto. Suppose, for example, that we could devise a better way of educating young people. Then our de facto education practice is not optimific. In that case, every schoolchild, every teacher, every administrator, and every parent who sends his or her child to school is performing a morally wrong act. The act is wrong, according to B_2, because it is not permitted by the rules of some practice we don't know about, don't believe in, and might not even be able to understand. Doesn't that seem absurd?

In short, the defects of interpretation B are very much like the defects of Brandt's ideal-moral-code theory. Under this view, we are required to act in ways that would be useful, even if in fact our society has not recognized or set up the relevant institutional framework, and even if our actions will be useless and detrimental as things now stand. Thus, it appears that interpretation B is as implausible as interpretation A, although for different reasons.

By way of conclusion, it must be emphasized that it is not at all clear that Rawls meant to affirm either interpretation A or interpretation B. Hence, the difficulties with those views may not pose any problem for the view he really meant to affirm. In that case, however, we must acknowledge that it is not easy to see what Rawls might have meant.

General Conclusions on Rule Utilitarianism

In general, rule utilitarianism seems to involve two rather plausible intuitions. In the first place, rule utilitarians want to emphasize that moral rules are important. Individual acts are justified by being shown to be in accordance with correct moral rules. In the second place, utility is important. Moral rules are shown to be correct by being shown to lead, somehow, to the maximization of utility. So the two intuitions are these. First, rules play an essential role in the determination of the normative status of acts. Second, utility plays an essential role in the determination of the normative status of rules. Rule utilitarianism, in its various forms, tries to combine these intuitions into a single, coherent criterion of morality. Since these basic intuitions are initially attractive, there is substantial plausibility to the rule-utilitarian approach.

In spite of this plausibility, it seems to be extraordinarily difficult to develop these ideas into a clear and acceptable doctrine. For if we proceed in the manner of primitive rule utilitarianism, we seem to overemphasize utility. It turns out that the rules make no difference at all. The only morally relevant consideration is the utility of the act, as compared with the utility of its alternatives. Hence, our rule-utilitarian insight turns out to have degenerated into a form of act utilitarianism. Since the basic motivation here is to improve upon act utilitarianism, this is a disappointment.

If we attempt to develop the rule-utilitarian insights in such a way as to avoid overemphasizing utility, we may fall into conventionalism. That is, we may end up saying that right acts are acts in accordance with actually accepted rules. Our interpretation A of Rawls is an example of this sort of problem. Such a view is hardly a form of utilitarianism at all, since the utility of an action (or of a rule, for that matter) seems to end up having no relevance to its normative status. But, what's worse, this form of conventionalism seems to be an extremely implausible view. For it apparently rules out the obvious possibility that there might be some de facto moral code that requires acts that in fact are not morally right.

Finally, if we attempt to develop rule utilitarianism in the manner of Brandt, we end up with a theory according to which people ought to act in conformity to some ideal set of rules—rules that would produce a lot of utility if they were believed. This happens in Brandt's theory and in our interpretation B of Rawls. The basic problem with this approach seems to be that such ideal rules may not fit very well into the actual pattern of behavior current in a society. These rules may require people to act in ways that would be useful if everyone cooperated, but that are in fact useless, since others are not going to cooperate. Thus, this approach, though in many ways the most promising of the three, seems to generate a lot of extremely unlikely results.

Hence, many commentators would say that the initial attractiveness of rule utilitarianism is misleading. They would say that no matter how we try to develop it, rule utilitarianism still turns out to be unacceptable. Such a pessimistic view may be too harsh. Perhaps it is possible to develop a form of rule utilitarianism that is clear and precise, and yet avoids all three of the pitfalls we have discussed. At present, however, it appears that this has not yet been done.

NOTES

1. An impressive discussion of this and other forms of rule utilitarianism can be found in David Lyons, *Forms and Limits of Utilitarianism* (Oxford: Oxford University Press, 1965).

2. Brandt's theory is advanced in two of his papers: "Toward a Credible Form of Utilitarianism," in *Morality and the Language of Conduct*, ed. Hector-Neri Castañeda and George N. Nakhnikian (Detroit: Wayne State University Press, 1963); and "Some Merits of One Form of Rule Utilitarianism," in *Mill: Utilitarianism with Critical Essays*, ed. Samuel Gorovitz (Indianapolis: Bobbs-Merrill, 1971), pp. 324–44.

3. Brandt, "Some Merits," in *Mill*, ed. Gorovitz, p. 332.

4. *Ibid.*, p. 331.

5. *Ibid.*, pp. 331–32.

6. *Ibid.* p. 331.

7. *Ibid.*

8. John Rawls, "Two Concepts of Rules," in *Mill*, ed. Gorovitz, pp. 175–94.

9. *Ibid.*, p. 175.

10. *Ibid.*, p. 185.

11. Views of this sort are discussed in greater detail in Chapter 11.

6

Egoism

Egoism, as a theory in normative ethics, can best be understood as the view that everyone ought to promote his own self-interest. In other words, the egoist holds that one acts in a morally acceptable way if and only if one acts in such a way as to secure the greatest possible benefit for oneself. So, if egoism is true, you are morally obligated to do whatever you can to help yourself, and I am morally obligated to do all I can to help myself. Unless it is ultimately to my benefit, I have no moral reason to perform acts that benefit you. Similarly, unless it is ultimately to your benefit, you have no moral reason to perform acts that benefit me. Hence, egoists make a sort of consistent selfishness their basic moral principle.

Quite a few people behave in such a way as to suggest that they believe in something like egoism, but among professional philosophers egoism has not fared well. Some philosophers claim that egoism, straightforward as it may seem, is self-contradictory. Others admit that it is consistent, but they argue that it is false. Finally, some hold that it is not a moral doctrine at all. Before we can evaluate any of these objections to egoism, we have to consider just what the egoist means to affirm.

What Is Egoism?

Egoism has been formulated in a variety of ways. Some of these formulations, if taken at face value, lead to some rather odd results.[1] So we should be careful to state the theory in as plausible a form as can be found. To do this, we can make use of some of the technical terms we introduced in our discussion of act utilitarianism.

In the first place, we assume that egoism is a doctrine about the normative status of act-tokens, rather than act-types. That is, when we speak of an act, what we have in mind is a particular, concrete, non-repeatable act such as the first walk on the moon, the signing of the Declaration of Independence by John Hancock, or the last telling of a lie by you. Each such act token has an agent—the person who performs it—and it has a time—the time at or during which it is performed.

Second, we assume that when an agent acts, she always selects her act from a set of alternatives. The alternatives to what someone actually does on some occasion are the other acts she could have done on that occasion instead of the one she in fact did.

Third, we assume that every action that occurs has some consequences. Consequences may be near or remote—it doesn't matter. They are later events that occur as a result of the action. Among the consequences of an action are episodes of pleasure and episodes of pain. According to act utilitarianism, the normative status of an act is determined by its utility—the result of subtracting the total amount of pain in the consequences from the total amount of pleasure in the consequences. Thus, according to act utilitarianism, it doesn't matter who feels the pleasure or who feels the pain. If an act causes some pleasure, then that pleasure is included when we determine the total number of hedons the act causes. If it causes some pain, then the dolors of that pain are included when we determine the utility of the act. *Whose* pleasure and pain is irrelevant, under act utilitarianism.

As we have seen, egoism is the view that each person should promote his own self-interest. Understood in terms of pleasure and pain, this would mean that each person should seek to maximize the balance of *his own* pleasure over *his own* pain.

It is easy to misunderstand this doctrine, so let us formulate it with some care. We can say that the *agent utility* of an action is the amount of pleasure the agent would feel as a result of his action minus the amount of pain the agent would feel as a result of his action. In other words, it is the result of subtracting the total number of dolors the agent would feel as a result of the action from the total number of hedons the agent would feel as a result of the action. To see how this concept works, let us consider an example.

Suppose a girl decides to run away and join the circus. She gets a lot of short-term pleasure as a result of doing this. She's thrilled to meet the performers, and she is excited by the prospect of traveling all over the country. However, as time passes she begins to feel lonely and unhappy. She discovers that the circus life is not for her. To make the case a bit more concrete, let us suppose that she feels exactly 100 hedons of pleasure during her first week with the circus, but that she feels 500 dolors of pain in the months that follow. If she feels no other pleasures or pains as a result of running away to the circus, then the agent utility of this act is −400. The fact that her parents were grief-stricken, the fact that her boyfriend was somewhat relieved, and the fact that her dog was rather sad are all utterly irrelevant here. These pleasures and pains were not felt by the agent of the act. They were felt by her parents, her boyfriend, and her dog. Hence, they have no direct bearing on the agent utility of her action. We can thus define agent utility as follows:

D_1:   The agent utility of an act is the result of subtracting the sum of the doloric values of all the episodes of pain felt by the agent of the act as a result of the act, from the sum of the hedonic values of all the episodes of pleasure felt by the agent of the act as a result of the act.

If it is more convenient, we can think of the agent utility of an act in the following way. Consider all the pleasure the act would cause for its agent. Consider all the pain the act would cause for its agent. Subtract the pain from the pleasure. The result is the agent utility of the act.

Making use of this concept of agent utility, we can formulate a fairly clear version of egoism: an act is morally right if and only if it maximizes agent utility. That is, one acts rightly if and only if he produces the greatest balance of pleasure over pain for himself that he can. Following the pattern of U_7 (see Chapter 2), we can state the main principle of egoism as follows:

E_1:   An act is morally right if and only if no alternative to that act has higher agent utility than it has.

Formulated as E_1, egoism is a form of *consequentialism*, the view that the normative status of an act depends upon its consequences. In this respect, egoism is like act utilitarianism. Furthermore, E_1 is a form of *hedonism*, the view that the normative status of an act depends upon how much pleasure and how much pain it would produce. In this respect too, E_1 is similar to act utilitarianism. However, E_1 makes the normative status of each act depend only on the amounts of pleasure and pain the agent of the act would feel, rather than upon the total amounts of pleasure and pain. Thus, this version of egoism is sometimes called *individualistic hedonism*, whereas act utilitarianism is called *universalistic hedonism*.

Some Common Misconceptions about Egoism

Sometimes egoism is misunderstood to be the view that each of us should try to gain the maximum of pleasure for ourselves in the short run. That is, we should indulge in as much immediate self-gratification as we can.

According to this view, we should eat, drink, and be merry today and forget about tomorrow's hangover. E_1 certainly does not have any such implication. E_1 does not imply that acts yielding immediate pleasure to the agent are to be preferred to acts yielding delayed pleasure to the agent. To see which of your acts really has the highest agent utility, you must look far into the future. You must consider the long-run consequences of what you propose to do, as well as the short-run consequences. A pain you feel nine months from now may serve to neutralize a pleasure you feel tonight. Thus, egoism is often said to be a doctrine of "enlightened self-interest."

Egoism is sometimes thought to imply that one ought never to act altruistically. That is, it is sometimes thought that if egoism is true, then one is never morally obligated to perform an act that will benefit other people. This is a very serious misunderstanding of egoism, and it should be cleared away. In order to see why egoism does not rule out altruism (of a sort), consider the following case. A very wealthy man is wondering what to do with some of his excess money. He realizes that there are basically only two ways in which he can spend it. On the one hand, he can spend it all on things that will give pleasure to no one other than himself. He can buy a yacht, some exotic automobiles, and some incredibly expensive jewelry. On the other hand, he can spend the money on something that will give pleasure to others. He can contribute a fully furnished and equipped library to the college of his choice.

Egoism does not imply that the rich man should buy the yacht and the other trinkets. Rather, it implies that he should spend the money in whichever of the two ways will, in the long run, give him the greatest satisfaction. He may enjoy giving things to others, or he may enjoy having a library named after himself, or he may be the sort of person who takes great pride in receiving an honorary degree from the college of his choice. In any of these cases, it may turn out that he would gain the greater personal happiness, in the long run, from giving the money to the college. In this case, egoism implies that he morally ought to give the money to the college. Thus, the act required by egoism may be extremely generous and even altruistic.

However, it is essential to recognize that according to egoism, what makes his charitable act morally right is *not* its charitableness, or its high overall utility. The fact that it makes others happy is, in itself, morally irrelevant. What makes the act morally right, according to egoism, is the fact that it maximizes the happiness of the agent of the act. In the example described, it just so happened that the act that makes the rich man happy also makes others happy. But the happiness of the others is only incidentally relevant to the morality of the act, according to egoism. So egoism allows us to perform altruistic actions—provided that such actions are ultimately in our own self-interest.

It is also worth pointing out that *egoism*, the normative theory presently under consideration, has very little to do with *egotism*. If a person consistently exaggerates his own importance, insists that he should be the center of attention, or otherwise reveals himself to have an inflated ego, he may be considered an egotist. So egotism is an annoying character trait. Egoism, on the other hand, is a moral theory, stating alleged necessary and sufficient conditions for the moral rightness of actions. It should be clear that egoism and egotism are logically unrelated. A person can be an egoist without being an egotist, and a person can be an egotist without being an egoist.

The term "egoism" is sometimes used to refer to a normative theory that is quite different from our E_1. This theory is in some ways quite grotesque, but there is good reason to take careful note of it. For it sometimes happens that people confuse this rather grotesque doctrine with the more typical form of egoism. In order to avoid this confusion, we should reflect on this other view, which may be stated as follows:

E_2:   An act is morally right if and only if no alternative would produce a greater balance of pleasure over pain for me.

E_2 entails that when I act, I am supposed to try to maximize my own pleasure-minus-pain. In this respect, E_2 is indistinguishable from E_1. However, E_2 entails that when anyone other than me acts, he or she is supposed to try to maximize *my* pleasure-minus-pain, too. Here we see a profound difference between E_1 and E_2. For according to E_1, each other person is supposed to try to maximize *his own* or *her own* pleasure-minus-pain.

E_2 is not a very plausible view. It entails that a person acts rightly only if he does as much as he can to benefit me, Fred Feldman. After I die, nothing will be morally forbidden and nothing will be morally required. For after I die, no act will benefit me more than any other. Every act will have a "Feldman-utility" of zero. Surely, no one other than me would have any interest in E_2, and if I believed this view I would be an egotist indeed!

But of course I don't mean to leave you out. Consider this schema:

E_3:   An act is morally right if and only if no alternative would produce a greater balance of pleasure over pain for————.

If you write your name in the blank in E_3, the result will be a possible moral theory. That theory would be as implausible as E_2. Furthermore, if you believed in that theory, you would be as much of an egotist as I would be if I believed in E_2. Although some philosophers have spent a considerable amount of time discussing doctrines such as these, they surely do not deserve very much attention. So let us forget about these rather silly forms of pseudoegoism and return to genuine egoism, E_1.

Egoism and Act Utilitarianism

Given one fairly plausible assumption, we can show that E_1 is incompatible with U_7, our version of act utilitarianism. This is of some interest, since some moralists find it easy to confuse the two doctrines.

Suppose a person is faced with the following situation. He is a collector of Renaissance paintings, and he is visiting a country church in Italy. On the wall hangs a beautiful old painting. The collector could easily steal it. If he were to steal the painting, let us suppose, he would not be caught, and he would subsequently gain great pleasure from looking at it in his secret gallery back home. He would not feel any pangs of guilt, since he is so obsessed with art as to be indifferent to morality. Thus, it seems that we can assign high agent utility to his act of stealing the painting. On the other hand, since he would be disgusted with himself if he were to refrain from stealing the painting, and since he would gain no pleasure from this act, we can assign low agent utility to his act of refraining from stealing the painting.

As should be evident, the people who use the church, and art lovers everywhere, will be deeply saddened by the theft of the painting. They will be much happier if it remains where it is. Thus, if we consider all of their pleasures and pains in addition to those of the collector, we find that the overall utility of theft is very low, whereas the overall utility of nontheft is fairly high. We can tabulate these results as follows:

act	overall utility	agent utility
a_1—stealing the painting	$-10,000$	$+500$
a_2—not stealing the painting	$+5,000$	-100

Assuming that a_1 and a_2 have no other alternatives, we can easily see that U_7 yields the result that a_1 would be wrong and that a_2 would be right. This follows from the fact that no alternative to a_2 has higher overall utility than a_2 has, whereas some alternative to a_1 does have a higher overall utility than a_1 has. On the other hand, it should also be clear that E_1 yields the contrary result. Since a_1 has the highest agent utility of the set, E_1 implies that a_1 is right and that a_2 is not right. Thus, we have a case in which the results generated by act utilitarianism differ from those generated by egoism. Hence, in this type of case the two theories are incompatible.

The only important assumption in this argument is this: we have assumed that it is possible for there to be a set of alternatives in which an act having the highest agent utility does not have the highest overall utility. That is, we have assumed that it is possible for there to be a case in which the act that is most beneficial to the agent is not the act that is most beneficial to society as a whole. If this assumption is correct, as it seems to be, then act utilitarianism is inconsistent with egoism. An act that is right according to the former theory may turn out to be wrong according to the latter.

Now that we have come to a clearer understanding of the nature of egoism, and have seen that it is distinct from a standard form of act utilitarianism, we should turn to the question of its truth. What reason is there to believe that egoism is true? What arguments have been given in favor of this normative theory?

Arguments for Egoism

Sometimes it is alleged that many of the problems our society faces arise as a result of a sort of misguided altruism. Well-intentioned people try to help others, but they succeed only in making things worse. For example, missionaries go to a tropical island to show the "backward natives" a "better way of life." As a result, some have argued, the natives suffer, disease and dissatisfaction become rampant, and the tropical paradise is destroyed. People have also argued that if we refrained from extending charity to others, the others would learn to fend for themselves, and everyone would be happier as a result. In general, then, it has been claimed that society as a whole would be better off if each of us devoted his energies to bettering his own status rather than meddling in the affairs of others.

It is easy to see how this view leads to egoism. For if self-interested acts in fact lead to the betterment of humanity as a whole, then self-interested acts are obviously morally right. However, if self-interested acts are all morally right, then egoism is true—for egoism is the doctrine that an act is morally right if and only if it maximizes the agent's self-interest. Therefore, egoism is true. This argument can be stated somewhat more clearly:

Closet Utilitarian Argument

(1) If people act in such a way as to maximize their own self-interest, then humanity will be better off as a whole.

(2) People ought to act in whatever way will lead to the betterment of humanity as a whole.

(3) Therefore, people ought to act in such a way as to maximize their own self-interest; in other words, egoism is true.

This argument is called the "closet utilitarian argument" because, as should be obvious, although it is designed to establish egoism, it presupposes the basic principle of act utilitarianism. A close look at the second premise will reveal that it is simply a disguised version of the act-utilitarian principle. To say that people should act in the way that results in humanity being better off is just to say that people should always act in such a way as to secure the greatest happiness for all concerned. If happiness is understood in terms of pleasure and pain, this is equivalent to requiring that we always maximize utility. Thus, to say, as (2) does, that people should always act in whatever way would lead to the betterment of humanity as a whole is just to say that an act is morally right if and only if it has at least as much utility as any of its alternatives. And this is act utilitarianism.

Thus, people who use the closet utilitarian argument are in a rather odd position. They purport to be arguing for egoism. Yet their argument presupposes a form of act utilitarianism. People who argue in this way are apparently not clear in their own minds about what makes right acts right. On the one hand they may feel, first, that what makes right acts right is that they have maximal overall utility. They may feel, second, that if we were all a bit more selfish, we would, almost accidentally, manage to do these morally right actions. In this case, their moral theory is basically utilitarian. They just happen to hold the subsidiary, empirical view that selfish acts tend to have high utility. On the other hand, people who use the closet utilitarian argument may really believe in egoism. In this case, they would feel that what makes right acts right is that they maximize *agent* utility. In this case, the appeal to the betterment of humanity as a whole would have to be considered an irrelevant rhetorical device. After all, according to egoism, such considerations are supposed to be given no moral weight.

In any case, this argument for egoism seems very weak. For one of its premises seems to be a form of act utilitarianism. In light of the problems we have already encountered with act utilitarianism, any such premise must be regarded as controversial at best. Furthermore, people who have rejected act utilitarianism and want to defend egoism surely cannot appeal consistently to act utilitarianism as a premise in their argument for egoism!

Another problem with the closet utilitarian argument arises from its first premise. We have already discussed this problem in the section on egoism and act utilitarianism. When we compared these two theories, we considered the question of whether acts with maximal agent utility always have maximal overall utility. We found that there is no good reason to suppose that this is the case. It is apparently possible for some agent to be faced with an alternative set in which the act that would be most in his own interest is not the same as the act that would be most in the interest of humanity as a whole. If this indeed can happen, then (1) of the closet utilitarian argument is false.

It appears, then, that both premises in the closet utilitarian argument are false. We surely have no proof of egoism here. Let us turn to another argument that has been used to bolster egoism.

Traditionally, egoism has been said to follow from the combination of an alleged fact about human motivation and an alleged fact about moral obligation. Let us consider the claim about motivation first. It is sometimes said that whenever a person acts, he is motivated to act by a desire for some sort of satisfaction. If the person didn't desire any satisfaction, he would have no reason to do anything, and hence would not do anything. Furthermore, it might be said that whenever a person acts, he acts in such a way as to secure for himself the greatest amount of satisfaction he can. If "satisfaction" is understood as "agent utility," this doctrine becomes the doctrine that each person always chooses to act in such a way as to maximize agent utility.

If we take this doctrine about motivation to be a fundamental law of psychology, a law that expresses a necessary feature of human motivation, we obtain a thesis that might be called "psychological egoism." It can be formulated as follows:

> PE: A person can perform an act only if that act has at least as much agent utility as any alternative.

Understood in this way, psychological egoism implies that it is impossible for anyone to perform a certain act if some alternative to that act would be more beneficial to him in terms of pleasure and pain. I simply cannot do anything other than maximize my own self-interest. Thus, we have our alleged fact about human motivation.

The alleged fact about moral obligation is that no one is morally obligated to perform an action if he cannot in fact perform it. If an action is impossible, it is not morally required. This is sometimes put by saying that "ought" implies "can." In other words, if you ought to do something, then you can do it. This principle may be stated as follows:

> K: A person is morally obligated to perform an action only if he can perform that action.

We call this principle "K" in honor of Immanuel Kant, who is often said to be the first major philosopher to recognize the importance of K.

It has been claimed that PE and K together entail E_1. The argument would look something like this: According to PE, people cannot do anything other than what maximizes their own self-interest. But if people cannot do anything other than what maximizes their own self-interest, then, according to K, they are not obligated to do anything other than what maximizes their own self-interest. But to say that they are not obligated to do anything other than what maximizes their own self-interest is just to say that it is right for them to maximize their own self-interest. Thus, an act is right if and only if it maximizes the agent's self-interest. In other words, E₁ is true.

The main points of this argument can be put as follows:

Motivation Argument

(1) A person can perform an act only if that act has at least as much agent utility as any alternative.

(2) A person is morally obligated to perform an act only if he can perform it.

(3) If a person can perform an act only if that act has at least as much agent utility as any alternative, and if a person is morally obligated to perform an act only if he can perform it, then it is right for a person to perform an act if and only if it has at least as much agent utility as any alternative.

(4) Therefore, it is right for a person to perform an act if and only if it has at least as much agent utility as any alternative; in other words, egoism is true.

When put in this rather stark form, the problems with the argument may become clearer. In fact, it should be clear that both (1) and (3) are false. If we reflect on (1), the thesis of psychological egoism, we should see that it is simply preposterous. For according to this doctrine, it is impossible for anyone to perform any action that fails to maximize his own self-interest. It might be reasonable to claim that in general, people would like to perform actions that are in their own interest. That is, it might be reasonable to maintain that each person wants to perform that action, from each alternative set, that has the highest agent utility. Maybe we are all selfish at heart. However, given the fact that most of us, most of the time, don't have the faintest idea which of our alternatives has the highest agent utility, it would be an extraordinary stroke of good luck if we always succeeded in performing just that act. Surely, even if we all want to be maximally selfish, we sometimes accidentally do something that benefits others more than it benefits us.

The third premise of our argument is false too. Psychological egoism and the Kantian dictum do not entail ethical egoism. To show that PE and K do not entail E₁, we need to describe a case in which PE and K are both true but E₁ is false. This is not too difficult. First, let us suppose that on some occasion, some agent, Smith, has two alternatives open to him. He can do either *a* or *b*. These two alternatives are equal in agent utility. Let us also suppose that psychological egoism is true in this situation. That is, we acknowledge that Smith cannot fail to maximize agent utility. In this particular case, of course, it does not make much difference, since his alternatives are equal in agent utility. In any case, Smith can do a and he can do b, but he can't do both together. PE is assumed to be true. Next, suppose that if either alternative were obligatory (which neither in fact is), Smith would be able to perform it. Smith is not morally required to do anything he is unable to do. Hence the Kantian dictum, K, is also true in this imaginary situation.

It should be clear that even if we grant all this, we can still consistently imagine cases in which a would be morally right and b would be morally wrong. Perhaps this results from the effects of a and b on others. In any case, this shows that E_1, our version of egoism, would be false, since E_1 entails that any act with maximal agent utility, such as b, is morally right. The assumption that E_1 is false, therefore, is compatible with the assumption that PE and K are true. Hence, PE and K do not entail E_1. Thus, line (3) of the motivation argument must also be rejected.

In light of these problems, we must conclude that neither of the two main traditional lines of defense for egoism is successful. Perhaps egoism cannot be shown to be true. Can it be shown to be false?

Arguments against Egoism

One of the most important classical arguments against egoism is the one presented by G. E. Moore in *Principia Ethica*.[2] Moore claimed that egoism is self-contradictory, and hence not an acceptable moral doctrine. Let us consider Moore's argument.

Moore begins by formulating a version of egoism that is rather different from our E_1. He puts it this way: "Each man ought rationally to hold: my own greatest happiness is the only good thing that there is; my actions can only be good as means, in so far as they help me win this."[3] Moore proceeds to argue that egoism, so formulated, is self-contradictory:

> What egoism holds, therefore, is that *each* man's happiness is the sole good—that a number of different things are *each* of them the only good thing. This is an absolute contradiction! No more complete and thorough refutation of any theory could be desired.[4]

Some commentators may feel that Moore's argument, even if successful, is irrelevant. After all, they might claim, what he calls "egoism" is utterly unlike what we call "egoism." Even if he has shown that the target of his criticism is "an absolute contradiction," he has not shown any defect in E_1. However, a closer look at Moore's argument will show that Moore is really not as far off the mark as he may seem to be.

First, we must recall that egoism, as we are understanding it, is the view that an act is right if and only if it maximizes agent utility. Thus, an act of mine is right if and only if it maximizes my utility. Following Moore, we can reason as follows: If egoism is true, then the only thing that makes any act of mine right is the fact that doing it would maximize my happiness. But if the only thing that makes an act of mine right is the fact that it would maximize my happiness, then my being happy is the only good thing. Therefore, if egoism is true, my being happy is the only good thing.

However, if egoism is true, then the only thing that makes any act of yours right is the fact that it would maximize your happiness. But if the only thing that makes an act of yours right is the fact that it maximizes your happiness, then your being happy is the only good thing. Hence, if egoism is true, then your being happy is the only good thing.

Putting these conclusions together, we get the result that if egoism is true, then your being happy is the only good thing, and my being happy is also the only good thing. Since your being happy is different from my being happy, it is impossible for both of them to be the only good thing. Hence, egoism is false.

Understood in this way, Moore's argument is valid. Given its premises, the argument shows that egoism is not true. So let's consider these premises, to see whether any of them is false.

The weakest link in the argument appears to be the following claim:

(1) If the only thing that makes an act of mine right is the fact that it maximizes my happiness, then my being happy is the only good thing.

To simplify our discussion, let us refer to the antecedent of this claim as "(a)":

(a) The only thing that makes an act of mine right is the fact that it maximizes my happiness.

The consequent of (1) is, from a logical point of view, composed of two parts:

(b) My being happy is a good thing.
(c) Nothing other than my being happy is a good thing.

What (1) says, then, is that (a) implies both (b) and (c). But it appears that this is not true. For in the first place, (a) does not imply (b). It could be claimed that my being happy is not a good thing at all, even though (a) is true. Rather, what is a good thing, it might be said, is my *making* myself happy. In other words, when a person makes himself happy, it is not his being happy that is intrinsically good, but his making himself happy that is intrinsically good. This would make egoism an odd sort of hedonism, but, so understood, the view would be consistent.

Also, it could be claimed that even though (a) is true, (c) is false. It could be maintained that there are many good things that simply have no relevance to my action—perhaps because I am incapable of producing, or even helping to produce, any of them. Such things, it could be said, never contribute toward the rightness of my actions, even though each of them, in itself, is a good thing.

We have seen that the falsity of both (b) and (c) is compatible with the truth of (a). Hence, (a) does not imply that my happiness is the only good thing. Therefore, (1) is false. For this reason, we must reject .Moore's argument against egoism. Moore hasn't shown that egoism entails that each person's being happy is the only good thing.

Another interesting argument against egoism is presented by Kurt Baier.[5] Baier attempts to show that egoism has some absurd consequences. He describes a case in which two individuals, K and B, are seeking the same goal. In each case, achieving the goal would maximize the agent's self-interest. Obviously, however, they cannot both achieve the goal. If B achieves the goal, then B must thwart K's efforts. If K is to achieve it, then K must thwart B's efforts. Baier claims that egoism has inconsistent results in this case. For, on the one hand, egoism entails that B ought to achieve the goal. This follows from the fact that achieving the goal would maximize B's self-interest. To do this, however, B must thwart K's efforts. Hence, B ought to thwart K's efforts. On the other hand, egoism entails that K ought to achieve the goal; after all, it would maximize his own self-interest. Since no one ought to thwart anyone's efforts to do what he ought to do, it follows that B ought not to thwart K's efforts to achieve the goal. Putting these results together, we see that egoism entails that B ought to thwart K's efforts, and that B ought not to thwart K's efforts. This is impossible, and so egoism must be false.

Although Baier's argument is interesting, it is not entirely conclusive. The argument makes essential use of this general moral principle: "No one ought to thwart anyone's efforts to do what he ought to do." We may state this principle more clearly:

(T)   If S_1 is morally obligated to do a, then it is not the case that S_2 is morally obligated to thwart S_1's efforts to do a.

Principle (T) plays an essential role in the argument. Without it, Baier has no way to show that B ought not to thwart K's efforts to achieve the goal. Baier must show this if he is to show that egoism yields an inconsistency in the imagined case.

But is (T) true? Some would say that (T) is false. Indeed, many movies and novels are based upon the assumption that (T) is false. Consider, for example, the age-old tale of two soldiers locked in mortal combat. Each is committed to fighting for his country, and so each is morally bound to try to thwart the other's efforts to do his duty. If (T) were true, such examples would be impossible. More prosaic cases can be described. Suppose Smith has promised to buy a certain toy for his little son and Jones has promised to buy the same toy for her daughter. Suppose there is only one such toy left in the store. In order to do his duty, Smith must thwart Jones's efforts to do her duty, and vice versa. If we reflect on (T), we will see that it is inconsistent with quite a lot of our moral experience. Thus, Baier's argument, which depends upon (T), is unsound. It does not refute egoism.[6]

Baier used principle (T) in his argument against egoism. But it is interesting to note that (T) conflicts not only with egoism, but also with act utilitarianism, under a fairly plausible interpretation. To see this, suppose again that there are two agents, K and B, and that each has a set of alternatives. Suppose that the best of K's alternatives is *a*, and the best of B's alternatives is *b*. By "best" here, we mean "having the highest overall utility." Suppose, finally, that it is impossible for both *a* and *b* to be performed. In this case, according to act utilitarianism, K is obligated to do *a*, and thus thwart B's efforts to do his duty, *b*. Hence, even under act utilitarianism principle (T) must be rejected.

Is Egoism a Moral Doctrine?

Some philosophers have attempted to show that egoism is not a moral doctrine at all. Though perhaps admitting that each of us has a good reason to select the act that will maximize our own self-interest, they have claimed that this "good reason" is not a *moral* reason. They say that egoism is acceptable as a doctrine of *prudence*, but not as a doctrine of morality. Hence, they will perhaps be willing to accept a principle such as this:

E_4: An act is prudent if and only if no alternative has higher agent utility.

But they reject E_1.

What reason is there for maintaining that E_1 is not a moral doctrine at all? Some commentators have claimed that egoists cannot consistently promulgate their view. From this, it has been inferred that the egoist's view is not a moral doctrine at all. This argument is fairly complex, but it merits close attention.[7]

First, let us introduce a technical term that plays an important role in the argument. This term is *consistently promulgatable*. Roughly, we can say that an alleged moral doctrine is consistently promulgatable if it is possible to teach that doctrine to others without performing an action judged by that doctrine to be wrong. Or, more succinctly:

D_1:   Doctrine D is consistently promulgatable =df. it is possible to promulgate D without violating D.

The argument now runs as follows: If someone, S, convinces others that E_1 is true, then they will act in accord with E_1. If they act in accord with E_1, then their actions will be directed toward the maximization of their own self-interest. If their actions are directed toward the maximization of their own self-interest, they will undoubtedly do things that will be injurious to S. Hence, S's act of convincing them that E_1 is true turns out in the long run to be injurious to S. Thus, S's act of convincing others that E_1 is true is itself not in accord with E_1. Therefore, E_1 is not consistently promulgatable. Since every moral theory is consistently promulgatable, E_1 is not a moral theory.

The main points of this argument can be put as follows:

Promulgation Argument

(1) If anyone promulgates E_1, he thereby fails to maximize agent utility.

(2) If anyone fails to maximize agent utility, he violates E_1.

(3) Therefore, if anyone promulgates E_1, he violates E_1; that is, E_1 is not consistently promulgatable.

(4) Every moral doctrine is consistently promulgatable.

(5) Therefore, E_1 is not a moral doctrine.

The argument proceeds in two stages. First, we use premises (1) and (2) to establish (3). Then we use (3) and (4) to establish (5). So, the independent premises are (1), (2), and (4). Line (3) is not the conclusion of the argument, but it follows validly from the preceding lines. Line (2) should be accepted, since under E_1 we must in fact always maximize agent utility. Thus, our attention should be directed toward the remaining independent premises, (1) and (4).

Line (1) looks implausible. What reason is there to maintain that whenever anyone promulgates E_1, he thereby fails to maximize agent utility? Couldn't there be a case in which someone promulgates E_1 and in so doing benefits himself? For example, suppose I promise to give you one million dollars if you will agree to spend thirty seconds promulgating E_1. Suppose you then spend thirty seconds trying to convince your grandmother that E_1 is true. At the end of this time I give you the money, as I promised I would. Surely, in a case such as this, promulgating E_1 does maximize agent utility. There is nothing else you could have done instead that would have been more in your interest. Just as surely, a case such as this is possible. Hence, (1) is not true.

Equally serious problems beset (4). There is no good reason to suppose that every moral doctrine is consistently promulgatable. For example, some one might hold this as a moral doctrine:

(P)   It is never right to promulgate anything.

Admittedly, (P) is a weird doctrine, and it is surely untrue. But couldn't someone accept it as a moral doctrine? Nevertheless, (P) cannot be promulgated without being violated. In light of this, we must conclude that the promulgation argument is not conclusive. We have yet to see a successful argument against egoism.

The Refutation of Egoism

The most direct way to refute egoism is simply to point out some of its consequences. If we reflect on these consequences impartially, we will see that egoism is false. Consider the following case. A man is the treasurer of a large pension fund. He is entrusted with the job of keeping track of and investing the money deposited by the workers. When a worker retires, the worker is entitled to draw a weekly sum from the fund. Suppose the treasurer discovers that it will be possible for him to use all the money for his own selfish pleasure without being caught. Perhaps he wants to buy a large yacht and sail to a South Sea island, there to live out his days in idleness, indulgence, procreation, and, in a word, enjoyment. Since there is no extradition treaty between the South Sea island and the United States, he can get away with it.

Let us also suppose that if the treasurer does abscond with the funds, hundreds of old people will be deprived of their pensions. They will be heartbroken to discover that instead of living comfortably on the money they had put into the pension fund, they will have to suffer the pain and indignity of poverty.

We can now see the essentials of the case. The treasurer has two main alternatives. He can steal the money, or he can leave it where it belongs. The first alternative will be more beneficial to him, but it will be very harmful to the workers. The second alternative will be harmless. So his alternatives and their agent utilities are:

a_1—stealing the money   +10,000
a_2—leaving the money where it is   −3

Obviously, a_1 has far higher agent utility than its alternative, a_2. E_1 is the view that an act is morally right if and only if it has at least as much agent utility as any alternative. Hence, E_1 entails that a_1 is morally right and a_2 is not morally right. This is clearly incorrect. For a_1 is not morally right.

It is cruel and selfish. Thus, E_1 is not true. This argument may be outlined as follows:

Pension Argument

(1) If E_1 is true, a_1 in the example is morally right.

(2) a_1 in the example is not morally right.

(3) Therefore, E_1 is not true.

This argument decisively refutes egoism, as do an enormous number of other arguments along the same lines. Our conclusion, then, is that egoism can be formulated in such a way as to be a consistent moral doctrine. Nevertheless, when so formulated, it simply is not true.

NOTES

1. A good example is the formulation proposed by William Frankena in his *Ethics* (Englewood Cliffs, N. J.: Prentice-Hall, 1963), p. 18. Frankena suggests that egoism consists of the view that (a) an act is right if and only if it is in the *agent's* self-interest, and (b) an act is right if and only if it is in the self-interest of anyone evaluating the act. It is no wonder that Frankena finds this view to be implausible.

2. G. E. Moore, *Principia Ethica* (Cambridge: Cambridge University Press, 1903), pp. 96–102.

3. *Ibid.*, p. 97.

4. *Ibid.*, p. 99.

5. Kurt Baier, *The Moral Point of View*, abridged ed. (New York: Random House, 1965), pp. 93–96.

6. These objections to Baier's argument are very similar to ones developed by Jesse Kalin in "Baier's Refutation of Egoism," *Philosophical Studies*, 22 (1971), 74–78.

7. An argument along these lines can be found in Brian Medlin, "Ultimate Principles and Ethical Egoism," *The Australasian Journal of Philosophy*, 35 (1957), 111–18. See especially Part Two of this paper.

7

Kant I

Sometimes our moral thinking takes a decidedly nonutilitarian turn. That is, we often seem to appeal to a principle that is inconsistent with the whole utilitarian standpoint. One case in which this occurs clearly enough is the familiar tax-cheat case. A person decides to cheat on his income tax, rationalizing his misbehavior as follows: "The government will not be injured by the absence of my tax money. After all, compared with the enormous total they take in, my share is really a negligible sum. On the other hand, I will be happier if I have the use of the money. Hence, no one will be injured by my cheating, and one person will be better off. Thus, it is better for me to cheat than it is for me to pay."

In response to this sort of reasoning, we may be inclined to say something like this: "Perhaps you are right in thinking that you will be better off if you cheat. And perhaps you are right in thinking that the government won't even know the difference. Nevertheless, your act would be wrong. For if everyone were to cheat on his income taxes, the government would soon go broke. Surely you can see that you wouldn't want others to act in the way you propose to act. So you shouldn't act in that way." While it may not be clear that this sort of response would be decisive, it should be clear that this is an example of a sort of response that is often given.

There are several things to notice about this response. For one, it is not based on the view that the example of the tax cheat will provoke everyone else to cheat too. If that were the point of the response, then the response might be explained on the basis of utilitarian considerations. We could understand the responder to be saying that the tax cheater has miscalculated his utilities. Whereas he thinks his act of cheating has high utility, in fact it has low utility because it will eventually result in the collapse of the government. It is important to recognize that the response presented above is not based upon any such utilitarian considerations. This can be seen by reflecting on the fact that the point could just as easily have been made in this way: "Of course, very few other people will know about your cheating, and so your behavior will not constitute an example to others. Thus, it will not provoke others to cheat. Nevertheless, your act is wrong. For if everyone were to cheat as you propose to do, then the government would collapse. Since you wouldn't want others to behave in the way you propose to behave, you should not behave in that way. It would be wrong to cheat."

Another thing to notice about the response in this case is that the responder has not simply said, "What you propose to do would be cheating; hence, it is wrong." The principle in question is not simply the principle that cheating is wrong. Rather, the responder has appealed to a much more general principle, which seems to be something like this: If you wouldn't want everyone else to act in a certain way, then you shouldn't act in that way yourself.

This sort of general principle is in fact used quite widely in our moral reasoning. If someone proposes to remove the pollution-control devices from his automobile, his friends are sure to say "What if everyone did that?" They would have in mind some dire consequences for the quality of the air, but their point would not be that the removal of the pollution-control device by one person will in fact cause others to remove theirs, and will thus eventually lead to the destruction of the environment. Their point, rather, is that if their friend would not want others to act in the way he proposes to act, then it would be wrong for him to act in that way. This principle is also used against the person who refrains from giving to charity; the person who evades the draft in time of national emergency; the person who tells a lie in order to get out of a bad spot; and even the person who walks across a patch of newly seeded grass. In all such cases, we feel that the person acts wrongly not because his actions will have bad results, but because he wouldn't want others to behave in the way he behaves.

A highly refined version of this nonutilitarian principle is the heart of the moral theory of Immanuel Kant.[1] In his *Groundwork of the Metaphysic of Morals*,[2] Kant presents, develops, and defends the thesis that something like this principle is the "supreme principle of morality." Kant's presentation is rather complex; in parts, it is very hard to follow. Part of the trouble arises from his use of a rather unfamiliar technical vocabulary. Another source of trouble is that Kant is concerned with establishing a variety of other points in this little book, and some of these involve fairly complex issues in metaphysics and epistemology. Since our aim here is simply to present a clear, concise account of Kant's basic moral doctrine, we will have to ignore quite a bit of what he says in the book.

Kant formulates his main principle in a variety of different ways. All of the members of the following set of formulations seem to have a lot in common:

> I ought never to act except in such a way that I can also will that my maxim should become a universal law.[3]
>
> Act only on that maxim through which you can at the same time will that it should become a universal law.[4]
>
> Act as if the maxim of your action were to become through your will a universal law of nature.[5]
>
> We must be able to will that a maxim of our action should become a universal law—this is the general canon for all moral judgment of action.[6]

Before we can evaluate this principle, which Kant calls the *categorical imperative*, we have to devote some attention to figuring out what it is supposed to mean. To do this, we must answer a variety of questions. What is a maxim? What is meant by "universal law"? What does Kant mean by "will"? Let us consider these questions in turn.

Maxims

In a footnote, Kant defines *maxim* as "a subjective principle of volition."[7] This definition is hardly helpful. Perhaps we can do better. First, however, a little background.

Kant apparently believes that when a person engages in genuine action, he always acts on some sort of general principle. The general principle will explain what the person takes himself to be doing and the circumstances in which he takes himself to be doing it. For example, if I need money, and can get some only by borrowing it, even though I know I won't be able to repay it, I might proceed to borrow some from a friend. My maxim in performing this act might be, "Whenever I need money and can get it by borrowing it, then I will borrow it, even if I know I won't be able to repay it."

Notice that this maxim is *general*. If I adopt it, I commit myself to behaving in the described way *whenever* I need money and the other conditions are satisfied. In this respect, the maxim serves to formulate a general principle of action rather than just some narrow reason applicable in just one case.[8] So a maxim must describe some general sort of situation, and then propose some form of action for the situation. To adopt a maxim is to commit yourself to acting in the described way whenever the situation in question arises.

It seems clear that Kant holds that every action has a maxim, although he does not explicitly state this view. When we speak of an action here, we mean a concrete, particular action, or *act-token*, rather than an *act-type*. Furthermore, we must distinguish between genuine actions and what we may call "mere bodily movements." It would be absurd to maintain that a man who scratches himself in his sleep is acting on the maxim "When I itch, I shall scratch." His scratching is a mere bodily movement, and has no maxim. A man who deliberately sets out to borrow some money from a friend, on the other hand, does perform an action. And according to our interpretation of Kant, his action must have a maxim.

It would be implausible to maintain that before we act, we always consciously formulate the maxim of our action. Most of the time we simply go ahead and perform the action without giving any conscious thought to what we're doing, or what our situation is. We're usually too intent on getting the job done. Nevertheless, if we are asked after the fact, we often recognize that we actually were acting on a general policy, or maxim. For example, if you are taking a test, and you set about to answer each question correctly, you probably won't give any conscious thought to your maxim. You will be too busy thinking about the test. But if someone were to ask you to explain what you are doing and to explain the policy upon which you are doing it, you might then realize that in fact you have been acting a maxim. Your maxim might be, "Whenever I am taking an academic test, and I believe I know the correct answers, I shall give what I take to be the correct answers." So a person may act on a maxim even though she hasn't consciously entertained it.

In one respect, the maxim of an action may be inaccurate: it does not so much represent the actual situation of the action as it does the situation the agent takes himself to be in. Suppose, for example, that I have a lot of money in my savings account but I have forgotten all about it. I take myself to be broke. When I go out to borrow some money from a friend, my maxim might be, "When I am broke and can get money in no other way, I shall borrow some from a friend." In this case, my maxim does not apply to my actual situation. For my actual situation is not one in which I am broke. Yet the maxim does apply to the situation I take myself to be in. For I believe that I am broke, and I believe that I can get money in no other way. So it is important to recognize that a maxim is a general policy statement that describes the sort of situation the agent takes himself to be in when he performs an action, and the sort of action he takes himself to be performing. In fact, both the situation and the action may be different from what the agent takes them to be.

Another point about maxims that should be recognized is this. Externally similar actions may in fact have radically different maxims. Here is an elaborated version of an example given by Kant that illustrates this point.[9] Suppose there are two grocers, Mr. Grimbley and Mr. Hughes. Mr. Grimbley's main goal in life is to get rich. After careful consideration, he has decided that in the long run he'll make more money if he gains a reputation for treating his customers fairly. In other words, he believes that "honesty is the best policy—because it pays." Hence, Mr. Grimbley scrupulously sees to it that every customer gets the correct change. When Mr. Grimbley gives correct change to a customer, he acts on this maxim:

M_1: When I can gain a good business reputation by giving correct change, I shall give correct change.

Mr. Hughes, on the other hand, has decided that it would be morally wrong to cheat his customers. This decision has moved him to adopt the policy of always giving the correct change. He doesn't care whether his honest dealings will in the long run contribute to an increase in sales. Even if he were to discover that honesty in business dealings does *not* pay, he would still treat his customers honestly. So Mr. Hughes apparently acts on some maxim such as this:

M_2: When I can perform a morally right act by giving correct change, I shall give correct change.

Mr. Grimbley's overt act of giving correct change to a customer looks just like Mr. Hughes's overt act of giving correct change to a customer. Their customers cannot tell, no matter how closely they observe the behavior of Mr. Grimbley and Mr. Hughes, what their maxims are. However, as we have seen, the actions of Mr. Grimbley are associated with a maxim radically different from that associated with the actions of Mr. Hughes.

For our purposes, it will be useful to introduce a concept that Kant does not employ. This is the concept of the *generalized form* of a maxim. Suppose I decide to go to sleep one night and my maxim in performing this act is this:

M_3: Whenever I am tired, I shall sleep.

My maxim is stated in such a way as to contain explicit references to me. It contains two occurrences of the word "I." The generalized form of my maxim is the principle we would get if we were to revise my maxim so as to make it applicable to everyone. Thus, the generalized form of my maxim is this:

GM_3: Whenever anyone is tired, he will sleep.

In general, then, we can represent the form of a maxim in this way:

M: Whenever I am ———, I shall ———.

Actual maxims have descriptions of situations in the first blank and descriptions of actions in the second blank. The generalized form of a maxim can be represented in this way:

GM: Whenever anyone is ———, she will ——.

So much, then, for maxims. Let us turn to our second question, "What is meant by universal law?"

Universal Law

When, in the formulation of the categorical imperative, Kant speaks of "universal law," he seems to have one or the other of two things in mind. Sometimes he seems to be thinking of a *universal law of nature*, and sometimes he seems to be thinking of a *universal law of freedom*.

A *law of nature* is a fully general statement that describes not only how things are, but how things always *must* be. Consider this example: If the temperature of a gas in an enclosed container is increased, then the pressure will increase too. This statement accurately describes the behavior of gases in enclosed containers. Beyond this, however, it describes behavior that is, in a certain sense, necessary. The pressure not only *does* increase, but it *must* increase if the volume remains the same and the temperature is increased. This "must" expresses not logical or moral necessity, but "physical necessity." Thus, a law of nature is a fully general statement that expresses a physical necessity.

A *universal law of freedom* is a universal principle describing how all people ought to act in a certain circumstance. It does not have to be a legal enactment—it needn't be passed by Congress or signed by the president. Furthermore, some universal laws of freedom are not always followed—although they should be. If in fact it is true that all promises ought to be kept, then this principle is a universal law of freedom: If anyone has made a promise, he keeps it. The "must" in a statement such as "If you have made a promise, then you must keep it" does not express logical or physical necessity. It may be said to express moral necessity. Using this concept of moral necessity, we can say that a universal law of freedom is a fully general statement that expresses a moral necessity.

Sometimes Kant's categorical imperative is stated in terms of universal laws of nature, and sometimes in terms of universal laws of freedom. We will consider the "law of nature" version, since Kant appeals to it in discussing some fairly important examples.

Willing

To will that something be the case is more than to merely wish for it to be the case. A person might wish that there would be peace everywhere in the world. Yet knowing that it is not within his power to bring about this wished-for state of affairs, he might refrain from willing that there be peace everywhere in the world. It is not easy to say just what a person does when he wills that something be the case. According to one view, willing that something be the case is something like commanding yourself to make it be the case. So if I will my arm to go up, that would be something like commanding myself to raise my arm. The Kantian concept of willing is a bit more complicated, however. According to Kant, it makes sense to speak of willing something to happen, even if that something is not an action. For example, we can speak of someone willing that everyone keep their promises.

Some states of affairs are impossible. They simply cannot occur. For example, consider the state of affairs of your jumping up and down while remaining perfectly motionless. It simply cannot be done. Yet a sufficiently foolish or irrational person might will that such a state of affairs occur. That would be as absurd as commanding someone else to jump up and down while remaining motionless. Kant would say of a person who has willed in this way that his will has "contradicted itself." We can also put the point by saying that the person has willed inconsistently.

Inconsistency in willing can arise in another, somewhat less obvious way. Suppose a person has already willed that he remain motionless. He does not change this volition, but persists in willing that he remain motionless. At the same time, however, he begins to will that he jump up and down. Although each volition is self-consistent, it is inconsistent to will both of them at the same time. This is a second way in which inconsistency in willing can arise.

It may be the case that there are certain things that everyone must always will. For example, we may have to will that we avoid intense pain. Anyone who wills something that is inconsistent with something everyone must will, thereby wills inconsistently.

Some of Kant's examples suggest that he held that inconsistency in willing can arise in a third way. This form of inconsistency is a bit more complex to describe. Suppose a person wills to be in Boston on Monday and also wills to be in San Francisco on Tuesday. Suppose, furthermore, that because of certain foul-ups at the airport it will be impossible for her to get from Boston to San Francisco on Tuesday. In this case, Kant would perhaps say that the person has willed inconsistently.

In general, we can say that a person wills inconsistently if he wills that p be the case and he wills that q be the case and it is impossible for p and q to be the case together.

The Categorical Imperative

With all this as background, we may be in a position to interpret the first version of Kant's categorical imperative. Our interpretation is this:

CI_1:   An act is morally right if and only if the agent of the act can consistently will that the generalized form of the maxim of the act be a law of nature.

We can simplify our formulation slightly by introducing a widely used technical term. We can say that a maxim is *universalizable* if and only if the agent who acts upon it can consistently will that its generalized form be a law of nature. Making use of this new term, we can restate our first version of the categorical imperative as follows:

CI_1':   An act is morally right if and only if its maxim is universalizable.

As formulated here, the categorical imperative is a statement of necessary and sufficient conditions for the moral rightness of actions. Some commentators have claimed that Kant did not intend his principle to be understood in this way. They have suggested that Kant meant it to be understood merely as a necessary but not sufficient condition for morally right action. Thus, they would prefer to formulate the imperative in some way such as this:

CI_1'':   An act is morally right only if its maxim is universalizable.

Understood in this way, the categorical imperative points out one thing to avoid in action. That is, it tells us to avoid actions whose maxims cannot be universalized. But it does not tell us the distinguishing feature of the actions we should perform. Thus, it does not provide us with a criterion of morally right action. Since Kant explicitly affirms that his principle is "the supreme principle of morality," it is reasonable to suppose that he intended it to be taken as a statement of necessary and sufficient conditions for morally right action. In any case, we will take the first version of the categorical imperative to be CI_1, rather than CI_1''.

It is interesting to note that other commentators have claimed that the categorical imperative isn't a criterion of right action at all. They have claimed that it was intended to be understood as a criterion of correctness for *maxims*.[10] These commentators might formulate the principle in this way:

CI_1''':   A maxim is morally acceptable if and only if it is universalizable.

This interpretation is open to a variety of objections. In the first place, it is not supported by the text. Kant repeatedly states that the categorical imperative is the basic principle by which we are to evaluate actions.[11] Furthermore, when he presents his formulations of the categorical imperative, he generally states it as a principle about the moral rightness of action. Finally, it is somewhat hard to see why we should be interested in a principle such as CI_1'''. For it does not constitute a theory about right action, or good persons, or anything else that has traditionally been a subject of moral enquiry. CI_1, on the other hand, competes directly with act utilitarianism, rule utilitarianism, and other classical moral theories.

In order to gain a better insight into the workings of the categorical imperative, it may be worthwhile to compare it with a doctrine with which it is sometimes confused—the golden rule. The golden rule has been formulated in a wide variety of ways.[12] Generally, however, it looks something like this:

> GR: An act is morally right if and only if, in performing it, the agent refrains from treating others in ways in which he would not want the others to treat him.

According to GR, then, if you wouldn't want others to lie to you, it is wrong to lie to them. If you would want others to treat you with respect, then it is right to treat others with respect.

Kant explicitly rejects the view that his categorical imperative is equivalent to the golden rule.[13] He points out a number of respects in which the two doctrines differ. For one, GR is not applicable to cases in which only one person is involved. Consider suicide. When a person commits suicide, he does not "treat others" in any way; he only "treats himself." Hence, when a person commits suicide, he does not treat others in ways in which he would not want the others to treat him. Therefore, under GR, anyone who commits suicide performs a morally right act. CI_1, on the other hand, may not yield this result. For if a person commits suicide, he does so on a maxim, whether other people are involved or not. Either his maxim is universalizable, or it is not. If it is not, CI_1 entails that his action is not right. If it is, CI_1 entails that his action is right. In this respect, CI_1 is clearly distinct from GR.

Kant also hints at another respect in which the two doctrines differ. Suppose a person considers herself to be utterly self-sufficient. She feels that she has no need of aid from others. GR then has nothing to say against her refraining from extending any kindness to others. After all, she has no objection to being treated in this unkind way by them. So GR entails that her behavior is morally right. CI_1, on the other hand, has no such consequence. Whether this person is willing to be mistreated by others or not, it may still be irrational of her to will that it be a law of nature that no one help anyone else. If so, CI_1 rules out uncharitableness, whether the agent likes it or not.

Similar considerations apply to masochists, whose behavior is not adequately guided by GR. After all, we surely don't want to allow the masochist to torture others simply on the grounds that he wouldn't object to being tortured by them! The unusual desires of masochists do not pose any special threat to CI_1.

So the main difference between GR and CI_1 seems to be this: According to GR, what makes an act right is the fact that the agent would not object to "having it done to himself." This opens the door to incorrect results in cases in which the agent, for some unexpected reason, would not object to being mistreated. According to CI_1, what makes an act right is the fact that the agent's maxim in performing it can be universalized. Thus, even if he would not object to being mistreated by others, his mistreatment of them may be wrong simply because it would be *irrational* to will that everyone should mistreat others in the same way.

Kant's Four Examples

In a very famous passage in Chapter II of the *Groundwork*, Kant presents four illustrations of the application of the categorical imperative.[14] In each case, in Kant's opinion, the act is morally wrong and the maxim is not universalizable. Thus, Kant holds that his theory implies that each of these acts is wrong. If Kant is right about this, then he has given us four positive instances of his theory. That is, he has given us four cases in which his theory yields correct results. Unfortunately, the illustrations are not entirely persuasive.

Kant distinguishes between "duties to self" and "duties to others." He also distinguishes between "perfect" and "imperfect" duties. This gives him four categories of duty: "perfect to self," "perfect to others," "imperfect to self," and "imperfect to others." Kant gives one example of each type of duty. By "perfect duty," Kant says he means a duty "which admits of no exception in the interests of inclination."[15] Kant seems to have in mind something like this: If a person has a perfect duty to perform a certain kind of action, then he must *always* do that kind of action when the opportunity arises. For example, Kant apparently holds that we must always perform the (negative) action of refraining from committing suicide. This would be a perfect duty. On the other hand, if a person has an imperfect duty to do a kind of action, then he must at least *sometimes* perform an action of that kind when the opportunity arises. For example, Kant maintains that we have an imperfect duty to help others in distress. We should devote at least some of our time to charitable activities, but we are under no obligation to give all of our time to such work.

The perfect/imperfect distinction has been drawn in a variety of ways—none of them entirely clear. Some commentators have said that if a person has a perfect duty to do a certain action, a, then there must be someone else who has a corresponding right to demand that a be done. This seems to be the case in Kant's second example, but not in his first example. Thus, it isn't clear that we should understand the concept of perfect duty in this way. Although the perfect/imperfect distinction is fairly interesting in itself, it does not play a major role in Kant's theory. Kant introduces the distinction primarily to insure that his examples will illustrate different kinds of duty.

Kant's first example illustrates the application of CI_1 to a case of perfect duty to oneself—the alleged duty to refrain from committing suicide. Kant describes the miserable state of the person contemplating suicide, and tries to show that his categorical imperative entails that the person should not take his own life. In order to simplify our discussion, let us use the abbreviation "a_1" to refer to the act of suicide the man would commit, if he were to commit suicide. According to Kant, every act must have a maxim. Kant tells us the maxim of a_1: "From self-love I make it my principle to shorten my life if its continuance threatens more evil than it promises pleasure."[16] Let us simplify and clarify this maxim, understanding it as follows:

$M(a_1)$: When continuing to live will bring me more pain than pleasure, I shall commit suicide out of self-love.

The generalized form of this maxim is as follows:

$GM(a_1)$: Whenever continuing to live will bring anyone more pain than pleasure, he will commit suicide out of self-love.

Since Kant believes that suicide is wrong, he attempts to show that his moral principle, the categorical imperative, entails that a_1 is wrong. To do this, of course, he needs to show that the agent of a_1 cannot consistently will that $GM(a_1)$ be a law of nature. Kant tries to show this in the following passage:

> . . . a system of nature by whose law the very same feeling whose function is to stimulate the furtherance of life should actually destroy life would contradict itself and consequently could not subsist as a system of nature. Hence this maxim cannot possibly hold as a universal law of nature and is therefore entirely opposed to the supreme principle of all duty.[17]

The general outline of Kant's argument is clear enough:

Suicide Example

(1) $GM(a_1)$ cannot be a law of nature.

(2) If $GM(a_1)$ cannot be a law of nature, then the agent of a_1 cannot consistently will that $GM(a_1)$ be a law of nature.

(3) a_1 is morally right if and only if the agent of a_1 can consistently will that $GM(a_1)$ be a law of nature.

(4) Therefore, a_1 is not morally right.

In order to determine whether Kant really has shown that his theory entails that a_1 is not right, let us look at this argument more closely. First of all, for our purposes we can agree that the argument is valid. If all the premises are true, then the argument shows that the imagined act of suicide would not be right. CI_1, here being used as premise (3), would thus be shown to imply that a_1 is not right.

Since we are now interested primarily in seeing how Kant makes use of CI_1, we can withhold judgment on the merits of it for the time being.

The second premise seems fairly plausible. For although an irrational person could probably will almost anything, it surely would be difficult for a perfectly rational person to will that something be a law of nature if that thing could not be a law of nature. Let us grant, then, that it would not be possible for the agent to consistently will that $GM(a_1)$ be a law of nature if in fact $GM(a_1)$ could not be a law of nature.

The first premise is the most troublesome. Kant apparently assumes that "self-love" has as its function, the stimulation of the furtherance of life. Given this, he seems to reason that self-love cannot also contribute sometimes to the destruction of life. Perhaps Kant assumes that a given feeling cannot have two "opposite" functions. However, if $GM(a_1)$ were a law of nature, self-love would have to contribute toward self-destruction in some cases. Hence, Kant seems to conclude, $GM(a_1)$ cannot be a law of nature. And so we have our first premise.

If this is Kant's reasoning, it is not very impressive. In the first place, it is not clear why we should suppose that self-love has the function of stimulating the furtherance of life. Indeed, it is not clear why we should suppose that self-love has any function at all! Second, it is hard to see why self-love can't serve two "opposite" functions. Perhaps self-love motivates us to stay alive when continued life would be pleasant, but motivates us to stop living when continued life would be unpleasant. Why should we hold this to be impossible?

So it appears that Kant's first illustration is not entirely successful. Before we turn to the second illustration, however, a few further comments may be in order. First, some philosophers would say that it is better that Kant's argument failed here. Many moralists would take the following position: Kant's view about suicide is wrong. The act of suicide out of self-love, a_1, is morally blameless. In certain circumstances suicide is each person's "own business." Thus, these moralists would say that if the categorical imperative did imply that a_1 is morally wrong, as Kant tries to show, then Kant's theory would be defective. But since Kant was not entirely successful in showing that his theory had this implication, the theory has not been shown to have any incorrect results.

A second point to notice about the suicide example is its scope. It is important to recognize that in this passage Kant has not attempted to show that suicide is always wrong. Perhaps Kant's personal view is that it is never right to commit suicide. However, in the passage in question he attempts to show only that a certain act of suicide, one based on a certain maxim, would be wrong. For all Kant has said here, other acts of suicide, done according to other maxims, might be permitted by the categorical imperative.

Let us turn now to the second illustration. Suppose I find myself hard-pressed financially and I decide that the only way in which I can get some money is by borrowing it from a friend. I realize that I will have to promise to repay the money, even though I won't in fact be able to do so. For I foresee that my financial situation will be even worse later on than it is at present. If I perform this action, a_2, of borrowing money on a false promise, I will perform it on this maxim:

$M(a_2)$:   When I need money and can get some by borrowing it on a false promise, then I shall borrow the money and promise to repay, even though I know that I won't be able to repay.

The generalized form of my maxim is this:

$GM(a_2)$:   Whenever anyone needs money and can get some by borrowing it on a false promise, then he will borrow the money and promise to repay, even though he knows that he won't be able to repay.

Kant's view is that I cannot consistently will that $GM(a_2)$ be a law of nature. This view emerges clearly in the following passage:

> . . . I can by no means will a universal law of lying; for by such a law there could properly be no promises at all, since it would be futile to profess a will for future action to others who would not believe my profession or who, if they did so over-hastily, would pay me back in like coin; and consequently my maxim, as soon as it was made a universal law, would be bound to annul itself.[18]

It is important to be clear about what Kant is saying here. He is not arguing against lying on the grounds that if I lie, others will soon lose confidence in me and eventually won't believe my promises. Nor is he arguing against lying on the grounds that my lie will contribute to a general practice of lying, which in turn will lead to a breakdown of trust and the destruction of the practice of promising. These considerations are basically utilitarian. Kant's point is more subtle. He is saying that there is something covertly self-contradictory about the state of affairs in which, as a law of nature, everyone makes a false promise when in need of a loan. Perhaps Kant's point is this: Such a state of affairs is self-contradictory because, on the one hand, in such a state of affairs everyone in need would borrow money on a false promise, and yet, on the other hand, in that state of affairs no one could borrow money on a false promise—for if promises were always violated, who would be silly enough to loan any money?

Since the state of affairs in which everyone in need borrows money on a false promise is covertly self-contradictory, it is irrational to will it to occur. No one can consistently will that this state of affairs should occur. But for me to will that $GM(a_2)$ be a law of nature is just for me to will that this impossible state of affairs occur. Hence, I cannot consistently will that the generalized form of my maxim be a law of nature. According to CI_1, my act is not right unless I can consistently will that the generalized form of its maxim be a law of nature. Hence, according to CI_1, my act of borrowing the money on the false promise is not morally right.

We can restate the essentials of this argument much more succinctly:

Lying-promise example

(1) $GM(a_2)$ cannot be a law of nature.

(2) If $GM(a_2)$ cannot be a law of nature, then I cannot consistently will that $GM(a_2)$ be a law of nature.

(3) a_2 is morally right if and only if I can consistently will that $GM(a_2)$ be a law of nature.

(4) Therefore, a_2 is not morally right.

The first premise is based upon the view that it would somehow be self-contradictory for it to be a law of nature that everyone in need makes a lying promise. For in that (allegedly impossible) state of affairs there would be promises, since those in need would make them, and there would also not be promises, since no one would believe that anyone was really committing himself to future payment by the use of the words "I promise." So, as Kant says, the generalized form of the maxim "annuls itself." It cannot be a law of nature.

The second premise is just like the second premise in the previous example. It is based on the idea that it is somehow irrational to will that something be the case if in fact it is impossible for it to be the case. So if it really is impossible for $GM(a_2)$ to be a law of nature, then it would be irrational of me to will that it be so. Hence, I cannot consistently will that the generalized form of my maxim be a law of nature. In other words, I cannot consistently will that it be a law of nature that whenever anyone needs money and can get some on a false promise, then he will borrow some and promise to repay, even though he knows that he won't be able to repay.

The third premise of the argument is the categorical imperative. If the rest of the argument is acceptable, then the argument as a whole shows that the categorical imperative, together with these other facts, implies that my lying promise would not be morally right. This would seem to be a reasonable result.

Some readers have apparently taken this example to show that according to Kantianism, it is always wrong to make a false promise. Indeed, Kant himself may have come to this conclusion. Yet if we reflect on the argument for a moment, we will see that the view of these readers is surely not the case. At best, the argument shows only that one specific act of making a false promise would be wrong. That one act is judged to be wrong because its maxim allegedly cannot be universalized. Other acts of making false promises would have to be evaluated independently. Perhaps it will turn out that every act of making a false promise has a maxim that cannot be universalized. If so, CI_1 would imply that they are all wrong. So far, however, we have been given no reason to suppose that this is the case.

Other critics would insist that Kant hasn't even succeeded in showing that a_2 is morally wrong. They would claim that the first premise of the argument is false. Surely it could be a law of nature that everyone will make a false promise when in need of money, they would say. If people borrowed money on false promises rarely enough, and kept their word on other promises, then no contradiction would arise. There would then be no reason to suppose that "no one would believe he was being promised anything, but would laugh at utterances of this kind as empty shams."[19]

Let us turn, then, to the third example. Kant now illustrates the application of the categorical imperative to a case of imperfect duty to oneself. The action in question is the "neglect of natural talents." Kant apparently holds that it is wrong for a person to let all of his natural talents go to waste. Of course, if a person has several natural talents, he is not required to develop all of them. Perhaps Kant considers this to be an imperfect duty partly because a person has the freedom to select which talents he will develop and which he will allow to rust.

Kant imagines the case of someone who is comfortable as he is and who, out of laziness, contemplates performing the act, a_3, of letting all his talents rust. His maxim in doing this would be:

$M(a_3)$:   When I am comfortable as I am, I shall let my talents rust.

When generalized, the maxim becomes:

GM(a₃):   Whenever anyone is comfortable as he is, he will let his
                      talents rust.

Kant admits that GM(a₃) could be a law of nature. Thus, his argument in
this case differs from the arguments he produced in the first two cases.
Kant proceeds to outline the reasoning by which the agent would come
to see that it would be wrong to perform a₃:

> He then sees that a system of nature could indeed always subsist under
> such a universal law, although (like the South Sea Islanders) every man
> should let his talents rust and should be bent on devoting his life solely to
> idleness, indulgence, procreation, and, in a word, to enjoyment. Only he
> cannot possibly *will* that this should become a universal law of nature or
> should be implanted in us as such a law by a natural instinct. For as a
> rational being he necessarily wills that all his powers should be developed,
> since they serve him, and are given him, for all sorts of possible ends.[20]

Once again, Kant's argument seems to be based on a rather dubious
appeal to natural purposes. Allegedly, nature implanted our talents in us
for all sorts of purposes. Hence, we necessarily will to develop them. If
we also will to let them rust, we are willing both to develop them (as we
must) and to refrain from developing them. Anyone who wills both of
these things obviously wills inconsistently. Hence, the agent cannot consistently will that his talents rust. This, together with the categorical
imperative, implies that it would be wrong to perform the act, a₃, of
letting one's talents rust.
     The argument can be put as follows:

Rusting-Talents Example

     (1) Everyone necessarily wills that all his talents be developed.
     (2) If everyone necessarily wills that all his talents be developed,
then the agent of a₃ cannot consistently will that GM(a₃) be a law of
nature.
     (3) a₃ is morally right if and only if the agent of a₃ can consistently
will that GM(a₃) be a law of nature.
     (4) Therefore a₃ is not morally right.

     This argument seems even less persuasive than the others. In the
quoted passage Kant himself presents a counterexample to the first
premise. The South Sea Islanders, according to Kant, do not will to
develop their talents. This fact, if it is one, is surely inconsistent with the
claim that we all necessarily will that all our talents be developed. Even if
Kant is wrong about the South Sea Islanders, his first premise is still
extremely implausible. Couldn't there be a rational person who, out of

idleness, simply does not will to develop his talents? If there could not be such a person, then what is the point of trying to show that we are under some specifically moral obligation to develop all our talents?

Once again, however, some philosophers may feel that Kant would have been worse off if his example had succeeded. These philosophers would hold that we in fact have no moral obligation to develop our talents. If Kant's theory had entailed that we have such an obligation, they would insist, then that would have shown that Kant's theory is defective.

In Kant's fourth illustration the categorical imperative is applied to an imperfect duty to others—the duty to help others who are in distress. Kant describes a man who is flourishing and who contemplates performing the act, a_4, of giving nothing to charity. His maxim is not stated by Kant in this passage, but it can probably be formulated as follows:

> $M(a_4)$: When I'm flourishing and others are in distress, I shall give nothing to charity.

When generalized, this maxim becomes:

> $GM(a_4)$: Whenever anyone is flourishing and others are in distress, he will give nothing to charity.

As in the other example of imperfect duty, Kant acknowledges that $GM(a_4)$ could be a law of nature. Yet he claims once again that the agent cannot consistently will that it be a law of nature. He explains this by arguing as follows:

> For a will which decided in this way would be in conflict with itself, since many a situation might arise in which the man needed love and sympathy from others, and in which, by such a law of nature sprung from his own will, he would rob himself of all hope of the help he wants for himself.[21]

Kant's point here seems to be this: The day may come when the agent is no longer flourishing. He may need charity from others. If that day does come, then he will find that he wills that others give him such aid. However, in willing that $GM(a_4)$ be a law of nature, he has already willed that no one should give charitable aid to anyone. Hence, on that dark day, his will will contradict itself. Thus, he cannot consistently will that $GM(a_4)$ be a law of nature. This being so, the categorical imperative entails that a_4 is not right.

If this is Kant's reasoning, then his reasoning is defective. For we cannot infer from the fact that the person *may* someday want aid from others, that he in fact already is willing inconsistently when he wills today that no one should give aid to anyone. The main reason for this is that that dark day may not come, in which case no conflict will arise. Furthermore, as is pretty obvious upon reflection, even if that dark day does arrive, the agent may steadfastly stick to his general policy. He may say, "I didn't help others when they were in need, and now that I'm in need I don't want any help from them." In this way, he would avoid having inconsistent policies. Unless this attitude is irrational, which it does not seem to be, Kant's fourth example is unsuccessful.

More Examples

It should be clear, then, that Kant has not provided us with a clear, persuasive example of the application of the categorical imperative. In light of this, some may feel that the categorical imperative is a worthless doctrine. Such a harsh judgment would probably be premature. For in the first place, Kant surely would have been worse off if he had succeeded in showing that suicide, or letting your talents rust, are invariably wrong. The normative status of these acts is hardly as obvious as Kant suggests. In the second place, the failure of Kant's illustrations may be due in part to his choice of some rather strange maxims, and to the fact that he presupposed some questionable views about the purposes of nature. Let us attempt to develop a more plausible illustration of the application of the categorical imperative.

In attempting to develop such an example, we should turn to the sort of case in which the categorical imperative stands the greatest chance of working correctly. This would be a case in which an agent proposes to take unfair advantage of his neighbors. It would be a case in which others, out of regard for the common good, have generously refrained from performing a certain kind of act, even though many of them might like to do such an act. Our agent, however, finds that he can get away with the act. The crucial feature of this case is that the agent cannot consistently will that the others act in the way he proposes to act. For if they all were to try to act in this way, that would destroy his opportunity for so acting.

Here is a good example of this sort of case. Primarily out of laziness, Miss Perkins, a college student, buys a term paper for her ethics course and submits it as her own work. Miss Perkins deals with a skillful term paper manufacturer, so she is assured of getting a very high grade. There is no chance that she will be found out. Most of us would say that regardless of its utility, Miss Perkins's act is morally wrong. She should not deceive her instructor and take advantage of her fellow students in this way. What does the categorical imperative say?

Let us call Miss Perkins's act of submitting the phoney term paper "a_5," and let us suppose that her maxim in performing a_5 is:

$M(a_5)$: When I need a term paper for a course and don't feel like writing one, I shall buy a term paper and submit it as my own work.

The generalized form of her maxim is:

$GM(a_5)$: Whenever anyone needs a term paper for a course and doesn't feel like writing one, she will buy one and submit it as her own work.

According to Kant's doctrine, a_5 is morally right only if Miss Perkins can consistently will that $GM(a_5)$ be a law of nature. So to see if a_5 is right, we must determine whether Miss Perkins can consistently will that everyone needing a term paper but not feeling like writing one should submit a store-bought one.

It is reasonable to suppose that Miss Perkins cannot will that $GM(a_5)$ be a law of nature. For consider what would happen if $GM(a_5)$ were a law of nature, and everyone needing a term paper but not feeling like writing one were therefore to submit a store-bought one. Clearly, college instructors would soon realize that they were reading work not produced by their students. The instructors would have to deal with the problem—perhaps by resorting to a system under which each student would be required to take a final oral exam instead of submitting a term paper. If some such alteration in the course requirements were instituted, Miss Perkins would lose her opportunity to get a good grade by cheating. Thus, she surely does not will that any such change in the system should occur. She prefers to have the system remain as it is. Since it is clear that some such change would occur if $GM(a_5)$ were a law of nature, Miss Perkins cannot consistently will that $GM(a_5)$ be a law of nature. Thus, according to CI_1, her act is not right.

The essentials of this example are simple. Miss Perkins wills that the system remain as it is—thus providing her with the opportunity to take advantage of her instructor and her fellow students. She recognizes that if everyone were to submit a store-bought term paper, the system would be changed. Hence, she cannot consistently will that everyone should submit a store-bought term paper. In other words, she cannot consistently will that $GM(a_5)$ be a law of nature. CI_1, together with this fact, entails that a_5 is morally wrong.

One of the most troubling aspects of this example is that it is pretty easy to see how the categorical imperative can be short-circuited. That is, it is pretty easy to see how Miss Perkins can make Kant's doctrine yield the result that her act is morally right. She needs only to change her maxim in a fairly trivial way:

$M(a_6)$:   When I need a term paper for a course, and I don't feel like writing one, and no change in the system will occur if I submit a store-bought one, then I shall buy a term paper and submit it as my own work.

$M(a_6)$ differs from $M(a_5)$ in only one respect. $M(a_6)$ contains the extra phrase "and no change in the system will occur if I submit a store-bought one." But this little addition makes a big difference to the argument. We found that Miss Perkins could not consistently will that $GM(a_5)$ be a law of nature. For if she willed that $GM(a_5)$ be a law of nature, she would, indirectly, will that the system be changed. But she already willed that the system remain as it is. However, no such argument applies to $GM(a_6)$. For it appears that if $GM(a_6)$ were a law of nature, the system would not be changed. Apparently, then, Miss Perkins can consistently will that $GM(a_6)$ be a law of nature. Hence, according to CI_1, her act of submitting a store-bought term paper, if performed under $M(a_6)$ rather than under $M(a_5)$, would be morally acceptable. This seems wrong.

The categorical imperative, interpreted as CI_1, yields incorrect results in another sort of case too. Consider a man who has a large amount of money in a savings account. He decides that he will wait until the Stock Market Index reaches 1000 and then take all of his money out of the bank. This act seems quite acceptable from the moral point of view. However, it seems that CI_1 yields the odd result that the act is morally wrong. Let us consider why this is so.

We can call the man's act of removing his money from the bank "a_7." The maxim of a_7 is:

$M(a_7)$:   When the Stock Market Index reaches 1000, I shall withdraw all my money from the bank.

The generalized form of $M(a_7)$ is:

$GM(a_7)$:   Whenever the Stock Market Index reaches 1000, everyone shall withdraw all of their money from the bank.

It should be clear that the man cannot consistently will that $GM(a_7)$ be a law of nature. For banks have loaned out most of the money deposited in them. If everyone came to withdraw their savings from their bank, banks would soon run out of money. Not everyone can withdraw simultaneously. Hence, $GM(a_7)$ cannot be a law of nature. Thus, the agent cannot consistently will that it be so. CI_1 entails, together with this fact, that it would not be right for the man to withdraw his own money under this maxim. Surely, there is something wrong with a moral theory that has this result.

This same problem arises in any number of cases. Whenever, for some irrelevant reason, an otherwise innocent maxim cannot be universalized, CI₁ yields the result that the act is wrong. So if a person acts on the maxim, for example, of not becoming a doctor, he acts wrongly. For he surely could not will that *everyone* should refrain from becoming a doctor. As a rational being, he recognizes that there must be some doctors. Similarly, if a person acts on the maxim of always using adequate contraceptive devices when engaging in sexual intercourse, she acts wrongly, according to this interpretation of CI₁. For if everyone were to do what she does, there would soon be no human race at all. This, Kant would think, is something no rational agent can consistently will.

These absurd results show that there is a very deep problem with CI₁. The problem, in general, is that there are many different reasons why a maxim may fail to be universalizable. Some of these reasons have nothing whatever to do with morality. Yet, as far as can be discerned from the text of the *Groundwork*, Kant nowhere attempts to distinguish between innocent-but-nonuniversalizable maxims, on the one hand, and evil-and-nonuniversalizable ones, on the other. Without such a distinction, CI₁ yields obviously incorrect results in innumerable cases.

So we can conclude that there are very serious problems with CI₁. Perhaps CI₁ is not an adequate interpretation of Kant's categorical imperative. Perhaps a more adequate version of that doctrine would not have these unsatisfactory results. However, if CI₁ is not Kant's theory, then it is very hard to see what Kant's theory might be.

NOTES

1. Immanuel Kant (1724–1804) is one of the greatest Continental philosophers. He produced quite a few philosophical works of major importance. The *Critique of Pure Reason* (1781) is perhaps his most famous work.

2. Kant's *Grundlegung zur Metaphysik der Sitten* (1785) has been translated into English many times. All references here are to Immanuel Kant, *Groundwork of the Metaphysic of Morals*, translated and analysed by H. J. Paton (New York: Harper & Row, 1964).

3. Kant, *Groundwork*, p. 70.

4. *Ibid.*, p. 88.

5. *Ibid.*, p. 89.

6. *Ibid.*, p. 91.

7. *Ibid.*, p. 69n.

8. In some unusual cases, it may accidentally happen that the situation to which the maxim applies can occur only once, as, for example, in the case of successful suicide. Nevertheless, the maxim is general in form.

9. Kant, *Groundwork*, p. 65.

10. See, for example, Robert Paul Wolff, *The Autonomy of Reason* (New York: Harper & Row, 1973), p. 163.

11. This is stated especially clearly on p. 107 of the *Groundwork*.

12. For an interesting discussion of various formulations of the golden rule, see Marcus Singer, "The Golden Rule," in *The Encyclopedia of Philosophy*, ed. Paul Edwards (New York: Macmillan; Free Press, 1967), Vol. 3, pp. 365–67.

13. Kant, *Groundwork*, p. 97n.

14. *Ibid.*, pp. 89–91.

15. *Ibid.*, p. 89n.

16. *Ibid.*, p. 89.

17. *Ibid.*

18. *Ibid.*, p. 71.

19. *Ibid.*

20. *Ibid.*

21. *Ibid.*, p. 91.

8

Kant II

In light of the conclusions reached in the preceding chapter, it may seem that Kant's categorical imperative is unacceptable as a moral theory. So far, however, we have considered only the first formulation of the categorical imperative. Kant presents several other principles, each of which he says is a formulation of the same doctrine. Perhaps when Kant says that these other principles are formulations of the same doctrine, what he means is that each of these other principles is extensionally equivalent to CI_1. In any case, we should look into these other versions of the categorical imperative to see whether we can find in any of them a more plausible moral theory.

The Formula of the End in Itself

We can draw a broad distinction between things that are good as means, and things that are good as ends. The distinction emerges clearly enough if we select some good thing and ask why it is good. Take sunlight. Sunlight is surely a good thing. But why is it good? Some would say that sunlight is good because, among other things, it makes plants grow, and it is a good thing that plants grow. But why is it good that plants grow? It is good that plants grow, it could be maintained, because without plants there would be no life on the earth, and it is good that there is life. But why is it good that there is life? Life, many would say, is good in itself. Its goodness does not arise as a result of what it leads to, or contributes to. It is good not because of its results, but because of itself. If these reflections about life are correct, then we can say that sunlight is good as a *means*, whereas life is good as an *end*. Another way to put this would be to say that sunlight is extrinsically good, whereas life is intrinsically good. Still another way to put it would be to say that sunlight is a means, whereas life is an end in itself.

We can define "means" in terms of "end in itself":

D_1: x is a means =df. there is something, y, that is an end in itself, and x contributes, directly or indirectly, to the existence of y.

Thus, according to D_1, sunlight is a means, since it contributes to the existence of life, which we are assuming to be an end in itself. If life is an end in itself, then money, health, education, and abundant natural resources may be taken to be good as means. Each of these things contributes to life, something that may be good in itself.

Philosophers have disagreed about what in fact is an end in itself. Mill and others have said that pleasure is the only thing that is an end in itself. G. E. Moore claimed that the love of beauty is an end in itself. Others have said that knowledge, virtue, and pleasure are all ends in themselves. Perhaps we would not go too far wrong if we said, following Moore, that a thing is an end in itself if and only if it would still be good even if it existed in complete isolation.

Kant claims that "rational nature exists as an end in itself."[1] By this, he seems to mean that all rational beings, including people, are ends in themselves. In other words, every person is intrinsically good. From this, Kant infers that it can never be morally right to treat any person merely as a means. That is, it is never morally right to treat a person as if he were simply a useful object for your own purposes. This view, which is the second version of the categorical imperative, is stated by Kant in a variety of ways:

> Act in such a way that you always treat humanity, whether in your own person or in the person of any other, never simply as a means, but always at the same time as an end.[2]
>
> A rational being, by his very nature an end and consequently an end in himself, must serve for every maxim as a condition limiting all merely relative and arbitrary ends.[3]
>
> So act in relation to every rational being (both to yourself and to others) that he may at the same time count in your maxim as an end in himself.[4]

Let us understand Kant to be saying in these passages that one ought never to act in such a way as to treat anyone merely as a means. In other words:

CI_2:   An act is morally right if and only if the agent, in performing it, refrains from treating any person merely as a means.

According to CI_2, there is a moral prohibition against treating anyone merely as a means. We should recognize that CI₂ does not rule out treating a person as a means. That is, CI₂ must not be confused with this rather implausible view:

> *CI₂′*: An act is morally right if and only if, in performing it, the agent refrains from treating any person as a means.

CI₂′ rules out any act in which the agent treats anyone as a means. But this is absurd, since we use other people as means to our ends all the time, and we cannot avoid doing so. A student uses his teacher as a means to gaining an education; a teacher uses her students as a means to gaining a livelihood; a customer in a restaurant uses his waiter as a means to gaining his dinner. None of these acts is ruled out by CI₂. For in each of these cases the agent of the act may also treat the others involved, *at least in part*, as ends in themselves. Thus, although these acts would violate a preposterous principle such as CI₂′, it is not clear that they would have to violate the more plausible principle, CI₂. For as we are understanding it, this second version of the categorical imperative only rules out treating persons *merely* as means.

CI₂ embodies an important moral insight, one that many would find plausible. It is the idea that it is wrong to "use" people. People are not mere objects, to be manipulated to serve our purpose. We cannot treat people as we treat wrecked cars, or wilted flowers, or old tin cans. Such things can be thrown out or destroyed when we no longer have any use for them. People, on the other hand, have dignity and worth, and must be treated accordingly.

Thus, what CI₂ says seems fairly plausible. Nevertheless, many moral philosophers would be uneasy about the claim that CI₂ is a formulation of "the supreme principle of morality." Can it really be the case that *all* wrong action is action in which people are used merely as means? Can all of our moral obligations be seen as obligations to treat people as ends? Some philosophers, admitting that it is important to treat people with respect, will deny that CI₂ captures the whole of our moral obligation. Others may even have their doubts about the acceptability of the insight embodied in CI₂, even if that insight were interpreted rather generously. Thus, it would be useful to see why Kant thinks CI₂ is true.

An Argument for CI₂

Kant suggests what seems to be a fairly interesting argument for CI₂. First, he points out that if there is something that is good as an end in itself, then that thing will provide a "ground of a possible categorical imperative."[5] By this, Kant seems to mean that if there is something that is good as an end in itself, then there is a true moral principle to the effect that this thing, whatever it may be, ought to be treated as if it were good as an end in itself. This seems reasonable.

Then Kant tries to show that people are ends in themselves. If he can succeed in establishing this point, then he will have a simple argument to show that people ought to be treated as ends in themselves. From this, it is not a very great step to the conclusion that an act is morally right if and only if the agent, in performing it, refrains from treating any person merely as a means.

Kant's argument that people exist as ends in themselves is rather complex, but the main thrust of it appears in the following passage:

> Persons . . . are not merely subjective ends whose existence as an object of our actions has a value *for us*: they are *objective ends*—that is, things whose existence is in itself an end, and indeed an end such that in its place we can put no other end to which they should serve *simply* as means; for unless this is so, nothing at all of *absolute* value would be found anywhere. But if all value were conditioned—that is, contingent—then no supreme principle could be found for reason at all.[6]

We can simplify what appears to be Kant's argument as follows:

People-are-Ends Argument

(1) If people are not ends in themselves, then nothing is an end in itself.

(2) If nothing is an end in itself, then there is never any reason to act in one way rather than in any other.

(3) There is sometimes a reason to act in one way rather than in another.

(4) Therefore, people are ends in themselves.

In this form, the argument is valid. Furthermore, at least two of the premises seem quite plausible. The second premise asserts that if nothing is an end, then no act is preferable to any other. This may seem odd, but it makes sense. To see why, consider, if you can, a state of affairs in which nothing is an end in itself. If there is nothing that is an end in itself, then there is nothing that is a means. For according to D$_1$, to say that something, x, is a means is just to say that there is some end in itself, y, such that x contributes to the existence of y. With no end, there can be no means. Thus, if there is nothing good as an end in itself, then there is nothing good either as an end or as a means. Hence, in these circumstances there would be nothing good at all. But if nothing is good at all, there can be no good reason to prefer any action to any other action. In this way, we can see that if there is nothing good as an end, then there is no reason to act in one way rather than in any other. This establishes (2).

Premise (3) is pretty straightforward. If we grant that some alternatives are morally preferable to others, then we must grant (3). The only person who would deny (3) is one who rejects morality altogether. Surely, the views of such a person may be ignored here.

Thus, the whole argument seems to turn on premise (1). It is clear that Kant affirms (1). He explicitly says that people are "objective ends," and he goes on to say that "unless this is so, nothing at all of absolute value will be found anywhere."[7] Yet it is not easy to see why Kant maintains this view. Isn't it possible that people are not ends in themselves, but that pleasure, for example, is? Some moralists would deny that people are ends in themselves, but would maintain that beautiful objects are ends in themselves. Others would say that people are good only as means, since the things that are good as ends are one and all mental states that exist only if there are people. In order to establish (1), Kant has to show that all such views are mistaken. He has to show that if people are not intrinsically good, then nothing is. Without some persuasive argument, it is not easy to accept this premise.

So Kant's argument is rather weak. He hasn't shown that people are ends in themselves. Nevertheless, many people would agree with Kant on this point. They would say that whether it can be proved or not, people are in fact ends in themselves. If this view is correct, it would of course be reasonable to maintain that people ought to be treated with the respect and consideration due to things of such great value.

Problems for CI₂

The greatest problem for CI₂ is not, however, the lack of a convincing proof. Nor is it that CI₂ is subject to obvious counter-examples. Rather, the main difficulty with CI₂ is that its meaning is never made sufficiently clear. The most troublesome concept in this version of the categorical imperative is the concept of "treating someone merely as a means." It is pretty clear that if you own and mistreat slaves, then you treat them as means. But what about some more typical cases? What about a patron in a diner who grunts out his order to the waitress without even looking at her? What about a "freeloader" who lives with relatives? What about a factory owner who pays minimum wages and refuses to install safety equipment? Are these people treating others merely as means? Suppose the patron smiles and leaves a tip. Suppose the freeloader offers to do some work around the house. Suppose the factory owner gives a bonus at Christmas. Would they still be treating others merely as means? Would they be treating them, in part, as ends in themselves? It is very hard to tell.

When a concept is left unclear, one way to gain some clarification is by looking closely at the author's examples. Often, the examples will shed light on the more important general concept. Fortunately, Kant has given several examples of the application of CI_2. Close consideration of these may help to clarify the intent of the principle. The examples are the same ones Kant discussed in connection with CI_1.

The first example is the man who contemplates committing suicide. As we saw previously, Kant's view is that suicide in this particular case would be wrong. Hence, he tries to show that the contemplated act would violate CI_2:

> If he does away with himself in order to escape from a painful situation, he is making use of a person merely as a means to maintain a tolerable state of affairs till the end of his life. But man is not a thing—not something to be used merely as a means: he must always in all his actions be regarded as an end in himself. Hence I cannot dispose of man in my person by maiming, spoiling, or killing.[8]

Kant's point here seems to be that if the man were to commit suicide, then he would be using himself merely as a means to the end of making his life tolerable until its end. If this is Kant's point, it certainly seems quite strained. Surely, the man could claim that in order to treat himself as an end, he must commit suicide. For if he does not commit suicide, he will suffer. And, he could insist, it is not appropriate for a person who is an end in himself to suffer.

So Kant's comments on this example are not very helpful. He does not say anything that gives us a new insight into the concept of treating someone merely as a means. Hence, we turn to the second example.

Kant's comments on the second example are more revealing. This is the case of the lying promise. Kant suggests that the man who makes the lying promise is "intending to make use of another man merely as a means to an end he does not share."[9] Kant goes on to point out the other man "cannot possibly agree with my way of behaving to him."[10] Kant's point here seems to be this: The man to whom the lie is told does not want to be used in the way the liar uses him. If he knew what was going on, he would refuse to lend the money. Thus, the liar is using him merely as a means. For this reason, his act is in violation of CI_2, and so is wrong.

Understood in this way, Kant's comments suggest a definition of what is meant by saying that a person, A, treats a person, B, merely as a means:

D_2:   A treats B merely as a means =df. A treats B in such a way that if B knew all about it, B would not want A to treat him in that way.

Thus, if you do not agree to being treated in a certain way, then if I treat you in that way I use you merely as a means. I use you for my purposes, but not for your own. Hence, according to CI₂, I act wrongly.

This line of reasoning may be plausible, but it leads to unacceptable results in a wide variety of cases. A large group of these cases have a similar pattern: B wants to do something morally wrong. A prevents B from doing this wrong act. According to D₂, A is then using B merely as a means, since B would not agree to A treating him in that way. According to CI₂, then, A is acting wrongly. This seems absurd.

Let us consider an example. Suppose B is planning to steal A's motorcycle. A learns of B's plans and decides to chain his motorcycle to a lamppost, thereby making it impossible for B to achieve his goal. Surely, if B knew what A was doing, B would not agree to it. B would not want A to chain up the motorcycle. For if A's motorcycle is chained, B cannot steal it. According to D₂, therefore, in chaining the motorcycle A is using B merely as a means. This, together with CI₂, entails that A's act of chaining the motorcycle is morally wrong. This result is surely incorrect.

As long as we interpret "treating a person merely as a means" according to D₂, it will not be clear how this problem can be avoided. It appears, then, that we should not accept this second account of the crucial concept. It does not provide us with a plausible view about what Kant might have meant. Let us consider the next example to see if we can find a more helpful suggestion.

The third example is the case of the person who decides to let all his talents rust. Kant thinks this is morally wrong, and so he tries to show that to so act would be to violate CI₂. Kant's comments on this case appear to be somewhat misdirected, however. Instead of trying to show that the man who lets his talents rust thereby treats himself merely as a means, Kant claims that he fails to "harmonize with" and "promote" humanity as an end in itself (whatever that may mean). The relevance of these comments is not clear. For CI₂ does not require us to "harmonize with" or "promote" humanity as an end in itself. It requires us only to refrain from treating people merely as means.

Since the third example is rather questionable anyway, let us move on and try to find some illumination in the final example. This is the example of the man who refuses to give to charity. Kant's comments here are more helpful. He apparently holds that the man who refuses to give to charity thereby acts wrongly. His error is that he fails to "agree positively with humanity as an end in itself."[11] If the man were to have done this, Kant suggests, he would have had to try, as much as he could have, to "further the ends of others."[12] Kant claims that since other people are ends in themselves, we act rightly only if we make their ends our own. This is an interesting idea, so let us examine it more closely.

Kant's comments on the final example suggest another interpretation of what is meant by "A treats B merely as a means." Kant explicitly says that we must further the ends of others. By this he seems to mean that unless we try, as much as we can, to see to it that others achieve their goals, we are not treating them as ends in themselves. We are treating them merely as means. Thus, if another person is trying to be happy, we must not only refrain from making him unhappy, we must try to help him become happy. The man who gives nothing to charity obviously violates this requirement. He treats those who need aid merely as means. We can define this concept as follows:

D_3:   A treats B merely as a means =df. B has some goal, and A could help B achieve that goal, but A refrains from doing so.

When we combine CI_2 with D_3, we seem to get the correct result in the charity case. Those who need charity have a certain goal—happiness. The agent can help them to achieve that goal, but he decides to refrain from doing so. Hence, according to D_3, he treats them merely as means. But CI_2 says that one acts rightly only if he treats no one merely as a means. So, in this case CI_2 entails that the man who refuses to give charity does not act rightly. His selfish act is morally wrong. This result seems acceptable.

However, the problem with D_3 should be obvious. It is, in effect, the same as the problem with D_2. If other people want, for example, to destroy the environment, then according to D_3, we must help them to achieve their misguided goal; otherwise, we are treating them merely as means. Thus, CI_2 and D_3 entail that if we refrain from helping such people to destroy the environment, we are acting wrongly. This seems preposterous.

So the trouble with D_3 is that, together with CI_2, it requires us to help others to achieve their goals, whatever those goals may be. If the others have morally acceptable goals, this may seem to be a reasonable doctrine. But if the goals of the others are morally wrong, then it is absurd to insist that we should try to help them to achieve these goals. Yet this is just what D_3 and CI_2 require.

Before we leave CI_2, we may find it worthwhile to consider one final proposal. Kant does not make this proposal himself, but some sympathetic readers may find hints of it in the *Groundwork*. The basic idea is that there are some goals that it is rational for a person to have, and others that it is irrational for a person to have. For example, it might be said that it is rational for a person to have happiness as his goal, whereas it is irrational of him to have the destruction of the environment as his goal. Perhaps Kant would say that we are under no moral obligation to help others achieve irrational goals, but if another person is attempting to achieve a rational goal, then we should "make his end our own."

One way to develop this idea would be as follows. First, we must introduce a new definition:

D_4:   A treats B merely as a means =df. B has some rational goal, and A can help B achieve that goal, but A refrains from doing so.

The difference between D_3 and D_4 is small, but significant. According to D_3, we treat another person merely as a means if we fail to help him achieve his goal, whatever that goal may be. According to D_4, we treat him merely as a means if we fail to help him achieve a rational, or reasonable, goal. Thus, the concept defined in D_4 may be more promising.

When we combine D_4 with CI_2, we get what may seem to be a more plausible moral doctrine. For under this interpretation, CI_2 requires us only to help others to achieve their *rational* goals. So there would be no need to help another person to destroy the environment, or commit a crime. On the other hand, there would be a need to help another to become happy—assuming that it is rational for that person to want to become happy.

Although the use of D_4 helps to make this version of the categorical imperative somewhat more successful, very great problems remain. For one, it often happens that there are several different persons who might benefit from one person's action. For example, suppose a man has an unbreakable piece of candy that he can give to either of two twins, Jean and Joan. If he gives the candy to Jean, he will make her happy. This will help Jean to achieve a rational goal she has. However, if he gives the candy to Jean, he will not be helping Joan to achieve a rational goal she has, for he will fail to help her to become happy. Similarly, if he gives it to Joan, he will fail to help Jean achieve a rational goal. Thus, according to D_4, whichever twin the man helps, he treats the other merely as a means. CI_2, then, implies that his act of giving the candy is morally wrong.

The general point should be clear. I can help each of many different persons achieve his rational goals. However, I cannot simultaneously help *all* of these individuals achieve their rational goals. I must choose some to help and some to ignore. According to D_4, it would follow that I have to treat some of them merely as means. CI_2 then yields the inevitable result that I act wrongly. This seems much too severe.

The second main problem with D_4 is that it makes use of a rather obscure concept—the concept of a "rational goal." If you think about it for a minute, you will see that where ultimate goals are concerned, it is hard to distinguish the rational from the irrational. Normally, we would say that a person who aims to collect a large amount of money is pursuing a rational goal, whereas a person who aims to collect a large number of bent nails is pursuing an irrational goal. But what is the difference? If each can gain happiness from his collection, why is one more rational than the other? Perhaps the only rational goal is happiness itself.

It is interesting to note that if we assume that happiness is the only rational goal, and if we also assume that Kant's view is the more moderate view that we should do the most we can to help other people achieve their rational goals, then Kant's view becomes indistinguishable from act utilitarianism. Of course, there is nothing in Kant's writing to suggest that he ever made either of these assumptions. With these reflections, we have strayed quite far from Kant's text. Perhaps it would be better to avoid such speculations.

It appears, then, that CI$_2$ is not a very successful principle. The insight behind it is vague, although plausible. There surely is something morally objectionable about using people. However, Kant's discussion of this view does not do enough to clarify this vague insight. Whether we interpret "A treats B merely as a means" according to D$_2$, D$_3$, or D$_4$, CI$_2$ yields obviously incorrect results in many cases. Until some more plausible account of the meaning of CI$_2$ is proposed, we must conclude that it is not an acceptable moral doctrine.

The Formula of Autonomy

Kant presents a third version of the categorical imperative. He claims that this version follows from the first two, although he does not prove that this is the case. Some of his comments about the third version are rather important, and so we should consider what he has to say. Before we turn to these comments, however, we need to review some background.

Kant makes a sharp distinction between acts done out of inclination, on the one hand, and acts done out of a sense of duty, on the other. When Kant speaks of inclination, he seems to have in mind such things as the desire for pleasure, the desire for power, the desire for respect, the fear of injury, and the fear of death. Anyone whose act is motivated by one of these factors is acting out of inclination. Kant claims that any act done out of inclination, no matter how useful it may be, lacks real moral worth. Even if duty requires a person to act in a certain way, his act is morally worthless if he does it not because it is his duty, but because he has some other inclination. To see the impact of this Kantian doctrine, consider two individuals, each of whom loves his neighbors. Imagine that the first loves his neighbors primarily because he enjoys their company. The second, on the other hand, loves his neighbors because he believes it to be the right thing to do. Kant would say that the first man's love is morally worthless.[13] It springs from a desire for pleasure. Kant would describe such love as "pathological." The second man's love has more value. It springs from a sense of duty.

Of course, a man might love his neighbors both because he enjoys their company and because he thinks it is right to love them. In such a case, it would be hard to tell whether his love has moral worth. Perhaps Kant's test would be this: If the man were to love his neighbors even after ceasing to enjoy their company, then his love would be based primarily on his sense of duty. Hence, it would have moral worth. In other words, an act has moral worth only if it is motivated by a sense of duty strong enough to produce the act even in the absence of all inclination.

This doctrine has some important consequences. Consider, for example, a person who genuinely believes that if he is bad he will go to hell. He believes hell to be a place of eternal torment, and the thought of going there frightens him silly. Suppose, furthermore, that he is moved by this fear to try scrupulously to avoid all wrong action. Such a person, Kant would say, acts primarily out of fear of punishment. In this case, his act is motivated not by his sense of duty, but by an inclination. For this reason, according to Kant, his actions are morally worthless.

It is not entirely clear why Kant holds that acts done out of inclination are morally worthless, but at one point he suggests an argument:[14] superficially right actions motivated by inclinations are right only by "mere accident." Kant's point in this argument seems to be this: Suppose a person is moved by inclination to perform an action that is superficially in accord with duty. If the circumstances had been slightly different, the same inclination might have moved the person to perform an act that violates her duty. Since it is only a matter of good luck that she acted correctly, her act lacks moral worth.

An example of this sort of case may make Kant's idea clearer. Suppose a man is moved by a desire for fame. He believes that he will be famous if he becomes a doctor. In no other way, he thinks, will he be able to become more famous. Since he wants to be famous, he decides to develop his talent for medicine. He works hard, and finally becomes well known as a great surgeon. Thus, he has developed a talent, as Kant thinks he should. Yet Kant would say that his act is morally worthless. It was motivated by an inclination—the desire for fame. This desire, if the circumstances had been different, could just as easily have led him to become a thief or a murderer. For if he had believed that he would become most famous as a thief, this very same inclination would have driven him to become one. So Kant would say that his act was right by "mere accident," and so lacks all moral worth.

Kant holds that there are only two main sorts of reasons why a person might choose to follow a principle, or law. On the one hand, he might follow the law out of inclination. That is, he might follow the law because he believes that doing so will help him to get something he wants, or avoid something he fears. On the other hand, he might follow the law because he conceives of himself as being the one who established it. In this case, his reason for following the law is not so much a desire for, or fear of, some result. Rather, it is that he thinks of the law as in some way his own. He made the law, and so he has a reason for following it.

It is important to be clear about this concept of "following a rule because it is my own." When we say that a person follows a law because it is his own, we do not mean to suggest that he follows it because he anticipates deriving some sort of pleasure from the recognition that he is following one of his own laws. If we understood this sort of action in this way, we would make it into a special case of acting out of inclination. Rather, we must say that when a person follows a law because it is his own, he follows it simply because he recognizes that he himself has established it as a rule; he feels it to be binding upon everyone, including himself, and he senses that it would be irrational to set up a rule and then not follow it. In such a case, the person's motivation cannot be a desire for pleasure, a fear of pain, or any other sort of inclination.

We can say that a person follows a law *autonomously* if he follows it primarily because he conceives of himself as being the one who established it. Thus, if a person acts in accord with a certain principle simply because it is his own principle—one that he established for himself—he is following that principle autonomously. Kant might say that such a person has "autonomy of the will." He follows self-made laws.

On the other hand, we can say that a person follows a law *heteronomously* if he follows it primarily because he believes that doing so will help him to satisfy some inclination. Thus, if I follow a law because I fear that I will be punished if I don't or because I hope to gain some pleasure from following it, then I follow it heteronomously. A person who consistently follows laws heteronomously can be said to have "heteronomy of the will." He follows laws not because he made them, but because of some inclination.

Given all this, Kant has to hold that we are morally obligated to follow laws autonomously. For there are only two ways of following laws—autonomously or heteronomously. Since acts done out of inclination have no moral worth, and since all acts done in accordance with laws followed heteronomously are done out of inclination, all such acts are morally worthless. Hence, we must act autonomously.

That this is indeed Kant's view is fairly evident in a few passages. Here is a particularly useful one. In it, Kant criticizes the views of previous moral philosophers.

> . . . when [these philosophers] thought of man merely as subject to a law (whatever it might be), the law had to carry with it some interest in order to attract or compel, because it did not spring as a law from *his own* will: in

order to conform with the law his will had to be necessitated by *something else* to act in a certain way. This absolutely inevitable conclusion meant that all the labour spent in trying to find a supreme principle of duty was lost beyond recall; for what they discovered was never duty, but only the necessity of acting from a certain interest. This interest might be one's own or another's; but on such a view the imperative was bound to be always a conditioned one and could not possibly serve as a moral law. I will therefore call my principle the principle of the *Autonomy* of the will in contrast with all others, which I consequently class under *Heteronomy*.[15]

Kant presents a number of different statements of the principle of autonomy. Some of them are hardly moral principles at all, and others are fairly clear statements of the view in question. Here are some examples:

> . . . the Idea *of the will of every rational being as a will which makes universal law*.[16]
> . . . every human will is a will which by all its maxims enacts universal law.[17]
> . . . act always on the maxim of such a will in us as can at the same time look upon itself as making universal law; . . .[18]
> . . . every rational being as an end in himself, must be able to regard himself as also the maker of universal law in respect of any law whatever to which he may be subjected.[19]

Kant states that "an action which is compatible with the autonomy of the will is permitted; one which does not harmonize with it is forbidden."[20] Hence, we may be justified in taking the principle of autonomy to be as follows:

> CI_3:   An act is morally right if and only if the agent, in performing it, follows some law autonomously.

In other words, your act is morally right if and only if you are motivated to perform that act primarily by the recognition that it is required by a rule that you have established for yourself, and for everyone else as well. If your act is motivated primarily by a fear of, or desire for, certain consequences, it is in violation of this version of the categorical imperative.

CI_3 is related quite closely to a Kantian view that might be called "the split personality doctrine." Kant seems to hold that each of us suffers from a kind of schizophrenia. Some of our actions are motivated by an aspect of our personality that can be called "reason"; other of our actions are motivated by another aspect of our personality, which can be called "desire." When our actions are motivated by reason, we act rationally. Furthermore, Kant apparently would maintain that all rational acts are morally right. When our actions are motivated by desire, then we act out of inclination. Such actions are morally worthless.

Thus, Kant's split-personality doctrine is very much like the traditional view that each person is somehow composed of warring parts —one part always pushing him toward immediate pleasures, the other part always urging him to act with reason and caution.

Kant maintains that if there were a being whose personality contained the reasonable part but not the lustful part, such a being would have a "holy will." It would always do the act that is morally right. No unruly desires would ever tempt it to sway from the straight and narrow path of morality. Interestingly, Kant says that there would be no moral commands for such a being. Nothing would appear to it as an imperative. Since it would always do the rational, morally right act, and since it would have no interest in doing anything else, there would be no point in urging such a being to do the morally right act.

Ordinary human beings do not have holy wills. Sometimes, moved by desires, we are tempted to do immoral acts. Thus, morality for us is a matter of commands, or *imperatives*. We are commanded, in effect, to master our inclinations. We are told to try, as far as we can, to follow the guidance of reason, not the urgings of desire. As Kant sees it, to follow the guidance of reason is to act in accordance with general principles your own reason has set up. Hence, to follow the guidance of reason is to act autonomously.

We can see now how the split-personality doctrine is related to CI_3. The doctrine entails that if we are to act morally, our reason must overcome our desire. This means that we must act according to the dictates of reason, rather than those of inclination. But to say that we act according to the dictates of reason is just to say that we act upon principles we have reasonably established for ourselves. In other words to act in accord with the dictates of reason is to act in accord with CI_3.

It is not easy to be sure about our evaluation of CI_3. On the one hand, it seems to be based upon a plausible insight. There is something especially worthy about a person whose acts are based upon principles he has established for himself, principles he would wish everyone to follow, regardless of consequences. Even when we do not share such principles, we have respect for the person who acts upon them. Such a person is a man or woman of principle, and CI_3 requires us to act as such an individual acts.

On the other hand, CI_3 seems to leave out a crucial factor—the content of the principles. Acting on self-made principles may be morally worthy, but it may be morally worthless too. For if the principles are worthless, then there is not much to be said for the acts one does in following them! A bigot, or a racist, may act out of respect for a self-made principle. But since his principle is so obviously distorted, his acts are wrong. Even if the bigot acts purely out of selfless respect for what he takes to be the moral law, we condemn his acts.

Conclusion

Kant's moral philosophy thus turns out to have some merits and some very great defects. Its merits are fairly clear. Kant has gathered together and defended a variety of extremely important moral insights. Upon examination, many of our deepest moral convictions will be found to rest upon these insights. Let us attempt to state some of these views.

Many of us would agree with Kant that there is something objectionable about a person who acts in a way in which he would not want others to act. A person who takes advantage of the forbearance of others, and thereby makes himself an exception to a rule he endorses for them, is an immoral person. This view, not adequately accounted for by the utilitarians, would strike many moralists as being essential to any adequate moral theory. Kant's first formulation of the categorical imperative seems to be an attempt to capture this view.

Another widely accepted doctrine is that in all our actions we must recognize the great intrinsic value of human life. Murder, slavery, and other forms of "using people" elicit our strongest moral disapproval. People are not merely things to be manipulated for one's personal ends. People are to be treated with respect. Kant's second formulation of the categorical imperative seems to be an attempt to capture this view.

Furthermore, Kant seems to be right in insisting that a person cannot be compelled to be moral. Each of us must recognize and accept the demands of morality for himself. A person who keeps his promises and pays his debts primarily because he feels compelled to do so in order to gain a good reputation may be harmless, but his behavior is surely not in keeping with our moral ideal. We have much greater respect for someone who keeps his promises because he recognizes for himself that it is right to do so. These ideas appear to be at least part of what Kant had in mind when he formulated the third version of the categorical imperative.

The great defect of Kant's moral philosophy is that he failed to develop any of these intuitions adequately. His presentation is so complex, his terminology so obscure, and his argument so confused that the careful reader is rarely confident that he knows precisely what Kant wants to say, or why he wants to say it. Even in our brief survey of some of Kant's most basic arguments and doctrines, we have found time and time again that his meaning is obscure. Unfortunately, with respect to many of these arguments and doctrines, it is very hard to develop a clear interpretation that is both plausible and recognizably Kantian in spirit. If we assume that moral philosophy is, among other things, an attempt to discover, clarify, and defend the truth about ethics, then we must conclude that Kant's work in moral philosophy, though extraordinarily rich and suggestive, is not entirely successful.

NOTES

1. Immanuel Kant, *Groundwork of the Metaphysic of Morals*, translated and analysed by H. J. Paton (New York: Harper & Row, 1964), p. 96.

2. *Ibid.*

3. *Ibid.*, p. 104.

4. *Ibid.*, p. 105.

5. *Ibid.*, p. 95.

6. *Ibid.*, p. 96.

7. *Ibid.*

8. *Ibid.*, p. 97.

9. *Ibid.*

10. *Ibid.*

11. *Ibid.*, p. 98.

12. *Ibid.*

13. Kant's concept of moral worth is somewhat troublesome. Some commentators have understood moral worth to be the same as moral rightness, or permissibility. According to this view, an act is morally worthy if and only if it is morally right. I am inclined to believe, however, that Kant's statements make slightly more sense if we understand moral worth in another way. According to this other view, not all morally right acts are morally worthy. Rather, an act is morally worthy if and only if (1) it is morally right, and (2) it is intrinsically morally good.

14. Kant, *Groundwork*, p. 79.

15. *Ibid.*, p. 100.

16. *Ibid.*, p. 98.

17. *Ibid.*

18. *Ibid.*, p. 100.

19. *Ibid.*, p. 105.

20. *Ibid.*, p. 107.

9

Kant and Rawls

In his extremely important book, *A Theory of Justice*,[1] John Rawls has suggested a novel and impressive interpretation of some of Kant's most difficult doctrines. According to Rawls, Kant belongs to the *contractarian* or *social-contract* tradition in moral philosophy. Since this way of looking at Kant is quite different from that presented in the preceding chapters, and since Rawls's theory is independently plausible, whether Kant held it or not, it will be worth our while to consider what Rawls has to say about Kant and the social-contract theory.

Before we proceed any further, two provisos are in order. First, it is important to recognize that Rawls does not present a whole moral theory. Rather, as the title of his book suggests, he is interested primarily in developing a theory of justice. Thus, although what we say here is suggested by Rawls, and is intended in large part to represent what he probably would say on these matters, Rawls himself did not formulate these views. He directed his attention to a substantially narrower issue than the one with which we are concerned. Our task in this chapter, then, is to attempt to describe a general moral theory that is, in its essentials, similar to the theory of justice developed by Rawls in *A Theory of Justice*.

Rawls would probably not object to our procedure, for he says that "the contractarian idea can be extended to the choice of more or less an entire ethical system, that is, to a system including principles for all the virtues and not only for justice."[2]

Our second proviso has to do with Rawls's claims about Kant. Rawls discusses several respects in which his own contractarian theory of justice is Kantian.[3] However, he does not go into great detail in any attempt to document these similarities. Indeed, he acknowledges that "some will want to read him [Kant] differently."[4] Yet it seems clear that Rawls's view, whether he would wish to insist on this point or not, does provide an interesting and insightful way of looking at some rather dark passages in Kant. My second provisio, then, is this: We must not assume that Rawls would make a sustained or serious effort to prove that Kant "really meant to hold" the Rawlsian social-contract theory we are about to discuss.

Traditional Social-Contract Theories

Traditionally, the social-contract theory has been a theory in political philosophy. It has been proposed as an account of the nature, origin, and justification of legal obligation. One of the most important classical elements of the theory is the concept of "the state of nature." People are said to be living in a state of nature if they have not yet banded together into a society. In this anarchic situation, there is no interfamilial cooperation at all. Each family must fend for itself. It is "a war of every man against every man."[5]

The most eloquent description of the state of nature is the one presented by Thomas Hobbes in his *Leviathan*:

> In such condition there is no place for industry, because the fruit thereof is uncertain: and consequently no culture of the earth; no navigation, nor use of the commodities that may be imported by sea; no commodious building; no instruments of moving, and removing, such things as require much force; no knowledge of the face of the earth; no account of time; no arts; no letters; no society; and which is worst of all, continual fear, and danger of violent death; and the life of man, solitary, poor, nasty, brutish, and short.[6]

According to the traditional contractarian political theory, the people who live in the state of nature may eventually come to realize that they would be much better off if they would learn to cooperate, and thereby call a truce to the war of every man against every man. In Hobbes's version of the theory, the people select some especially powerful person, or group of persons, and agree together to give their personal power or sovereignty, such as it may be, to that person or group. According to Hobbes, it is as if each person should say to each other person, "I authorize and give up my right of governing myself to this man, or to this assembly of men, on this condition, that thou give up thy right to him, and authorize all his actions in like manner."[7] Once this is done, the people are well on the road to creating a commonwealth, or as Hobbes calls it, "a great LEVIATHAN." In other words, they have begun to join together so as to form a society.

From this point on, the people are no longer in the state of nature. Rather, they are in the state of society. They have begun to assume legal obligations to one another, and to the society. The obligations, according to Hobbes, are based primarily on the fact that no matter how strong any individual citizen may be, the great leviathan is sure to be much stronger. Hence, the leviathan can force the citizen to act in ways that will be most beneficial to the society as a whole, regardless of any inclinations the citizen may have to the contrary.

Traditionally, the theory of the social contract has been a theory of the origin of the state, and of the source and justification of political and legal obligations. However, we can construct a rather naive and implausible moral theory on the same basis. According to this theory, our moral obligations are also based upon a social contract. But the contract here will have to be some sort of "moral contract." That is, it will have to be a mutual agreement among many people to join together as a society under a single moral code. The moral obligations of these original contractors, as well as those of their descendants in the society, will be the obligations imposed upon them by the originally agreed upon moral code.

In order to simplify our discussion, let us suppose that every act that is open to moral evaluation is performed in exactly one society. We can then say that if a is an act, then "a's society" is the society in which a would be performed. Next, we can say that the "contracted code" for a society is the moral code that the founders of that society originally agreed to abide by when they emerged from the state of nature. Using these abbreviations, we can state a very naive form of the moral version of the social-contract theory:

> *NSCT*:   An act, a, is morally right if and only if a is permitted by the contracted code for a's society.

In this form, the contractarian position is not very plausible. Among its many defects, the most striking is that it presupposes that every society has exactly one contracted code. Surely, however, there is no reason to suppose that for every society there is some moral code that was contracted for by the members of that society at some prehistoric convention. At any rate, there is no historical or anthropological evidence to support the idea that people once lived in a state of nature. If in fact people never did live in a state of nature, and never did enter into a social contract of the sort envisaged by Hobbes, then we must conclude that no society has a contracted moral code. If this is the case, then NSCT implies that no act is morally right. This apparently shows that NSCT is totally unacceptable.

The most natural way to deal with this problem and still retain the basic intuition of the social-contract viewpoint would be to move to what may be called the "hypothetical social-contract theory." According to this view, our moral obligations are determined by the moral code we would adopt if we were to contract together to live under a moral code.

Let us say that the "would-be contract code" for a society, S, at a time, t, is the code that the members of S would agree to live under if they were to contract together at t to live under a moral code. Now we can formulate a version of the hypothetical social-contract theory quite easily:

> *HSCT*:   An act, a, is morally right if and only if there is some moral code, C, such that C is the would-be contract code for a's society at the time of a's performance, and C permits a.

In other words, this theory permits us to act in such ways as are permitted by the moral code we would agree to live under if we were to have a great convention and agree to live under some moral code.

In this form, contractarianism does not imply that each society in fact has contracted to live under any moral code. Indeed, it doesn't imply that any society has ever contracted to do anything. Hence, HSCT avoids the most serious problem faced by its predecessor, NSCT. Nevertheless, HSCT does imply that the normative status of each act is the status assigned to it by the moral code that the members of the relevant society would choose to live under if they were to choose to live under some moral code. Hence, this hypothetical social-contract theory retains the basic contractarian intuition.

It is not easy to provide a definitive evaluation of HSCT. The problem here is that the theory is so vague. Until we are told more about the hypothetical circumstances in which the new code would be chosen, it is virtually impossible for us to determine which code would be chosen. This leads to serious obscurity. If, for example, we suppose that the choice of the moral code would be made by people who still retain all of their former moral beliefs, then it seems that the code that they would choose would be quite similar to the code they already have. In this case, the would-be contract code for the society would be the current moral code. Clearly, if this sort of thing can happen, HSCT reduces to a form of conventionalism. As we have already seen, this would be implausible.[8] On the other hand, if the people who make the choice of a new code are assumed to be devoid of moral beliefs at the time of the hypothetical moral contract, then it is hard to see how they could select any moral code at all. What would be their motivation for choosing any code? Thus, the main problem with HSCT is that it fails to provide a sufficiently clear account of the hypothetical choice situation. For this reason, it is simply not clear what code, if any, the members of the society would be inclined to choose. We need to be told more about the imaginary circumstances in which they would be permitted to make their selection.

Rawls and the Original Position

In *A Theory of Justice*, Rawls attempts to solve a version of this problem. In particular, he attempts to give a clear and detailed description of the circumstances in which we are to imagine that the selection of principles of justice is to occur. He says that people in these circumstances are in "the original position." He tries to show that the correct principles of justice are precisely the ones that would be selected by rational people if they were in the original position. Taking our cue from what Rawls says, we can propose what we may call "Rawlsian social-contract theory." Unlike the theory Rawls proposed, this will be a general normative theory, not just a theory of justice.

According to our Rawlsian social-contract theory, the normative status of each act is the status assigned to it by the moral code that would be selected by the members of a society if they were in the original position and were to choose a moral code to live under. This can be stated more succinctly. First, let us say that a moral code, C, is the "original-position would-be moral code for a society, S" if that code is such that if the members of S were in the original position and were to choose a moral code, then they would choose C. Now we can state our version of the Rawlsian theory:

> *RSCT*:   An act, *a*, is morally right if and only if there is some moral code, C, such that C is the original-position would-be moral code for *a*'s society, and C permits *a*.

Intuitively, the idea is this: If we want to decide the normative status of an act, *a*, we must first determine in what society *a* would be performed. Next, we try to imagine which moral code the members of that society would select to live under if they were to be in the original position and were to choose to live under some moral code. The normative status of the original act, *a*, is then determined by that code. If the code the members of that society would select says that *a* is permitted, then *a* is in fact morally right. If the code they would select says that *a* is not permitted, then *a* is in fact morally wrong. The actually current code in *a*'s society plays no role in our deliberations.

Obviously, if we are to understand why this theory constitutes a genuine improvement over NSCT and HSCT, we must give some careful consideration to what Rawls says about the original position. Otherwise, we really don't know what RSCT means. So our question is this: What are the circumstances such that if a code were selected in them, then it would have to be a "correct" moral code? In other words, what is "the original position"?[9]

Rawls lays down some rather severe requirements concerning the information available to those in the original position. In the first place, although each person in the original position knows general facts about human nature, none of them knows anything about his own particular circumstances in life. Thus, if you were in the original position and were forced to select a moral code for a society in which you would live, you would have to make this choice without any information about the social status, wealth, or prestige that you would have in the society. This "veil of ignorance" is designed to assure that your selection of a moral code will not be biased in favor of your own future interests. If there were no veil of ignorance governing these matters, each of us might be motivated to select a code that would favor our own future interests over those of our fellow citizens. For example, if you knew that you were going to be among the poorest people in the society, you might choose a moral code containing principles requiring very substantial welfare and charity for the poor. On the other hand, if you knew that you were going to be a very rich person in that society, you might incline toward a moral code allowing the rich to retain, protect, and enlarge their wealth. The veil of ignorance eliminates any such biased choosing.

A second requirement of those in the original position concerns their motivation. Each of them must be motivated to maximize his own welfare in the society to come. Thus, each of them is assumed to want to get as much of those things he considers to be good as is possible. This condition, together with the veil of ignorance, is designed to insure that those in the original position will have a decent respect for the interests of the individuals in the society to come. For if you want to insure that you will be well treated, and if you don't know what role you will be playing, then you will be motivated to insure that no matter what role you play, you will be relatively well treated. In effect, this insures that you will have a decent concern for the welfare of every member of the society to come. For all you know, he might be you! This theme in Rawls seems to echo Kant's insistence that we treat others at least in part as ends in themselves. We will consider this point later.

Finally, Rawls requires that those in the original position, clouded by the veil of ignorance but motivated to maximize their own welfare in the future society, make a rational selection of a moral code. In other words, their choice cannot be arbitrary or capricious. They cannot simply "flip a coin." They must choose their moral code in such a way as to reflect their rationality. The choice must be consistent with their motivation and with their knowledge. This requirement also echoes a Kantian theme. Somehow, morality involves rational choice. Whereas the role of rational choice is never made sufficiently clear in Kant, its place in Rawls's theory is explicit.

Rawls places two important constraints on the choice itself. First, he requires that those in the original position reach a unanimous decision concerning the code under which they shall live. So the final selection of the code may be the result of considerable compromise and negotiation. Rawls suggests that such bargaining could not be based upon any attempt on anyone's part to secure a selfish advantage. After all, no one knows the role he will play in the society to be governed by the moral code being selected. Hence, no one would bargain for a special advantage for his own role. Rawls suggests, then, that the only bargaining that could go on under these unusual circumstances would be bargaining directed toward a fairer and more rational moral code. This, of course, is all to the good.

The second constraint on the choice is that all parties to the contract must recognize that the code they select will be in effect in perpetuity. This constraint is designed to rule out frivolous or speculative choosing. Without some such constraint, those in the original position might opt for a system under which a few privileged individuals would live well and the others would live in poverty. They could reason that if they turn out to be among the poverty-stricken, they can always stage a revolution and overturn the system. Under the constraints Rawls has imposed, however, this sort of reasoning would be ruled out. Each person must choose with full recognition of the fact that the code selected in the original position is the code under which he and all his descendants will have to live. The social contract is thus viewed as a solemn agreement on the part of everyone concerned to abide by the selected rules forever. Each person must choose a code such that no matter how lowly his role in society may turn out to be, he will be assured sufficiently decent treatment that he will be able to live out his days without regrets about the moral code he helped select.

Rawls also places some constraints on the principles that may be selected by those in the original position. His discussion, once again, is directed primarily toward a choice of principles of justice, and so what he says is only a rough guide to our problem. Let us suppose that those in the original position would be asked to select exactly one complete and consistent moral code. We can think of such a code as being a set of rules, each of this form: "When in situation S, one ought to do an act of type A." Each such code will be complete, in that it prescribes a suitable action for every important sort of situation. And it will be consistent, in that it never prescribes two incompatible actions for the same situation. We must also suppose that these codes will be rather abstract. That way the choice of a code will not require detailed knowledge of the geographical, economic, or social conditions that will prevail in the society to come.

We can summarize this rough and abbreviated account of the original position by emphasizing the following essential facts about it:

1. Although those in the original position know general facts about

human nature, each of them is enveloped by a veil of ignorance concerning his own particular role and status in society.

2. Those in the original position are motivated to maximize their welfare—that is, the amount of things they consider good—in the society to come.

3. Those in the original position are rational. Their choice will not be frivolous, but will be consistent with their knowledge and motivation.

4. The agreement made by those in the original position to live under a certain code must be unanimous.

5. The parties to the agreement made in the original position understand that they are committing themselves to abide by the code in perpetuity.

6. The codes from which they select are complete and consistent.

7. The codes from which they select are relatively abstract.

Now, perhaps, we can understand the Rawlsian position more easily. The idea is that an act is morally right if and only if it is permitted by the moral code that the members of the society would choose if they were in the original position and were to choose a moral code. It is assumed, of course, that the code they would choose may be quite different from the code that in fact is already current in their society. Thus, according to this interpretation, RSCT is not a form of conventionalism. Rawls's view is also quite different from any form of utilitarianism we have considered, even though it is (remotely) possible that some people might choose utilitarianism if they were in the original position and had to choose a moral code to live under. The theory is different from utilitarianism because even if right acts happen to maximize utility, what makes them right is not the fact that they maximize utility. What makes right acts right, according to RSCT, is the fact that they are permitted by the original-position would-be codes for their societies.

The Rawlsian social-contract theory is clearly contractarian in its essentials. It is a well-developed form of the hypothetical social-contract theory. But whereas our relatively empty form of this view, HSCT, is disappointingly vague and uninteresting, Rawls's theory seems to be quite rich. Rawls has provided a clear and detailed account of the choice situation. This enables us to imagine more easily how we would choose if we were in that situation and were required to choose a moral code for ourselves.

Perhaps we can now begin to see some of the ways in which Rawls's view is a refinement and an elaboration of some Kantian themes. We should recall, first, that the concept of autonomy of the will plays an extremely important role in Kant's moral philosophy.[10] To say that a person follows a law autonomously is to say that he follows that law purely out of his recognition that he has established it for himself as a moral principle, and that it would be irrational to establish a moral principle and then not follow it. The third version of the categorical imperative, as interpreted in the preceding chapter, is this:

CI₃: An act is morally right if and only if the agent, in performing it, follows some law autonomously.

When we turned to an evaluation of CI₃, we found that it captured an important moral insight. This is the insight that there is something especially worthy about a person whose actions are based upon principles he has established for himself. This worthiness seems to be lacking in those whose actions are motivated by fear of punishment or anticipation of reward. Yet we also found that CI₃ does not account for an important element in this moral intuition. For CI₃ does not insure in any way that the autonomously followed principles will be good ones. A bigot, or fanatic of any sort, may act autonomously. Surely, we do not want to say that such people act rightly simply because they follow their own laws! Hence, in the end CI₃ seemed unsatisfactory.

This problem with CI₃ would be resolved, at least in part, if we were to understand the notion of autonomy in a slightly different way. We could say that a person has autonomy of the will when he is motivated to act in accord with principles he has rationally and impartially established for himself. If we think of a rational and impartial choice of principles as the sort of choice that occurs when the chooser is not biased in his own (or anyone else's) favor, when the chooser is rational, and when the chooser is concerned with choosing in such a way that no segment of society would be made to suffer needlessly as a result of his choice, then it should be clear that the choice made in the original position must be rational and impartial. Thus, if we think that an autonomous selection of principles involves a rational and impartial choice of those principles, then we will say that the choice made in the original position is autonomous. Those who act on principles thus chosen will be acting in accord with suitable self-made principles.

If we look at Kant in this Rawlsian way, we can see one manner in which a Kantian might attempt to answer the question raised earlier concerning CI₃. He can say that it is not enough merely to act on principles one has established for oneself. For if the choice of principles is defective, then one may be acting on self-made but inappropriate principles. One must act on principles one has established for oneself autonomously. That is, one must act on principles that would have been selected if one had done the selecting in the original position. When one acts on this sort of self-made principle, then one inevitably acts rightly. For then there is no way in which one could have selected a defective principle.

Thus, it should be clear that the Rawlsian social-contract theory is quite similar to Kant's principle of autonomy, if Kant's principle is interpreted in this way. Under each view, we are required to act in accord with principles we would select if we were to select rationally and impartially. In Rawls's theory, the original position provides a setting in which a rational and impartial choice would be made. Although some such view may be implicit in Kant, it is certainly not present as clearly. Kant does make clear, however, that one's choice of principles must be rational, and must not be influenced by what he calls "inclinations." Thus Rawls's theory may be seen as a refined and developed version of a possible interpretation of Kant's view.

Rawls explains his own view of the relation between his theory and Kant's in this passage:

> Kant held, I believe, that a person is acting autonomously when the principles of his action are chosen by him as the most adequate possible expression of his nature as a free and equal rational being. The principles he acts upon are not adopted because of his social position or natural endowments, or in view of the particular kind of society in which he lives or the specific things that he happens to want. To act on such principles is to act heteronomously. Now the veil of ignorance deprives the person in the original position of the knowledge that would enable them to choose heteronomous principles. The parties arrive at the choice together as free and equal rational persons knowing only that those circumstances obtain which give rise to the need for principles of justice. . . . To be sure, the argument for these principles does add in various ways to Kant's conception. . . . But I believe that this and other additions are natural enough and remain fairly close to Kant's doctrine.[11]

A second interesting connection between Kant and Rawls has to do with the Kantian "kingdom of ends." In the *Groundwork*, Kant admonishes us to "so act as if you were always through your maxims a law-making member in a universal kingdom of ends."[12] He also tells us that our own autonomously selected maxims ought to "accord with a possible kingdom of ends."[13] Yet Kant never tells us precisely what this possible kingdom of ends is supposed to be. Is it an ideal society in which everyone treats everyone else as an end? Or is it taken to be a genuine possibility toward which we should strive? What rules would it have? How would it be organized? How big could it be? Precisely what role does the conception of a kingdom of ends play in Kantian moral philosophy?

The Rawlsian concept of the original position may seem rather less sublime, but it is certainly clearer than the Kantian concept of the kingdom of ends. As an interpretation of Kant's notion, it seems to amount to this: Those in the original position are behind a limited veil of ignorance.

None of them knows which role he will play in the future society. Being rational, and being concerned with maximizing his own good, each person must choose moral principles in such a way that no matter what role he plays, he will not be shortchanged. As a result, his choice will be made in such a way as to insure a fair deal for the occupier, whoever he may be, of each role in the society. In other words, the constraints on the original position insure that each role occupier is treated as an end in himself. After all, each chooser must choose with the full realization that if he chooses in such a way as to shortchange someone, it may turn out that he has shortchanged himself!

Thus, Rawls has given us a rather interesting way of approaching the Kantian concept of the kingdom of ends. Of course, there are substantial differences here, too. One of the most striking is in the area of motivation. Rawls, almost by sleight of hand, puts us into a position in which our selfish motives force us, whether we like it or not, to treat others as ends. Each of us apparently wants to treat only himself as an end. But since we don't know which role we'll be playing, we must treat all role players as ends, just to be sure that we don't misuse ourselves. Kant would probably find this an unsatisfactory conception of the kingdom of ends. He would prefer that we treat others as ends simply out of respect for their dignity. If we treat them as ends because of some inclination, as Rawls apparently would have it, our acts lack moral worth.

In any case, the Rawlsian social-contract theory is clearly Kantian in spirit, and it suggests a way of understanding some of Kant's remarks about the kingdom of ends.

Evaluation of Rawls's Social-Contract Theory

Rawls's theory is of substantial interest from two rather different points of view. In the first place, it provides us with an exciting new way of understanding Kant. In the second place, it constitutes an inherently plausible moral theory, regardless of its accuracy as an interpretation of Kant.

It is hard to say whether Rawls's interpretation of Kant is ultimately successful. It seems clear that some of the similarities Rawls stresses are genuine. Yet it also seems that there remain some very substantial differences between Kant and Rawls. For one thing, it appears to be contrary to the spirit of Kantianism to assume that those in the original position would be motivated by a desire to maximize their own good. For according to Kant, our selection of moral principles should be made without regard to our desires for future goods or our fears of future evils. Thus, Rawls may be charged with having allowed too much inclination to creep into his characterization of the circumstances of moral choice. Another Kantian theme that seems to be absent in Rawls's theory is the idea that morally right action is action with a universalizable maxim. Kant held, at least some of the time, that logical consistency of the universalized form of the maxim is the criterion of moral rightness. This sort of criterion of morality is nowhere to be found in Rawls's theory.

Questions such as these concerning the adequacy of Rawls's interpretation of Kant may be of considerable interest to scholars specializing in the interpretation of Kant. However, for our present purposes it will be more useful to consider the question of whether Rawls's theory is independently worthy of belief. That is, regardless of its value as an interpretation of Kantian moral philosophy, does RSCT provide us with an adequate criterion of morality?

One troubling feature of this version of Rawls's theory is a feature it shares with Brandt's ideal-moral code theory.[14] The feature in question is this: The theory requires us to act in accord with a moral code that may be significantly different from the one actually current in our society. So even if a person does his very best to treat others as they think they should be treated, he may be acting wrongly. His error, according to RSCT, may be that he fails to make his actions accord with some moral code that neither he nor they believe in, and that they would not want established if they were to think about it. This surely seems odd.

A second problem with this theory (although probably not with Rawls's theory of justice) comes about as a result of the fact that the rightness of actions is tied down as it is to *societies*. Let us suppose that different societies may have different original-position would-be contract codes. Let us also suppose that a given individual may be in two different societies at the same time. An example of such a situation was given in our discussion of Brandt's theory.[15] Finally, let us suppose that some such individual performs an act that is permitted by the would-be code of one of his societies but prohibited by the would-be code of the other. Here we seem to have the makings of a case in which a given act is both right and wrong at the same time. If such a result can in fact be generated, it would prove that RSCT is false.

A defender of Rawls might insist that it is impossible for two different societies to choose different codes. Indeed, a defender of Rawls might insist that all reference to societies is out of place here anyway. However, RSCT is a development of the social-contract theory, and as such it is natural to construe it in terms of societies, as I have done. Under this version of Rawls's theory, it remains possible that different societies, even those having some members in common, might choose incompatible codes.

A final problem with RSCT is generated by the fact that only human beings are allowed to participate in the choice of the moral code for the society. Plants, animals, and inanimate objects don't have the opportunity to enter into the bargaining process. This may seem trivial, but it leads to a problem that many philosophers find quite vexing. It has lately come to be known as "the problem of human chauvinism."[16]

Many moralists have come to the conclusion that it is morally wrong to inflict needless pain on animals. Thus, they argue against inhumane treatment of laboratory animals and cruelty to sheep, cattle, and other animals raised for human consumption. Although such concern is not universal, it is quite widespread, and surely ought not to be ruled out without an argument by any moral theory. Yet RSCT seems to rule against the legitimacy of moral concern for nonhumans.

Since each of the choosers in the original position is human, and since each is assumed to be selfish, each will choose in such a way as to protect his own interest, in so far as that interest can be determined. The veil of ignorance insures that none will trample on the interests of others, since none knows "who he is." But the veil of ignorance is not so opaque as to blind the choosers to the fact that they won't be cows, or chickens, or sheep in the society to come. As selfish choosers and humans, they have no motivation to protect the interests of nonhumans. Hence, the code they select will not contain provisions protecting such creatures from needless pain. This seems unfortunate.

Such problems as these are of some interest, but none of them really strikes at the heart of what Rawls has said. For Rawls did not propose a total moral theory. He only proposed a theory about the basic principles of justice. None of these criticisms, then, should be taken to be a criticism of *A Theory of Justice*. That work must be considered on its own merits.

NOTES

1. John Rawls, *A Theory of Justice* (Cambridge, Mass.: Harvard University Press, 1971).

2. *Ibid.*, p. 17.

3. *Ibid.*, pp. 251–57.

4. *Ibid.*, p. 252.

5. Thomas Hobbes, *Leviathan*, in *English Philosophers from Bacon to Mill*, ed. E. A. Burtt (New York: Modern Library, 1939) p. 161.

6. *Ibid.*

7. *Ibid.*, p. 177.

8. For a discussion of conventionalism and some of its problems, see pp. 76–77; 163–67.

9. Rawls discusses the original position on pp. 118–92 of *A Theory of Justice*.

10. For a discussion of Kant's views on autonomy, see pp. 128–32.

11. Rawls, *A Theory of Justice*, p. 252.

12. Immanuel Kant, *Groundwork of the Metaphysic of Morals*, translated and analysed by H. J. Paton (New York: Harper & Row, 1964) p. 106.

13. *Ibid.*, p. 104.

14. See pp. 67–71.

15. See pp. 70–71.

16. This concept has been developed by Peter Singer in *Animal Liberation* (New York: A New York Review Book, 1975).

10

Ross's Formalism

In spite of their great differences, there may seem to be one major respect in which utilitarianism and Kantianism are very similar. Each theory attempts to provide a criterion of morally correct action, and in each case the criterion provided is *monistic*. That is, each theory provides a criterion that selects just one, relatively easy-to-identify characteristic, and asserts that all and only morally correct acts have that characteristic. Of course, the characteristic provided by utilitarianism is quite different from the characteristic provided by Kantianism. In this respect, the moral theory of W. D. Ross may be thought of as being quite unlike utilitarianism and Kantianism. Whereas those theories are monistic, Ross's theory seems to be *pluralistic*. That is, Ross claims that there are several distinct characteristics, not reducible to a single one, any of which may tend to make an act right.

Prima Facie Duty

The most fundamental concept in Ross's moral theory is the concept of *prima facie duty*. Sometimes Ross uses the expression "conditional duty" to refer to this concept. Ross explains the concept of prima facie duty as follows:

> I suggest "prima facie duty" or "conditional duty" as a brief way of referring to the characteristic (quite distinct from that of being a duty proper) which an act has, in virtue of being of a certain kind (e.g. the keeping of a promise), of being an act which would be a duty proper if it were not at the same time of another kind which is morally significant. Whether an act is a

duty proper or an actual duty depends on *all* the morally significant kinds it is an instance of.[1]

The fact that Ross has chosen the term "prima facie duty" may suggest that to say that an act is a prima facie duty is to say that "at first glance" it appears to be a duty. But Ross vigorously denies that this is what he has in mind. When he says that an act is a prima facie duty, he is not saying merely that it *appears* to be a duty, or that it could easily be supposed to be a duty. Rather, he wants to insist that when an act is a prima facie duty, this fact is an objective fact about that act, and not just an appearance.

Nor is it the case that to say that an act is a prima facie duty is simply to say that it is in fact obligatory. The property of being a prima facie duty is distinct from the property of being a duty, or of being what Ross calls a "duty proper."

Furthermore, when we say that an act is a prima facie duty, we are not saying that it is a duty of some special kind. For many acts are prima facie duties, but it would be utterly wrong to perform them. Thus, from the fact that an act is a prima facie duty, it does not follow that it is a duty.

It may be a bit unclear what Ross means when he says that an act is a prima facie duty. Perhaps the meaning of this term can be clarified by means of an example. Suppose all we know about some proposed act is that if it were performed, it would be a case of promise keeping. That is, someone has made a promise to someone else, and if he were to perform this act, it would be the keeping of that promise. Even if we know nothing else about the act, we may still be inclined to say that there is at least one moral reason in favor of performing it. Because it would be an act of promise keeping, it would seem to have at least one "right-making characteristic." Another way to put this point would be to say, following Ross, that the act in question is a prima facie duty.

Suppose, to continue the example, that the person who made the promise in fact promised to murder some innocent victim. In this case, as should be obvious, to keep the promise would be to murder the victim. Ross would say that the act of keeping the promise is nevertheless a prima facie duty. There is still at least one good moral reason in favor of performing it: it would be a case of promise keeping. On the other hand, there are some pretty good reasons for refraining from doing the act. For one, the performing of the act would result in severe injury to the innocent victim.

Ross says that the property of being a prima facie duty is a "parti-resultant property," whereas the property of being a duty proper is a "toti-resultant property." He explains this distinction by saying that we can determine that an act is a prima facie duty even if we know only a little about it. We need know only a *part* of its nature in order to find that it is a prima facie duty. But we must know the *totality* of its nature if we are to determine that it is a duty proper.

In the example, the act of promise keeping is a prima facie duty, and this results simply from a part of its nature. The part in question is the fact that the act would be a case of promise keeping. But that same act of promise keeping is surely not a duty proper. The act would in fact be wrong. The fact that an act is a duty proper arises not just in virtue of some part of its nature, but from its whole nature. When we consider the whole nature of the imagined act of murder (if we could do so), we discover that it is not a duty proper.

Ross lists the main kinds of prima facie duty. They are as follows:

1. The duties of *fidelity*: These are duties that arise as a result of promises, whether explicit or implicit. Any act that a person has committed himself to doing—whether by explicitly uttering the words "I promise," or in some other, more subtle way—is a prima facie duty. There is at least one good moral reason in favor of doing any such act. This is not to say, as our last example showed, that the act ought to be performed.

2. The duties of *reparation*: If someone has previously injured some other person, and can now perform some act that would serve to "make up" for that injury, then he has a prima facie duty to do so. The fact that the act would "repair" a past wrong provides a moral reason for doing such an act.

3. The duties of *gratitude*: If someone has previously performed a service for me, or has in any way benefited me, and I can now do some act that would serve to repay him for his past kindness, then I have a prima facie duty to do so. The moral reason for doing such an act is simply that it would tend to benefit someone who has previously benefited me.

4. The duties of *justice*: Here, Ross has in mind the fact that we have a moral reason to prevent unjust distributions of goods, if we have it in our power to do so. If I can prevent someone from getting more or less of a good thing than he deserves, I have a prima facie duty to do so. Or, if someone is already getting more or less than he deserves and I am in a position to set things right, then I have a prima facie duty to upset such an unjust distribution.

5. Ross thought that virtue, intelligence, and pleasure are all intrinsically good. Thus, he also thought that we should try, other things being equal, to see to it that others enjoy as much of these goods as they can. So if I can help to make others more virtuous, intelligent, or pleased, then I have a prima facie duty to do so. These are the duties of *beneficence*.

6. According to Ross, each of us has a prima facie duty to make himself more virtuous and intelligent, but we have no prima facie duty to give ourselves more pleasure. Thus, our prima facie duties to ourselves

are somewhat unlike our prima facie duties to others, according to Ross. This duty to become more virtuous and intelligent is called the duty of *self-improvement*.

7. The final class of prima facie duties are called the duties of nonmaleficence. We have at least one good moral reason to avoid injuring others, and so there is a prima facie duty to perform any act that would prevent or avoid an injury to another person.

Several of these kinds of prima facie duty are decidedly backward-looking. That is, the normative status of the act depends more upon what has happened in the past than on what will happen as a result in the future. This is especially obvious in the cases of fidelity, reparation, and gratitude. Thus, it would appear that a utilitarian would have a hard time explaining why we have any moral reason to perform such acts. According to the utilitarian view, as we saw earlier, the rightness of an act depends entirely on what would happen *after* its performance. But in Ross's view, acts in these categories are prima facie duties regardless of the amount of utility they would produce if performed. Their prima facie obligatoriness arises from what has come before, not from what will come after.

Another respect in which Ross's theory differs from utilitarianism is its treatment of justice. Ross claims that we have a prima facie duty to ensure that justice is done, regardless of the utility of doing so. The utilitarian can account for the morality of justice, if at all, only by claiming that doing justice produces more utility than any alternative. In this respect, it may appear, Ross's theory is somewhat preferable.

It should now be clear why Ross considers himself a pluralist. He has given us a list of seven different sorts of prima facie duties. Perhaps the list could be condensed a bit by combining gratitude, reparation, and justice, or by combining benevolence, self-improvement, and non-maleficence. But even if it could be condensed in some way, there would still remain several distinct categories of prima facie duty. Justice and benevolence, for example, seem to have no obvious common source of prima facie obligatoriness.

Ross's Theory

In spite of his apparent pluralism, Ross wants to provide us with a single statement of necessary and sufficient conditions for right action. Indeed, in one place he attempts to set out what he takes to be "the nature of the acts that are right." But before we consider Ross's statements, it might be useful to reflect a bit on some things he cannot say, and on why he cannot say them. This may serve to make clear why Ross states his view as he does, rather than in some apparently simpler way.

It would clearly be wrong to state Ross's view in any way such as this:

R_1: An act is morally right if and only if it is a prima facie duty.

Although it is of course true that in Ross's view every morally right act is a prima facie duty, it is equally obvious that many acts that are prima facie duties are not morally right. For example, if I have promised to murder someone, then my act of keeping that promise would be a prima facie duty, but surely it would not be right.

We might be tempted to make use of the concept of alternatives in order to resolve this sort of difficulty. Perhaps we would try:

R_2: An act is morally right if and only if it is a prima facie duty and none of its alternatives is a prima facie duty.

But R_2 is in fact only a very slight improvement over R_1. For in almost every morally interesting case, we find that we are faced with a conflict of prima facie duties. On the one hand, we have a moral reason to perform one of the alternatives. On the other hand, we have another moral reason to perform one of the other alternatives. We cannot do both actions, and in many cases only one of them is right.

Perhaps an example will make this clear. Suppose a man has some money and finds that he can spend it in two ways. On the one hand, he can use it to pay back a long-outstanding debt; on the other hand, he can use it to buy several cases of beer for his friends. Let us suppose that these are his only alternatives, and that they are incompatible. Notice, first, that his first alternative is a prima facie duty: if he pays back the debt, he fulfills a promise. His second alternative would also be a prima facie duty, since it would produce some innocent pleasure for some of his friends. Under R_2, neither of these acts would be right, since neither is the only prima facie duty from a set of alternatives. Each has an alternative that is also a prima facie duty. But surely it is possible that it would be right for the man to pay the debt and wrong for him to squander the money on beer. So R_2 is unacceptable.

One way in which we might attempt to deal with this problem is as follows: First, we could list Ross's prima facie duties in order of their relative importance. Perhaps the list would be the one Ross provided:

1. promise keeping
2. reparation
3. gratitude
4. justice
5. beneficence
6. self-improvement
7. nonmaleficence

Then we could claim that when two or more prima facie duties appear among the alternatives, the right act to perform is the one that is the highest ranking prima facie duty. For example, in the case last discussed, we had a conflict of prima facie duties. One alternative was a prima facie duty of promise keeping, and hence should be ranked first. The other alternative was a prima facie duty of beneficence, and hence would be ranked fifth. In this case, according to the view being suggested, the right act would be the act of promise keeping, and so the man should pay the old debt.

The proposal, then, is that we view Ross's theory as follows:

R_3: An act is morally right if and only if it is a prima facie duty and none of its alternatives is a higher ranking prima facie duty.

Although it might have some initial attractiveness, R_3 is an unacceptable theory. It can be seen to be defective in at least two different ways.

The first problem is that conflicts may exist among alternatives that are prima facie duties of the same rank. For example, suppose a man has promised his parents that he will attend their fiftieth wedding anniversary. But he has also promised a casual aquaintance that he will play tennis with him at the same time. The acts are incompatible alternatives, each is a prima facie duty, and each is a prima facie duty of the first rank. R_3 yields the result that either would be right, and that neither would be preferable to the other. Clearly, however, it might be right in this case for the man to honor his promise to his parents rather than his promise to the casual acquaintance. The obligation to the parents may outweigh the obligation to the friend. So, R_3 apparently can yield the wrong results in some cases.

A second problem with R_3 cuts even more deeply. If we reflect on the list of prima facie duties, we will soon be able to imagine cases in which the proposed ranking is inappropriate. In some cases, doing justice is more important than keeping a promise. For example, suppose a judge has promised to be very lenient in the sentencing of a political ally who has committed a serious crime. The judge should not keep the promise. Rather, he should see to it that justice is done. In other cases, it might be more important to keep a promise than it would be to insure a just distribution of goods. This would be most obvious in a case in which the goods in question are of slight value, the injustice minimal, and the promise very solemn. So there just isn't any reason to suppose that any single ranking of prima facie duties will be adequate to all cases. No matter how we order them, there will be cases for which the ranking will seem wrong.

Perhaps some will think that these problems can be overcome by combining Ross's theory with some ideas from utilitarianism. For example, it might be thought that we can improve Ross's theory by stating it in this way:

R_4:   An act is morally right if and only if it is a prima facie duty and no alternative prima facie duty has a higher utility than it has.

According to R_4, we select the prima facie duty that has the highest utility, and that will be the right act to perform.

It would be difficult to prove that R_4 is extensionally equivalent to act utilitarianism. Nevertheless, the two views yield very similar results. In fact, in every case in which act utilitarianism yields a wrong result and the relevant alternatives are prima facie duties, R_4 will yield the same wrong result.

To see why this is so, let us reconsider the punish-the-innocent case (see Chapter 4). Recall that the police chief had several main alternatives open to him. Among these were punishing an innocent man and continuing to search for the real killers. Each of these is a prima facie duty. The first, because it would cause a lot of pleasure, is a prima facie duty of beneficence. The second is a prima facie duty of justice, as well as of promise keeping. In this case, R_4 implies that since all of the alternatives are prima facie duties, the police chief should perform the act with the highest utility. In other words, R_4 implies that punishing the innocent man would be right in this case. As we saw earlier, however, most sensitive people find this result abhorrent.

Ross was aware of this problem, and he devoted considerable attention to its solution. Here is his answer:

> It is worth while to try to state more definitely the nature of the acts that are right. We may try to state first what (if anything) is the universal nature of *all* acts that are right. It is obvious that any of the acts that we do has countless effects, directly or indirectly, on countless people, and the probability is that any act, however right it may be, will have adverse effects (though these may be very trivial) on some innocent people. Similarly, any wrong act will probably have beneficial effects on some deserving people. Every act therefore, viewed in some aspects, will be prima facie right, and viewed in others, prima facie wrong, and right acts can be distinguished from wrong acts only as being those which, of all those possible for the agent in the circumstances, have the greatest balance of prima facie rightness, in those respects in which they are prima facie right, over their prima facie wrongness, in those respects in which they are prima facie wrong. Prima facie rightness and wrongness being understood in the sense previously explained. For the estimation of the comparative stringency of these prima facie obligations no general rules can, so far as I can see, be laid down.[2]

So, Ross seems to think that in every case, some of our prima facie duties are more "stringent" than others, although there are no general rules about this. That is, our obligation to perform one act is more binding upon us than our obligation to perform some of its alternatives. So it looks as if we can state Ross's actual theory in this way:

R_5:   An act is morally right if and only if it is a prima facie duty and no alternative is a more stringent prima facie duty.

A defender of Ross would say that R_5 generates the correct result in every case we have discussed. For example, in the case in which a man has promised to murder an innocent victim, Ross could say that there is a prima facie duty to keep the promise and a prima facie duty to break the promise. He could go on to claim that in this particular case, the prima facie duty to break the promise is more stringent than the prima facie duty to keep it. Thus, it is right to break the promise and avoid murdering the innocent victim.

A correct result is also yielded in the punish-the-innocent case. Here, the most stringent prima facie duty is the duty to see to it that justice is done. The prima facie duty to cause pleasure by punishing an innocent victim is far less stringent. Hence, it is not right to punish the innocent victim.

Problems for Ross

Let us now turn to some objections that may be raised against Ross's theory. One objection that has in fact been raised is that Ross's theory lacks "system" and "unity." It has been claimed that Ross has failed to provide us with a coherent, unified account of the nature of morally right action. Rather than giving us a single statement of what makes right acts right, he has provided us with a list of seven different sorts of action that are often right. This, it has been claimed, gives us no insight into the basic problem of normative ethics.

In his reply to this objection, Ross says that "loyalty to the facts is worth more than a symmetrical architectonic or a hastily reached simplicity."[3] This apparently means that Ross is willing to admit that his theory is unsystematic, but that he feels that this constitutes no defect in it. If in fact our moral obligations are somewhat unsystematic, then an adequate theory of them must reveal this lack of unity.

However, it seems that Ross was too quick to admit that his view lacks unity. What, after all, is meant by the claim that his view is unsystematic? If it means that Ross has failed to provide a single criterion of right action, then the objection is based on a misconception. For Ross has provided a single criterion of right action—it is stated in R_5. R_5 gives us a single statement of an (allegedly) necessary and sufficient condition for moral rightness. How could a normative theory be more "unified" or "coherent" than this?

Another objection may be more to the point. It might be said that if Ross's theory were true, no one would be able to determine what he ought to do. After all, Ross has not provided us with any way of telling which of two prima facie duties is the more stringent. Obviously, however, people sometimes do figure out their obligations. Hence, Ross's theory must be false.

Ross apparently feels that we have the ability to "see" or "intuit" the fact that there is a prima facie duty to keep promises, a prima facie duty to increase knowledge, virtue, and pleasure in others, and so forth. For this reason, he has been called an *intuitionist*. His intuitionistic thesis is that reflective, intelligent adults can intuit that there is a prima facie duty to perform actions of the seven kinds mentioned in his list. But Ross denies that this faculty of intuition enables us to know which of our prima facie duties, in any given case of conflict, is the most stringent. In fact, Ross's view is that we never do know for certain what we ought to do. So he would reply to the objection above by denying its second premise. For Ross, it is not so obvious that we often know what act is right.

This reply might suggest that Ross thinks that it doesn't matter what we do. After all, if we can't tell what we ought to do, why not just do what seems to be most fun? But of course Ross does not believe in any such thing. His view is that we must reflect very carefully when confronted with a difficult moral choice.

> . . . we are more likely to do our duty if we reflect to the best of our ability on the prima facie rightness or wrongness of various possible acts in virtue of the characteristics we perceive them to have, than if we act without reflection. With this greater likelihood we must be content.[4]

Ross also speaks of an alleged "sense of our particular duty in particular circumstances." He says that this sense is "highly fallible, but it is the only guide we have to our duty."[5] Some philosophers have questioned whether there is any such sense.

A final objection to Ross's theory may be raised. Many readers find Ross's view to be empty, trivial, or unenlightening. It seems to some of these people that all Ross has said is that an act is right if and only if it has at least as much rightness as any alternative. Surely, if this is all that Ross has said, then his view is indeed rather trivial.

One way to develop this objection would be to ask how we determined that Ross's theory always generates the right results. Why is it, for example, that in every case of moral conflict, the act that we think is obligatory is the very one that Ross thinks is the most stringent prima facie duty? How can he tell that it's not the case that some wrong act is, unfortunately, the most stringent prima facie duty? One suggestion is that the term "most stringent prima facie duty" is really just a complicated synonym for "obligatory act." If this is so, then it's no wonder that the obligatory act always turns out to be the most stringent prima facie duty!

Another way to develop this objection would be to ask what the terms "prima facie duty" and "stringent" are supposed to mean. For, as is obvious, these are the main terms by means of which Ross has stated his criterion of morally right action. Ross has explained that to say that an act is a prima facie duty is to say that it is "an act which would be a duty proper if it were not at the same time of another kind which is morally significant." This isn't terribly clear, but what it seems to suggest is this: An act is a prima facie duty provided that it has a tendency, perhaps overridden, to be right. It would be right to perform that act unless one of its alternatives were preferable. In other words, that act, a, is such that if there is no alternative, b, that would be preferable, then a is right. We can formulate this idea as follows.

D_1: a is a prima facie duty =df. if there is no alternative, b, such that it would be right to perform b instead of a, then it would be right to perform a.

Now we can attempt to formulate a definition of "stringent." This is a term that Ross does not define, but the idea is clear enough. The prima facie duty to perform a is more stringent than the prima facie duty to perform b if and only if it would be right to perform a instead of b. So the definition should perhaps be this:

D_2:   The prima facie duty to perform a is more stringent than the prima facie duty to perform b =df. it would be right to perform a instead of b.

Let us assume that these definitions do in fact capture Ross's concepts. Now we can reexamine R_5 to see exactly what it means. Recall that R_5 is as follows:

R_5:   An act is morally right if and only if it is a prima facie duty and no alternative is a more stringent prima facie duty.

According to our proposed definitions, what this means is that an act, a, is morally right provided that two conditions are satisfied. First, a has to be a prima facie duty. That is, a is such that if there is no alternative, b, such that it would be right to perform b instead of a, then a would be right. The second condition is that there must be no alternative to a that is a more stringent prima facie duty. According to D_2, this means that there is no alternative, b, that would be right to perform instead of a. When we put these two conditions together, we get something like this:

R_6: An act, a, is morally right if and only if (i) if there is no preferable alternative, then a is right; and (ii) there is no preferable alternative.

It should be obvious that R_6 is quite trivial. It tells us little more than that an act is right if and only if it is right. This is something we knew even before we began our study of normative ethics. By itself, however, this result does not show that Ross's theory is trivial. It only shows, if anything, that we cannot define "prima facie duty" and "stringent" in the manner proposed without trivializing the theory. The remaining problem is that it may be difficult to discover any better way to define these terms. If no adequate definitions can be found, then perhaps we should conclude that Ross's theory is either rather trivial or rather obscure.

NOTES

1. William David Ross, *The Right and the Good* (© Oxford University Press, 1930), pp. 19–20.Reprinted by permission of the Oxford University Press.

2. *Ibid.*, p. 41.

3. *Ibid.*, p. 23.

4. *Ibid.*, p. 32.

5. *Ibid.*, p. 42.

11

Relativism

Consider the following case. The Smith family invites the Jones family to dinner. After some small talk, Mr. Smith goes to the kitchen and returns with a huge platter on which there is a roasted pig with an apple in its mouth. "Let's dig in," he says. The Jones family is shocked. They don't know what to say. Finally, Mrs. Jones explains the problem. They don't eat meat. Out of deep moral conviction, the Jones family has adopted vegetarianism. However, they do not want to offend the Smiths, and so Mrs. Jones says that she respects the Smiths' right to eat meat. "After all," she says, "what's right for us may not be right for you." Everyone nods in agreement. This philosophical point seems to smooth over the moral disagreement. The problem is solved with the Smith family eating the pig and the Jones family eating the apple.

A closely related maxim appears in more serious contexts. For example, when people are traveling in foreign countries, they are often surprised by the customs of the natives. Suppose some travelers find that the natives of the country they are visiting own slaves. A native slave owner might appeal to this philosophical principle to avoid criticism: "What's right in your society may not be right in ours." If the visitors are tolerant, or if they wish to appear so, they may acknowledge the validity of this point: "Who are we to criticize your morals? After all, morals are relative."

In these cases and many others like them, we find people appealing to a doctrine that has come to be known as *relativism*. Many non-philosophers apparently believe that relativism in normative ethics is both true and important. In fact, however, there are many different interpretations of the relativistic principle. Because these interpretations are easily confused, it is a matter of some interest to attempt to distinguish them from one another. Having done this, we may begin to see which ones, if any, are true, and which ones, if any, are of philosophical significance.

Belief Relativism

Some forms of relativism are fairly complex, but belief relativism is simple. According to this view, when we say:

R_1: What's right for one person may not be right for another.

what we mean is:

R_2: It is possible that there is a kind of action, such that one person believes that actions of that kind are morally right and another person does not believe that actions of that kind are morally right.

So, for example, if Mrs. Smith believes that eating meat is morally right but Mrs. Jones does not believe that eating meat is morally right, then R_2 is true.

R_2 is a principle of *personal belief relativism*. It simply asserts that the moral beliefs of one person may be different from those of another person. This view is to be distinguished from a slightly more interesting view that may be called *societal belief relativism*. This is the view that the moral beliefs of one society may differ from those of another. This view is a little more complex, largely because there is some unclarity in the concept of a "society." It is not easy to give a precise and adequate definition of this term. Furthermore, even if we assume that we understand what a society is, we must face another problem. That problem arises from some obscurity in the notion of a society's beliefs. Strictly speaking, societies don't have any beliefs. But perhaps we can say, in an extended sense, that a society believes something if the vast majority of its members believe it. In other words, if the vast majority of members of society S believe that vegetarianism is morally required, then we can say that society S believes that vegetarianism is morally required.

Making use of this concept, we can formulate the doctrine of societal belief relativism as follows:

R_3: It is possible that there is a kind of action, such that one society believes that actions of that kind are morally right and another society does not believe that actions of that kind are morally right.

Not much needs to be said about the truth of R_3. It is true. If we grant that there are "societies," then we must also grant that R_3 is true. Surely, anyone who has the slightest acquaintance with the facts of anthropology would have to admit that moral beliefs differ from society to society.

Thus, belief relativism in general seems to be true. What's more important, however, is the question of whether belief relativism is of interest as a philosophical doctrine. Or, to put the question in another way, does the truth of belief relativism have any impact upon ethical theory? One way to answer this question is to formulate an interesting doctrine of *absolutism* and then consider whether belief relativism and absolutism conflict. If they conflict, then belief relativism may be of some interest.

We can say that absolutism is the view that there is one criterion of morality valid for all people at all times. In other words, it is the view that there is a single ultimate moral standard. This view may be understood in the following way. Consider this schema:

C: An act is morally right if and only if————.

If absolutism is true, then there is some way of filling in the blank in C that will result in C becoming a true statement. This way of filling in the blank must not trivialize C. That is, we can't put "it is morally right" in the blank. The result of doing that would be true, but trivial. We must fill in the blank with some nonmoral expression. So absolutism can be formulated as follows:

A: There is a way of filling in the blank in C that is nontrivial and
        results in C becoming a universally valid criterion of morality.

If act utilitarianism is true, then absolutism, as we are understanding it, is true as well. For if act utilitarianism is true, then we can write "it has at least as much utility as any alternative" in the blank in C. The result, if act utilitarianism is true, would be true. Hence, absolutism would be true. A similar conclusion could be reached if rule utilitarianism, the first categorical imperative, or any other criterion of morality were true. In any such case, there would be one feature that serves everywhere as a necessary and sufficient condition for moral rightness.

It should be evident that absolutism, understood as A, does not conflict with relativism, understood as either R_2 or R_3. From the fact that people's moral beliefs differ, we surely cannot infer anything about the existence of a single ultimate standard of morality. Indeed, R_2 and R_3 are compatible with the claim that everyone believes in the same ultimate standard. For example, it could be that Mrs. Jones and Mrs. Smith both believe that act utilitarianism is the ultimate standard of morality. However, Mrs. Jones believes that eating meat causes great suffering in hell, whereas Mrs. Smith believes that eating meat causes only pleasure (if it is properly cooked). Thus, though they agree about the ultimate principle of morality, they disagree about the morality of eating meat.

Even if people do not believe in the same ultimate standard, it cannot be inferred that there is no single ultimate standard. For example, if one person believes in one ultimate standard and another person believes in another incompatible standard, then we can infer only that at least one of these individuals is mistaken. From the fact that they have conflicting beliefs about what is the true criterion of morality, we surely cannot infer that there is no true criterion of morality. Thus, R₂ and R₃ are compatible with A. For this reason, it is hard to see why anyone would think R₂ and R₃ to be of philosophical interest.

Perhaps this helps to explain the impatience some philosophers feel when "relativistic" anthropologists start describing some of the unusual moral beliefs of some societies. The anthropologist points out that there is a tribe in Brazil whose members believe that it is morally right for a man to marry his horse, and morally wrong for a woman to appear in public with her nose exposed. The philosopher is uneasy. He recognizes that such a belief is rather weird, but he can't see the point of it all. Since the existence of such beliefs is compatible with the truth of act utilitarianism, the categorical imperative, Ross's theory, or any other criterion of morality, such beliefs have no direct bearing on the truth of absolutism. Without some special, rather unexpected argument, it is hard to see that such anthropological facts have any relevance to moral philosophy.

Conventionalism

Let us consider another interpretation of the doctrine that "what's right in one society may be wrong in another." One form into which this view could be developed is known as *conventionalism*. Roughly, conventionalism is the view that you should act in the way in which your society believes you should act. In other words, the moral conventions of one's society determine one's moral obligations. Since the moral conventions of one society may differ from those of another, this view yields the result that "what's right in one society may be wrong in another."

In order to state conventionalism adequately, we must make a few assumptions. First, we must assume that for every act there is exactly one society that is, in a sense, "the society in which the act is performed." If we don't make this assumption, then we will have a hard time saying *whose* conventions determine the normative status of the act. If we assume that each act occurs in exactly one society, then we can say that it is the conventions of *that* society that are relevant to the determination of the rightness of the act.

Second, we will assume that each society has a set of conventions, or general moral principles. We can assume that each such set of conventions is consistent: for each act, it assigns at most one moral evaluation. Thus, for any act you perform, your society's conventions will assign at most one of these values: "right," "wrong," or "obligatory." For the sake of convenience, we can also assume that the conventions are complete: for each act, they assign at least one normative status. Of course, a society may in fact be found to have an inconsistent or incomplete set of conventions. This point, though probably true, should not make a significant difference in the present context. Finally, we can say that an act is permitted by the conventions of a society if and only if the conventions assign the act the normative status of "right."

Now we can state one form of conventionalism:

> R_4: An act is morally right if and only if it is permitted by the conventions of its society.

Apparently, many people feel that something like R_4 is true. For many people insist that we ought to conform to the conventions of our own society. So, for example, if a man who lives in a society in which polygamy is practiced has more than one wife, a conventionalist would say that he acts rightly. On the other hand, the conventionalist would say that a polygamist in a monogamous society does not act rightly. For according to the conventionalist, "what's right in one society may not be right in another." This view has considerable intuitive appeal.

As we saw earlier, in connection with Rawls's version of rule utilitarianism, any theory relevantly similar to R_4 faces enormous difficulties. Perhaps the most serious of these is a conceptual problem. In order to state conventionalism in a coherent way, we have to assume that for each act, there is exactly one society that is, in some sense, "the society in which the act is performed." This assumption, however, is very implausible. Some of its difficulties can be seen by contemplating the fact that many acts involve persons who come from different societies. For example, consider a case in which a mugger in a big city attacks a visitor from a rural district in another state. The mugger may have little in common with the victim. They may speak different languages, eat different kinds of food, have different views about morality, and so on. Surely, two such persons are from radically different social backgrounds. Are they from different societies? Many people would say they are. Are they also from the same society? Many would agree to this as well. Which society, then, is the one in which the mugging is performed? It seems impossible to tell.

If a person is a member of many societies at once, then this problem arises even when an act of his involves no one but himself. Suppose a person, A, is a member of society S_1 and society S_2. The conventions of S_1 rule out suicide, but those of S_2 permit it. A commits suicide. Is his act right or wrong, according to R_4? Once again, it seems impossible to tell.

The deeper problem with R_4 is that the concept of "society" is itself so obscure. One way to illustrate this obscurity would be to ask this question: "What features must a group of people have in common in order to be members of the same society?" We can understand this question to be a request for a statement of necessary and sufficient conditions for comembership in the same society. A related question is this: "Under what circumstances will a group of people constitute a society?" Even the most cursory reflection on these questions will reveal the seriousness of the problem. People in the same society may speak the same language, or they may not. They may live near one another, or they may live far apart. They may have similar religious and moral views, or they may have divergent views in these areas. Given this obscurity in the concept of society, it would seem better to avoid this concept in our moral theory, if possible. Hence, we have a problem with R_4.

Let us assume that some resourceful sociologist can solve this problem. Let us assume that a clear, precise, and useful concept of society can be developed. What, then, shall we say about R_4?

One problem with R_4 has to do with intersocietal comparisons. Suppose society S_1 has a complete and consistent set of conventions, but suppose this set of conventions permits slavery, racism, exploitation of women and children, aggressive warfare, and self-pollution. Suppose society S_2 also has a complete and consistent set of conventions, but suppose that these conventions rule out slavery, racism, and the other evils allowed in S_1. Suppose the conventions of S_2 are based upon a respect for the dignity of all human beings, regardless of race, sex, or age. Surely, in such a case we want to be able to say that the second set of conventions is better than the first set. We want to be able to say that the members of S_2 are more advanced morally than the members of S_1.

Yet if a form of conventionalism such as R_4 is true, it is not clear that we can justifiably say any such thing. For if R_4 is true, then the members of S_1 act rightly if they follow the conventions of S_1, and the members of S_2 act rightly if they follow the conventions of S_2. Assuming that the members of each society follow their own conventions in equal measure, we must conclude that they perform an equal number of right acts. What more can we ask them to do? According to R_4, we cannot condemn the members of S_1 for failing to follow the conventions of S_2. For R_4 says they act rightly when they follow their own conventions. Nor can we condemn the conventions of S_1 for failing to be more like those of S_2. What would be the basis of any such condemnation?

Thus, if we accept conventionalism, we apparently lose the ability to make intersocietal moral comparisons. This seems to be a fairly serious loss.

An interesting special example of this problem may be called "the reformer's dilemma." Consider the case of an Old Testament reformer. He sees that his fellow citizens are living lazy, selfish, worthless lives. He recognizes that they have adopted a miserable set of moral conventions. In order to raise them out of their deplorable situation, he exhorts them to become more sensitive to their immorality. He urges them to reflect on the possibility that they may have adopted the wrong principles. Surely, we must admit that there is a chance that the reformer is right. Perhaps his society has adopted a worthless set of conventions. Perhaps the citizens would be better off if they followed his advice. Yet, if conventionalism is true, the reformer must be wrong. For according to R_4, the reformer's fellow citizens act rightly only if they follow the moral conventions of their society. Hence, when the reformer asks the citizens to follow some other rules, he is asking them to perform acts that are morally wrong. No matter how miserable their current conventions may be, no matter how reasonable the proposal of the reformer may be, R_4 entails that the citizens are right to follow their old rules, and that they would be wrong to follow the reformer's proposed rules. Thus, conventionalism turns out to be an extremely conservative moral doctrine.

We can formulate this argument in a fairly simple way. Let us say that a person "advocates moral reform" if and only if he claims that the moral conventions of his society permit actions that are in fact not right. Now we can offer the following argument:

The Reformer's Dilemma

(1) If R_4 is true, anyone who advocates reform is mistaken.

(2) Sometimes people who advocate reform are not mistaken.

(3) Therefore, R_4 is not true.

It is not clear how a conventionalist would respond to this argument. Perhaps (2) would be denied. In any case, this constitutes a puzzle for conventionalism.

For our purposes, however, another feature of R_4 may be of somewhat greater interest. It should be evident that R_4 is compatible with absolutism. But not only is R_4 compatible with absolutism, it entails that absolutism is true. Thus, if we allow R_4 to be our interpretation of relativism, then, in order to be logically consistent we must accept absolutism too.

The proof of this is simple enough. If R_4 is true, then there is a single ultimate standard of morality that is true everywhere. That standard is R_4 itself. But absolutism is defined as the doctrine that there is a single ultimate standard of morality. Hence, if R_4 is true, absolutism is true.

Perhaps some readers will feel that this proof is somewhat sophistical. They may insist that the proof works only because we have defined absolutism in an inadequate way. They may prefer to put the issue in these terms: Absolutism should be understood as the view that there is a single type of action that is everywhere morally right. Therefore, if absolutism is true, then a person acts rightly, regardless of his society, only if he performs actions of that specific kind. Relativism, however, entails that many different sorts of action may be right—it all depends upon the society. Hence, absolutism, properly understood, is incompatible with relativism.

Unfortunately, even if we understand absolutism in this way, R_4 still entails that absolutism is true. For if R_4 is true, then there is a single type of action that is everywhere morally right—that is, action that is in accord with the conventions of the society in which it is performed. We may say that all action of this type is "conventional." If absolutism is understood as the view that there is a single type of action that is everywhere morally right, then R_4 entails absolutism. This is because R_4 entails that conventional actions are everywhere morally right.

So even though conventionalism appears to be opposed to some sort of absolutism, in fact it is not opposed to absolutism in either of the two forms here considered. It may not be easy to formulate a clear version of absolutism that is in fact inconsistent with our conventionalistic doctrine, R_4.

Conceptual Relativism

Let us turn, finally, to a form of relativism that really does conflict with absolutism. Consider the following sentence:

(4) Boston is near.

Although there are circumstances in which (4) could be used intelligibly, in most circumstances (4) would seem incomplete. This becomes clear upon reflection on the question of whether (4) is true or false. If so asked, many people would say that it is impossible to tell whether (4) is true or false. They would wonder, "Near *what*?" Their intuition would be that (4) needs to be completed by adding the name of some other place. So if (4) is short for:

(5) Boston is near Marblehead.

then (4) is short for something true. But if (4) is short for:

(6) Boston is near Brest-Litovsk.

then (4) is short for something false. As it stands, however, many people would say that (4) is incomplete, and that by itself it is neither true nor false.

Another way to illustrate the incompleteness of (4) would be to ask whether Boston has the property of nearness. Many people would say that there is simply no such property as nearness. They would say that nearness is a relation. Boston stands in the relation of nearness to Marblehead, but it does not stand in this relation to Brest-Litovsk. It makes no sense to ask whether, in itself, Boston has nearness. Nearness to *what*? This way of putting the question is rather metaphysical, and the earlier way is rather linguistic, but they come to pretty much the same thing.

These points have a straightforward analogy in ethics. Some would say that "is morally right" is like "is near." These philosophers maintain that sentences of the form:

(7) That act is morally right.

are just as incomplete as (4). In itself, they would maintain, any such sentence is neither true nor false. In order to make the sentence express something true or false, it must be completed in some way such as:

(8) That act is morally right in contemporary American society.

or

(9) That act is morally right in Victorian English society.

This point can be put metaphysically, too. We can say that there simply is no such property as rightness. Rather, rightness is a relation between an act and a society. An act may be right relative to one society, and may be not right relative to another society. But no act is just plain right. This view, which is called *conceptual relativism*, is our final version of the relativistic doctrine that "what's right in one society may be wrong in another."

There are many, many occasions in which people say things like (7). The conceptual relativist must maintain that whenever someone says something like (7), his statement is short for something like (8) or (9). Usually, when a person says that an act is right, what he means is that it is right in his society. But in any case, he must have *some* society in mind;

or else his sentence is incomplete, and expresses neither truth nor falsity.

We can state this relativistic theory in two different ways. Put linguistically, it is as follows:

> R_5: Sentences of the form "act a is morally right" are either meaningless or else short for sentences of the form "act a is morally right in society S."

This same doctrine can be put more metaphysically as follows:

> R_6: There is no such property as "rightness." Rightness is a relation between acts and societies.

These forms of relativism do conflict with absolutism. For if either R_5 or R_6 is true, then there cannot be a criterion of morality. If R_5 is true, then any proposed criterion would be meaningless. For as we have understood the term, a criterion of morality contains the phrase "act a is right." According to R_5, this phrase does not make any sense by itself. Similarly, if R_6 is true, then there is no such property as rightness. In this case, there surely cannot be a significant criterion stating the necessary and sufficient conditions for an act to have rightness.

Conceptual relativism has some rather interesting consequences. One of the most striking of these is that it seems to rule out the possibility of intersocietal moral conflicts. To see how this happens, consider this case. Suppose a member of society S_1 is visiting in the land of society S_2. There he sees some members of S_2 poking out the eyes of another member of S_2, who has been found guilty of voyeurism. The man from S_1 is appalled. He claims that it is not right to be so harsh in punishing a crime as innocent as voyeurism. In S_1, peeping toms are merely required to pay a small fine. But the people from S_2 insist that the peeping tom deserves to be blinded. They say that their act is morally right.

Let us use the letter b as the name of the act of blinding the peeping tom. Now we can put the debate into simple terms. The man from S_1 says:

> (10) Act b is not morally right.

The people from S_2 say:

> (11) Act b is morally right.

This appears to be a straightforward case of moral conflict. The opinion of the visitor from S_1 seems to conflict with the opinion of the people from S_2; they have opposite views about the normative status of act b. However, if conceptual relativism is true, then there is no conflict. For if conceptual relativism is true, then sentence (10) is either meaningless or else short for:

(10′) Act b is not morally right in S_1.

And (11) is either meaningless or else short for:

(11′) Act b is morally right in S_2.

If either (10) or (11) is meaningless, then there is no conflict. So let us suppose that (10′) expresses more adequately what is really meant by (10), and that (11′) expresses more adequately what is really meant by (11).

It should be evident that (10′) and (11′) may be true together. There is no logical conflict between them. When the visitor from S_1 says (10′), he may be reporting the truth. At the same time, when the people from S_2 say (11′), they may be reporting the truth too. Hence, there is no logical conflict between the opinion of the man from S_1 and that of the people from S_2. This surely seems wrong.

So our argument is this:

No-Conflicts Argument

(1) If conceptual relativism is true, there is no conflict between the visitor from S_1 and the people from S_2.

(2) There is a conflict between the visitor from S_1 and the people from S_2.

(3) Therefore, conceptual relativism is not true.

This type of argument will be discussed in much greater detail in Chapter 12. For now, it may be sufficient to recognize that it provides a serious problem for the conceptual relativist. Anyone adopting either R_5 or R_6 must be prepared to deal with the issue of intersocietal moral conflict.

Conceptual relativism faces a few other problems. One of these is that it depends upon the concept of "society." If this concept is obscure or indefinable, then so much the worse for R_5 and R_6. Furthermore, conceptual relativism seems to rule out moral comparisons of societies. No clear sense can be attached to statements such as "Society S_1 is morally preferable to society S_2." In this respect, conceptual relativism is like conventionalism. Finally, a version of the reformer's dilemma can be applied to conceptual relativism.

The greatest problem with conceptual relativism, however, is much deeper than any of these. It must be recognized that conceptual relativism entails that there is no such property as moral rightness. Equivalently, it entails that no one has ever performed an act that is just plain morally right. We must not suppose that under this view, "nothing is right or wrong but thinking makes it so." For under this view, not even thinking can make an act right or wrong.

This gives rise to the problem of explaining what "right in society S" might mean. It cannot be defined as "believed by members of S to be right," since if there is no such property as rightness, then no one can believe anything to be right. Another way to put this is to point out that if sentences of the form "act *a* is morally right" are meaningless, then sentences of the form "S believes that act *a* is morally right" are also meaningless. Put most simply, if there is no such *property* as rightness, then the *relation* of rightness cannot be defined by reference to any such alleged *property* of rightness. How such a relation is to be defined is yet to be explained.

Relativism and Tolerance

It is often suggested that relativism in ethics is the natural development of an enlightened, tolerant attitude toward the various customs of divergent societies. Indeed, we sometimes find people arguing that since relativism is true, we should try to be less chauvinistic. Yet it is not entirely clear how relativism, in its different forms, bears on the question of whether we should be tolerant.

It should be clear that belief relativism, by itself, has no bearing whatever on tolerance. From the fact that people in different societies have different moral beliefs, nothing follows about the desirability of tolerance.

Conventionalism, formulated here as R4, does have consequences for tolerance. However, these consequences may not be what is expected. R4 says that an act is right if and only if it is permitted by the conventions of its society. Therefore, an act of tolerance is morally right, according to this doctrine, if and only if it is permitted by the conventions of its society. So if you live in a society in which tolerance is not particularly esteemed, you should not be tolerant. Indeed, you may be morally required, according to conventionalism, to be intolerant. On the other hand, if you live in a society whose conventions require tolerance, then conventionalism requires that you be tolerant.

Thus, there is no merit whatever to the following line of thought: "Since conventionalism is true, we should be more tolerant of the behavior of people in other societies. For they are only acting in accord with their own conventions, as they should." The correct response to this argument may be that if intolerance is required by the moral conventions of our society, conventionalism entails that we are acting rightly only if we treat those others intolerantly. Thus, it may be inconsistent to maintain both that conventionalism is true and that tolerance is universally right.

Conceptual relativism leads to a similar conclusion in regard to tolerance. The statement that tolerance is morally right is, according to this view, incomplete. It is either meaningless or else short for a statement of the form "tolerance is right in S_1." So if a conceptual relativist says:

(12) Tolerance is right.

then his own view entails that he must either complete his sentence or admit that he is talking nonsense. If he means that tolerance is right in society S_1, then perhaps he is right. If he means that tolerance is right in society S_2, then perhaps he is wrong. If he means that tolerance is just plain right, then according to his own view, he's talking nonsense. For under his view, there is no such thing as "just plain" rightness.

Thus, relativism does not imply that people should be more tolerant or that they should be less tolerant. In some forms, it implies nothing at all about tolerance. In other forms, it implies that we should be tolerant if and only if tolerance is required by the conventions of our society. In still other forms, it entails that tolerance is neither right nor wrong; it is only "right in S_1" or "wrong in S_2." So, no matter how it is understood, relativism does not entail that we should try to develop a more tolerant attitude toward the moral views of others.

These reflections on relativism have led us to consider some questions that belong more properly to the field of metaethics. For example, we have questioned whether "a is morally right" is a complete sentence by itself, or whether it needs to be expanded into something of the form "a is morally right in society S_1." Traditionally, this question has been construed as a question about the meaning, or logical form, of normative statements. As such, it is more properly studied in metaethics than in normative ethics. In order to pursue such questions in a more coherent way, we need to gain a clearer understanding of the nature of metaethics and some of its typical views. This is the objective of the next chapter.

Naturalism in Metaethics

Metaethics

There is a sense in which it would be correct to say that virtually every competent speaker of English knows the meaning of such terms as "good," "bad," "right," "wrong," and "obligatory." For virtually every competent speaker of English is able to use each of these words in an understandable manner, and is able to understand statements made by other competent speakers in which these words are used. It might be said, therefore, that there is really no serious problem about the meanings of such expressions, since even little children know what they mean.

But there is another sense of "know the meaning," such that it might not be correct to say that we all know the meaning of each of these terms. This becomes clear upon reflection on the fact that most of us would not find it easy to formulate a clear, precise, and acceptable definition of any of them. The situation here is similar to a situation in geometry. Most people know what the word "circle" means even before they begin to study geometry. That is, they can use the word in an understandable manner, and they can understand others who use the word correctly. However, many competent speakers of English would be at a loss if asked to give a clear, precise, and accurate definition of the word "circle." They might try to describe how circles look. Or perhaps they would mention some familiar objects that are circular. Doing these things, however, is not the same as defining "circle." To define "circle," we have to present a statement similar to this one:

D_1: x is a circle =df. x is a closed plane curve, equidistant at all points from a given point.

So when we say that many people do not know the meanings of "good," "bad," and the rest, we do not mean that they are unable to use these words competently, or that they cannot understand other competent speakers of English who use them. What we mean is that they cannot provide suitable definitions.

Some people might wonder about these definitions. Suppose it is true that many people cannot give adequate definitions of these moral terms. What difference does that make? If they can use the words, and can understand others who use them, why should they be concerned about giving definitions? Wouldn't that be just an intellectual game with no practical value? Couldn't they just as easily look the words up in the dictionary? Furthermore, what does all this have to do with philosophical questions about morality?

Different philosophers would answer these questions in different ways. Some might respond by saying that correct definitions of moral terms are of the greatest practical value. For as we all know, differences in moral values provide a rich source of hatred, conflict, and even war. If it could be discovered that these differences in values derive from differences in moral concepts, perhaps some of these conflicts could be resolved. Close attention to the meanings of the relevant moral terms might enable us to discover such differences in moral concepts.

Other philosophers might answer the questions above by pointing out that there are many serious, unsettled questions of morals. For example, is abortion morally wrong? Is death intrinsically evil? Is virtue as great a good as pleasure? Some of these questions are of obvious practical importance. Furthermore, until we come to an adequate understanding of the meanings of these questions, it seems unlikely that we will be able to discover acceptable answers. And we cannot fully understand the meanings of the questions, it might be claimed, until we can provide definitions of the terms appearing in them.

Still other philosophers might say that the attempt to find acceptable definitions of "good," "bad," "right," and the others is, after all, a sort of intellectual game not designed to achieve any practical end. It is an intellectual pursuit that people engage in primarily because they find it interesting and pleasant to do so. They are puzzled about the moral concepts, curious to know just what the terms mean, and willing to work hard at formulating adequate definitions of these meanings, even if the discovery and formulation of such definitions will not have any practical value. Their attitude toward philosophy is like the attitude of some composers toward their music, or of some poets toward their poetry. They find their work to be exciting and satisfying even if it has no practical payoff.

Definitions

Although more exhaustive categorizations might be proposed, for our purposes it may be sufficient to distinguish among three main kinds of definitions. Definitions of the first kind may be called *stipulative definitions*. A stipulative definition is not designed to report a preexistent fact about the meaning of a word. Rather, it is designed to create a convenient new abbreviation. For example, suppose we want to discuss some complicated feature of actions and there simply is no single word in the English language that expresses this feature. In such a case, we can introduce a new word and stipulate that it shall henceforward be used to express the complicated feature we want to talk about. A good example of this sort of procedure is the definition of "utility" that was presented in Chapter 2. We were interested in the amount of pleasure, minus the amount of pain, that a given act would produce if it were performed. We wanted a simple expression that would refer to this amount. So we introduced a stipulative definition of "utility."

It would be silly to object to a stipulative definition on the grounds that the word being defined really doesn't mean what the definition says it means. For the idea behind such a definition is not to report a fact about meaning. The idea is to create a convenient synonym. So we should object to a stipulative definition, if at all, only on the grounds that the abbreviation is inconvenient, hard to remember, or somehow misleading.

Obviously, however, not all definitions are merely stipulative. A lexicographer who presented stipulative definitions of all the words in his dictionary would produce a work of staggering uselessness. We look to the lexicographer to provide definitions that accurately report the ways in which competent speakers use words. When we look up the word "prorogue" in the dictionary, we do not want to be told that it would be fun to use "to prorogue" as a synonym for "to vote for a knave." We want to be told that "to prorogue," as used as a term of parliamentary procedure, means the same as "to adjourn." Let us call definitions of this second kind *lexical definitions*. These definitions are designed to provide an accurate account of the meaning of the term being defined, as it is used by competent speakers.

The philosophical puzzle about the meaning of "good" would not be solved by looking up "good" in a dictionary. For if you look in a dictionary, you may find a variety of synonyms for "good," such as "excellent," "superior," and "better than average." Such a definition would be useful to a person who does not know what "good" means, but who does know what "excellent" or "superior" means. However, such definitions would not adequately explain the meaning of "good" to someone engaged in a philosophical enquiry into the meaning of this word. One way to see this is to notice that if a person does not have the concept of goodness at all, it is unlikely that we can make him understand that concept simply by telling him that it is the same as the concept of excellence or superiority. Let us consider this in greater detail.

The philosophical puzzles about the meanings of "good," "bad," and the other moral terms can be solved only by providing what we can call an *analysis* or *analytical definition* of each of these terms. It is not easy to explain just what an analytical definition is, but we can state a number of requirements.

The first requirement is a formal requirement. Consider again our definition of "circle:"

D_1: x is a circle =df. x is a closed plane curve, equidistant at all points from a given point.

Notice, first, that the word to be defined, or the *definiendum*, appears on the left of the symbol "= df." This symbol may be read "means, by definition" or "is definitionally equivalent to." The *definiens*, or expression used to do the defining, appears on the right of the definition symbol. Our first requirement of an analytical definition, then, is that its definiens and definiendum be in the same language.

Notice, next, that we have not simply put the single word "circle" as the definiendum. We have put "x is a circle." The reason for this is simple. The word "circle" is used in such a way that the least complex complete sentences in which it can be used are of the form "x is a circle." Actual sentences may have names of circles instead of "x." In the definition, "x" is a variable, or place holder for these actual names. Some expressions, such as "taller," would need two variables, and so would look more like this: "x is taller than y." "Between" would need three variables, since the least complex complete sentences in which "between" occurs are of the form "x is between y and z." So the second requirement is that the word being defined must appear in the definiendum with the appropriate number of variables. Furthermore, the same variables must appear in the definiens.

In addition to these formal requirements, there are two main substantive requirements for adequate analytical definitions. The first is what we may call *immunity from counter-examples*, and the second is *enlighteningness*.

A counter-example to a definition is a case, whether actual or merely possible, in which the definiendum is true of something but the definiens is not true of that same thing, or vice versa. Consider the following incorrect definition:

> D_2: x is a table $=$ df. x is a piece of furniture consisting of a flat top supported by four legs.

We can say that "x is a table" is true of a thing, provided that the thing is a table. Another way to look at this point is as follows: First, we remove the "x" from "x is a table." Then we select some name of the thing in question, and put that name in place of the "x." If the resulting sentence is true, then "x is a table" is true of the thing.

Can we find anything of which "x is a table" is true, but of which "x is a piece of furniture consisting of a flat top supported by four legs" is not true? If so, that thing is a counter-example to D_2. Of course, it is easy to find counter-examples in this case—for instance, any three-legged table. Such a table is clearly a table, but it is not a piece of furniture consisting of a flat top supported by four legs. Thus, "x is a table" is true of such tables, but "x is a piece of furniture consisting of a flat top supported by four legs" is not. Hence, any such table is a counter-example to D_2. It shows that D_2 is a defective definition.

An important point to notice is that we can construct counter-examples even in cases in which there is no actual item of which one side is true and the other side is not. Consider this definition:

> D_3: x is a table $=$ df. x is a piece of furniture consisting of a flat top supported by less than 500 legs.

Perhaps there is in fact no table with more than 499 legs. Nevertheless, D_3 is open to counter-examples. Surely there *could be* an extraordinarily long cafeteria table with 500 legs. If so, such a table is a counter-example to D_3, and so D_3 is defective.

A correct definition is not open to counter-examples. D_1, for example, seems to be correct. For it is not possible for there to be a circle that is not a closed plane curve of the described kind, nor is it possible for there to be a curve of that kind that is not a circle. If this is correct, D_1 passes the first substantive requirement for analytical definitions. It is immune to counter-examples.

The second main substantive requirement of an analytical definition is enlighteningness. As we have seen, an adequate definition cannot be explicitly circular, as these are:

> D_4: x is a circle $=$ df. x is a closed plane figure shaped exactly like a circle.

> D_5: x is a table $=$ df. x is a piece of furniture that isn't anything other than a table.

Nor can an analytical definition be implicitly circular, as these are:

D_6: x is a circle =df. x is a closed plane figure of circular shape.

D_7: x is a table =df. x is a very tableish piece of furniture.

D_6 and D_7 are not explicitly circular, for in neither of them does the definiendum appear in the definiens. But they are almost as empty and trivial as D_4 and D_5. Almost anyone who wants to learn the meaning of "circle" or "table" would find these definitions unhelpful. It is unlikely that a person who does not understand the meaning of "circle" will understand the meaning of "circular shape." Similarly, it is unlikely that a person who does not understand the meaning of "table" will understand the meaning of "tableish." Any definition that is implicitly circular, as these are, is unenlightening, and so fails to pass the second substantive requirement for analytical definitions.

Another kind of unenlightening definition is the definition *per obscurius*. A definition is *per obscurius* if the terms used in the definiens are more obscure than those used in the definiendum. This is especially clear in those cases in which some term in the definiens would most naturally be defined by reference to the term in the definiendum. For example, if someone didn't know the meaning of "adjourn," it would probably be pointless to tell him that "adjourn" means the same as "prorogue."

If we assume a certain view about language, we can develop an interesting thesis about definitions. The view about language is this: Every independently meaningful expression expresses a property, concept, or *intension*. For example, the expression "x is a circle" expresses the property of being a circle, or circularity; "x is a table" expresses the property of being a table, or tableness; "x is red" expresses redness. The interesting thesis about definitions, then, is that in an adequate definition, the property expressed by the definiendum is the same as the property expressed by the definiens. For example, if definition D_1 is correct, then "x is a circle" expresses the same property as "x is a closed plane curve equidistant at all points from a given point." In other words, circularity is the same as being a closed plane curve equidistant at all points from a given point. And in still other words, for something to be a circle is the same as for it to be a closed plane curve equidistant at all points from a given point.

In light of all this, we can perhaps understand why some philosophers prefer to discuss metaethics as if it were primarily an investigation into the properties, or concepts, of goodness, rightness, wrongness, and so on, rather than an investigation into the meanings of the expressions "x is good," "x is right," and so on. These philosophers choose to enquire into the correct analysis of the property goodness, whereas others prefer to enquire into the correct definition of the expression "*x* is good." If we assume the view about meaning suggested above, we can see that these two enterprises are really not so different from each other. Indeed, it might be said that one represents the metaphysical approach and the other the linguistic approach to what is in fact just one problem.

Naturalism in Metaethics

Now let us turn to the main topic of this chapter, naturalism in metaethics. The main thesis of the naturalist, put in linguistic terms, is that "*x* is good" can be defined exclusively by use of some combination of naturalistic expressions. Put in metaphysical terms, the naturalist's view is that goodness can be analyzed purely by reference to some combination of naturalistic properties. This leaves a lot of questions to be asked and answered.

Perhaps the easiest way to explain what naturalism is, and at the same time to offer a suggestion about why anyone would believe in it, would be to present a view that naturalists want to reject. Then, by pointing out their objections to this view, we may begin to see what naturalists want to propose instead. The objectionable view may be called "antinaturalism." According to the antinaturalists (assuming there are some), goodness is a strange property. Good things have this property, but there is no scientific or observational method that can help us to determine whether or not a particular thing has it. That is, we cannot see, taste, or otherwise perceive the goodness of a thing, nor is there any sort of device that one can use to check for its presence. In these respects, goodness is unlike any natural property. For there is always some way to check a natural property for its presence. Some natural properties can be observed fairly directly. For example, we can see the redness of a red object and feel the sphericity of a spherical object. We can use a Geiger counter to test for radioactivity and a ruler to test for twelve-inchedness.

If two individuals disagree about whether or not a certain thing is good, they may be unable to come to any agreement. It may be that no amount of empirical study, or scientific observation, would serve to change their opinions. One holds that the thing in question has goodness, and the other holds that it does not have goodness. Only one of them is right, but there is simply no way to determine who it is.

The expression "*x* is good," according to antinaturalists, expresses this mysterious property of goodness. When we say that something is good, we ascribe goodness to it. According to the antinaturalists, we cannot define "*x* is good." All we can say, by way of explaining the meaning of this term, is that it expresses goodness—an unanalyzable, unobservable, undetectable property.

Naturalists find this view unacceptable. They feel that antinaturalism makes goodness too mysterious. How can there be a property whose presence is utterly undetectable? If it is undetectable, why do people have such strong opinions about which things have it? If "x is good" cannot be defined, and if it expresses an undetectable property, how do people ever come to know the meaning of "good"? How can we be sure that others mean what we mean when they use this term? Why do people get so worked up about those who refuse to predicate goodness of the things they think to be good? According to antinaturalism, these questions are apparently unanswerable.

So, naturalists have many reasons for rejecting antinaturalism. The basic reason, however, is that they feel that antinaturalism makes ethical language too mysterious, at best, and utterly meaningless, at worst. Consequently, naturalists want to claim that goodness can, after all, be tied down to what we can perceive, or feel. They want to say that the meaning of "x is good" can be explained by the use of terms that each express an ordinary, observable property. But which terms?

Different naturalists attempt to define "x is good" in different ways. Each thinks he has discovered the real meaning of the term, and each thinks that the other naturalists are wrong. But naturalists agree on two main points. First, "x is good" and the other moral terms can be defined. Second, none of the definitions needs to employ an irreducibly moral term; every one of them can ultimately be paraphrased entirely in terms of naturalistic expressions. In order to come to a clearer understanding of naturalism, let us consider one of the simplest naturalistic positions.

Perry's Theory

One pretty obvious fact about our use of the terms "good," "bad," and the rest is that we often find that things that are called good are things that people favor, like, want, approve of, or feel admiration for; things that are called bad are things that people disfavor, hate, reject, disapprove of, or feel contempt for. A simple metaethical view can be constructed on the basis of this fact.

We can distinguish between positive and negative interests. If a person favors, likes, or wants something, then he has a positive interest in that thing. If a person disfavors, hates, or rejects a thing, then he has a negative interest in that thing. These interests are to be understood as purely psychological facts. To want something, for example, is to *feel* a certain way about it and to be motivated to behave in certain ways with respect to it. To reject a thing is to *feel* in certain other ways about it and to be motivated to act in other ways toward it.

Although it is not clear that we must, or even can, define "x has a positive interest in y," there is one fact about this expression that must be understood. Our naturalistic definition of "x is good" is going to make use of this notion of positive interest. In order to avoid circularity, it is absolutely essential that we do *not* define "x has a positive interest in y" in terms of "x is good." Thus, we cannot define "interest" in any such way as this:

> D_8: x has a positive interest in $\dot{y}$ =df. x believes that y is good.

> D_9: x has a negative interest in y =df. x believes that y is bad.

Since we are attempting to formulate a naturalistic theory, we must be careful that our concept of interest is a genuinely naturalistic one. So we should see to it that if interest is defined at all, it is defined purely in terms of psychology or some other natural science. Thus, we may propose:

> D_{10}: x has a positive interest in y =df. x favors, likes, wants, approves of, or feels admiration for y.

> D_{11}: x has a negative interest in y =df. x disfavors, dislikes, rejects, or feels contempt or hatred for y.

Another way of defining "x has an interest in y" was proposed by Ralph Barton Perry, a philosopher generally recognized to be one of the leading proponents of the naturalistic theory we are about to consider. He attempted to avoid introducing circularity into his theory by defining "interest" in rather behavioristic terminology:

> The following is here proposed: interest is a train of events determined by expectation of its outcome. Or, a thing is an object of interest when its being expected induces actions looking to its realization or non-realization. Thus peace is an object of interest when acts believed to be conducive to peace, or preventive of peace, are performed on that account, or when events are selected or rejected because peace is expected of them.[1]

Perry's idea here seems to be that something is an object of someone's favorable interest provided that the person is motivated to try to bring the thing into existence; it is an object of someone's negative interest provided that the person is motivated to prevent it from coming into existence. Perry probably formulated these definitions with an eye toward avoiding circularity and insuring that his view would be genuinely naturalistic. However, the definitions are somewhat implausible as they stand, since someone surely could have a positive interest in a sunset, or a landscape, yet there really isn't much one can do to bring either of these things into existence.

Perry went on to define "x is valuable" in terms of interest:

> According to the definition of value here proposed, a thing—any thing—
> —has value, or is valuable, in the original and generic sense when it is the
> object of an interest—any interest. Or, whatever is object of interest is ipso
> facto valuable. Thus the valuableness of peace is the characteristic confer-
> red on peace by the interest which is taken in it, for what it is, or for any of
> its attributes, effects, or implications.[2]

We can make use of Perry's main idea and define "good" and "bad" naturalistically as follows:

D_{12}:   x is good (bad) =df. someone has a positive (negative) interest
       in x.

The naturalistic theory based on D_{12} is not quite the same as Perry's theory, but it is similar in many important respects. It is, in addition, independently worthy of some consideration.

One of the main objections that has been raised against Perry's view, and one that can be raised against D_{12} as well, is that it entails a contradiction. For it happens very frequently that two different persons have conflicting attitudes toward the same thing. For example, suppose two individuals see a movie, and one of them likes it and the other dislikes it. We can now prove, via D_{12}, both that the movie was good and that it was bad. For D_{12}, together with the fact that someone has a positive interest in the movie, entails that the movie is good, and D_{12}, together with the fact that someone has a negative interest in the movie, entails that the movie is bad. But isn't this a contradiction? How can the movie be both good and bad?

We should recognize that D_{12} does not directly entail that a thing can be both good and not good at the same time. That surely would be a contradiction. What the theory does entail is that if someone has a positive interest in a thing, that thing is good. If someone else has a negative interest in that same thing, then it is also bad. To say that it is both good and bad is different from saying that it is both good and not good. So this objection may misfire.

Nevertheless, "good" and "bad" are usually considered to be *contraries*. That is, something can be neither good nor bad, but nothing can be both good and bad. If our ordinary concepts of good and bad are in fact contraries, then D_{12} is unacceptable. For according to this definition, the concepts of good and bad are not contraries; that is, something can be both good and bad at the same time. This seems to constitute a very serious objection to the theory.

Another objection to D_{12} is that it seems incredibly generous. It makes it very easy for a thing to be good. All that is required is that someone, however depraved, have a positive interest in it. So if some maniac favors atomic war, then atomic war is good. If another maniac loves forest fires, then forest fires are good. Similarly, if some fool dislikes truth and beauty, then truth and beauty are bad. These are surely very implausible results. Surely we want our metaethical theory to allow for more discrimination than this!

The Ideal-Observer Theory

So let us turn to another theory, one that is somewhat like the theory we have been discussing but that lacks its obvious and serious drawbacks. This form of naturalism has been called *the ideal-observer theory*. Those who favor the ideal-observer theory may have been motivated to adopt it after reflecting on the defects of the theory last discussed. One defect of Perry's view is that it entails that something is good if anyone, no matter how immoral, has a positive interest in it. The other defect is that it takes into consideration the interests of everyone, and hence generates contrary judgments. Both of these defects can be resolved by severely restricting the class of persons whose interests are to count. Rather than counting everyone's interest equally, the ideal-observer theory counts the interest of only one person—a person with impeccable standards.

The basic idea behind the theory is that when we say that something is good, we are saying that if there were an "ideal observer," he would have a positive interest in that thing. To say that something is bad is to say that the ideal observer would have a negative interest in that thing. Obviously, the crucial concept here is the concept of the ideal observer, so let us now consider that topic.

We might formulate the ideal-observer theory by means of these two definitions:

> D_{13}: x is an ideal observer =df. x has a positive interest in all and only good things, and a negative interest in all and only bad things.

> D_{14}: x is a good (bad) =df. if there were an ideal observer, he would have a positive (negative) interest in x.

By itself, neither of these definitions is circular. However, if we propose to use them together, then circularity arises. For we are then attempting to define "good" by use of "ideal observer," and we are also attempting to define "ideal observer" by use of "good." The theory as a whole then amounts to the utter triviality that a thing is good provided that it would be approved by a person who approved of all and only good things, if there were such a person. So if we want the theory to be a genuine form of naturalism, we must provide a purely naturalistic account of what is meant by saying that someone is an ideal observer. We must describe the ideal observer without using words such as "good," "bad," "right," "wrong," and "obligatory." Can this be done?

One philosopher who has made this attempt is Roderick Firth.[3] He lists the following as essential features of the ideal observer:

1. He is omniscient with respect to nonethical facts.
2. He is omnipercipient.
3. He is disinterested.
4. He is dispassionate.
5. He is consistent.
6. He is normal in other respects.

Let us use this list rather than D_{13} as the definitive statement of the characteristics of the ideal observer.

The resulting theory, summarized in D_{14} and the list, seems to be a genuine improvement over Perry's theory. For this theory will apparently not generate contrary moral judgments, since there is only one interest that the ideal observer would have in each thing, if he were to exist. Nor will this theory generously allow that everything is good, for the ideal observer, if he were to exist, would surely not have a positive interest in everything—he would be more discriminating than that. Another good feature of the ideal-observer theory is that it accords well with the intuition that people would more readily come to agree on the truth of value judgments if they were more knowledgeable, imaginative, disinterested, dispassionate, consistent, and normal. Many of our differences seem to arise from our ignorance, shortsightedness, self-interest, emotionality, and inconsistency. Were these character defects to be removed, we might get along together much better—and each of us would be more like the ideal observer.

In spite of its strengths, the ideal-observer theory has been subjected to a number of very serious criticisms. Two main categories of criticism should be considered. The first has to do with the question of whether the theory is in fact a form of naturalism. It has been claimed that it is impossible to fully characterize the ideal observer without making some use of evaluative concepts, if only covertly. If this is so, the theory may become circular and it surely ceases to be a purely naturalistic theory. For now the account of the meaning of "good" is not given entirely in terms from natural science.

One specific source of trouble is the concept of disinterestedness. Does this mean that the ideal observer simply does not care about the events and actions he observes? Probably not, for if he doesn't care, he won't have any reason to adopt any attitude toward them. In this case, nothing is good or bad. Perhaps disinterestedness means that the ideal observer does not adopt any position of favoritism. But in this case, he will be barred from favoring the case of the victim over that of the mugger, and so he won't judge the mugger to be bad or the victim to be good. Undoubtedly, to be disinterested is to avoid *arbitrary* favoritism—that is, favoritism not based on good reasons. Here, at last, we have uncovered an evaluative term in the characterization of the ideal observer.

It is likely that careful thought about the other concepts used in the description of the ideal observer will reveal that several of them are covertly evaluative. For example, what is meant by "normal"? And what is it to be "dispassionate"? If these terms cannot be defined purely naturalistically, the theory ceases to be a form of naturalism and may start to be circular.

Another important objection to the ideal-observer theory is that it seems to be based on a rather implausible assumption. Defenders of the ideal-observer theory apparently assume that if ordinary people were changed so as to satisfy the requirements of omniscience, omnipercipience, disinterestedness, dispassionateness, consistency, and normality, then they would all agree about moral questions. But is this a reasonable assumption? It would seem that our cultural heritage has a great deal to do with our moral views. Suppose, for example, that a devout Puritan were changed so as to become an ideal observer. It seems that these intellectual and emotional changes could occur without seriously upsetting the Puritan's basic moral beliefs. He might still have a negative attitude toward loafing on the job, indiscriminate sexual behavior, and gluttony. Now consider a happy-go-lucky swinger, also modified so as to become an ideal observer. Isn't it reasonable to assume that even when his intellectual capacities are enlarged, he will still have a positive attitude toward some of the things the Puritan opposes? Even if the Puritan and the swinger were equally knowledgeable about nonethical facts, they might still disagree in their attitudes toward certain kinds of behavior. Notice, finally, that there would not have to be anything "abnormal" about either of them for this to happen.

If this sort of thing could happen, then the ideal-observer theory is in deep trouble. For the theory is phrased as if there would be just *one* ideal observer, if there were any. However, nothing in the theory leads to this result. For all we know, if there were an ideal observer, there would be dozens of them. If the preceding discussion is correct, these ideal observers could disagree among themselves in their attitudes toward the various kinds of activity they might observe. In this case, the theory seems to imply that such kinds of behavior would be both good and bad. Once again, contrary judgments may be forthcoming.

We can modify the theory so as to rule out this sort of possibility. We just define "good" and "bad" in terms of the attitudes of *one* ideal observer:

D_{15}: x is good (bad) =df. if there were exactly one ideal observer, he would have a positive (negative) attitude toward x.

Now, however, another problem arises. If there were exactly one ideal observer, would it be the modified Puritan, or the modified swinger? Each seems fully qualified to be an ideal observer, yet only one of them can be selected. Obviously, until the ideal-observer theory provides a systematic solution to this problem, it remains quite empty.

Subjective Naturalism

Another kind of naturalism has enjoyed a great deal of popularity, and it may avoid all of the problems we have encountered in the naturalistic theories already discussed. This is the theory that is often called *subjective naturalism*. It is based on the idea that when a person says that something is good, he is really not describing that thing so much as he is describing himself. Evaluative statements, according to this view, are really disguised statements about our own psychological states, and are not primarily about the objects they seem to be about.

Let us assume again that we can distinguish between positive and negative interests. When we speak of an interest, we do not mean a belief. For if we defined "x has a positive interest in y" as "x believes that y is good," our theory would become circular and nonnaturalistic. So an interest is a feeling, emotion, desire, or attitude, and not a belief.

We can now formulate a view that has often been called *naive subjective naturalism*:

NSN: For any person, S, if S says, "x is good (bad)," then S means what S would mean if S were to say, "I have a positive (negative) interest in x."

It should be noted that this statement of naive subjective naturalism is not a definition. We have not said what, according to naive subjective naturalists, "x is good" means. The reason for this is that according to this view, "x is good" means one thing when you say it and another thing when I say it. The meaning varies from speaker to speaker. For when I say that something is good, I mean that *I* have a positive interest in it. When you say that it is good, you mean that *you* have a positive interest in it. Hence, giving a formal definition of naive subjective naturalism would be a rather complicated business.

Naive subjective naturalism has often seemed very attractive. For it surely is reasonable to believe that when a person says that something is good, he likes, approves, wants, favors, or has some other positive interest in that thing. When a person says that something is bad, he very often has a negative interest in that thing. Naive subjective naturalism just takes these reasonable beliefs and elevates them to the status of definitions.

Nevertheless, there are several pretty obvious problems with this view. For one, it seems to allow too many things to be good. For example, suppose a drug addict has come to hate the drug to which he is addicted. He does not think that the drug is good. Nevertheless, he is addicted to the drug, and whether he wants to or not, he has an uncontrollable craving for it. In this case, since he has a desire for it, we must conclude that he has a positive interest in the drug. From this, it follows, according to naive subjective naturalism, that the addict would be telling the truth if he were to say, "This drug is good." For if he were to say this, he would mean that he has a positive interest in the drug—and he has.

What this example shows is that it would be useful to try to distinguish among interests. Some interests, such as the addict's, should not count. Others should. Precisely how this distinction is to be drawn is unclear.

Another problem with naive subjective naturalism is that it apparently requires too much intimacy with the things we evaluate. For example, suppose someone says:

(A) There are some good things I never thought of.

It appears that (A) might express a truth. This person is merely admitting that her personal experience of good things may be somewhat limited. She hasn't encountered, or reflected upon, every last one of them. But according to naive subjective naturalism, her statement really means the same as:

(B) There are some things (i) in which I have a positive interest, and (ii) of which I have never thought.

(B) seems to be self-contradictory. For it is surely impossible to have a positive interest in something (as we are understanding "positive interest") when you haven't even thought of that thing. Hence, it appears that (A) does not mean the same as (B). Otherwise, (A) would have to be self-contradictory too. So the argument is this:

Intimacy Argument

(1) If naive subjective naturalism were true, (A) would mean the same as (B).

(2) (A) does not mean the same as (B).

(3) Therefore, naive subjective naturalism is not true.

A more sophisticated form of subjective naturalism, one that is defended by Edward Westermarck, is designed to overcome both of these objections.[4] Westermarck attempts to isolate a class of emotions, which he calls the "retributive emotions." This class includes such emotions as revenge, anger, hatred, gratitude, and approval. Westermarck attempts to classify these emotions into two main subtypes. The "hostile retributive emotions" include revenge, anger, hatred, disapproval, among others. The "friendly retributive emotions" include gratitude, approval, love, and so forth.

Each of these subtypes is again divided. This division is into the "interested" and the "disinterested" emotions. A person feels an interested emotion when, for example, he wants revenge because he has personally suffered some injury, or when he feels gratitude for some personal benefit. Disinterested emotions are "assumed by those who feel them to be uninfluenced by the particular relationship in which they stand both to those who are immediately affected by the acts in question and to those who perform the acts."[5] The result is that we now have a four-way classification:

	Interested	Disinterested
Hostile	revenge, etc.	disapproval
Friendly	gratitude, etc.	approval

Westermarck's view is that the disinterested emotions are the specifically moral ones. When someone says that something is good, what he really means is that he has a tendency to feel disinterested friendly retributive emotion toward that thing. Similarly for "bad." So, Westermarck's main thesis may be formulated as follows:

> WSN: For any person, S, if S says, "x is good (bad)," then S means what S would mean if S were to say, "I have a tendency to feel disinterested friendly (hostile) retributive emotion toward objects similar to x."

This version of Westermarck's theory is not affected by either of the two objections to naive subjective naturalism that we discussed. In the first case, Westermarck would deny that the drug addict feels a *disinterested* friendly emotion toward the drug. He may feel a deeply *interested* desire to have it, but that has no bearing on the meaning of "good." As far as the addict's moral emotions are concerned, it is likely that he feels a strong disinterested hostile emotion toward the drug. Hence, the addict would speak the truth if he were to say that the drug is bad.

With respect to the second objection, Westermarck would point out that under his theory it is not required that one have the appropriate emotion toward the object being evaluated. All that is required is that one have a *tendency* to have that emotion toward objects *like* the one being evaluated. So if someone says that there are good things he never thought of, all he means, according to Westermarck, is that there are things similar to ones toward which he tends to feel approval, but of which he has never thought. This seems possible.

Westermarck's theory has been subjected to a remarkable variety of objections, but we will concentrate on just two. The first objection which is based on an argument proposed by A. C. Ewing in *The Definition of Good*,[6] turns on some alleged features of synonymous statements. It seems intuitively clear that if two statements have exactly the same meaning, then whatever suffices to prove one of them true should also suffice to prove the other one true. For example, if certain evidence proves that a figure drawn on a blackboard is a circle, then that same evidence also proves that that figure is a closed plane curve equidistant at all points from a given point. Since the two statements have the same meaning, how could the evidence prove the one without also proving the other?

Now consider two statements that, according to Westermarck's theory are supposed to have the very same meaning:

(A) I have a tendency to feel disinterested hostile retributive emotion toward actions similar to this act of premarital sexual intercourse.

(B) This act of premarital sexual intercourse is bad.

Suppose some rather conservative person, Smith, has made these two statements on some occasion. One thing that might serve to confirm statement (A) would be the results of an impartial, sustained, careful interview by an experienced psychologist. Perhaps the psychologist would use a polygraph, hypnosis, Rorschach tests, and other scientific means. By the use of such instruments, the psychologist could establish that when Smith affirmed statement (A), he was telling the truth. Smith really does have a tendency to get worked up when he thinks about premarital sex. But wouldn't it be ludicrous to suppose that this psychological evidence about Smith would serve in any way to support statement (B)? Smith's blood pressure or galvanic skin response has absolutely nothing to do with the morality of premarital sex. So it appears that the evidence that supports (A) does not support (B). Hence, (A) cannot mean the same as (B). Since (A) would mean the same as (B) if Westermarck's theory were true, Westermarck's theory is obviously not true.

The argument can be formulated as follows:

Different-Proof Argument

(1) If Westermarck's theory is true, then (A) means the same as (B).

(2) (A) can be confirmed by purely psychological evidence.

(3) (B) cannot be confirmed by purely psychological evidence.

(4) If (A) can be confirmed by purely psychological evidence but (B) cannot, then (A) does not mean the same as (B).

(5) Therefore, Westermarck's theory is not true.

This is a valid argument, and it seems to be quite persuasive. The most likely reply to it would be to deny (3). Westermarck, or a defender of his view, might insist that one *can* prove a moral judgment by appeal to psychological facts. Perhaps if we had a clearer insight into the nature of these judgments, we would not find this assertion so paradoxical. Perhaps it is only our ingrained adherence to some vague form of antinaturalism that makes us so unwilling to accept this assertion. It will be left to the reader to determine whether this possible response by Westermarck is adequate.

Another very important argument against subjective naturalism seems to be due to G. E. Moore. In his paper "The Nature of Moral Philosophy" Moore argued as follows:

> If this view be true, then when I judge an action to be wrong, I am merely making a judgment about my own feelings towards it; and when you judge it to be wrong, you are merely making a judgment about yours. And hence . . . when I judge of a given action that it was wrong, and you perhaps of the very same action that it was not, we are not in fact differing in opinion about it at all; any more than we are differing in opinion if I make the judgment "I came from Cambridge to-day" and you make the judgment "*I* did not come from Cambridge to-day."[7]

In this passage, Moore is not attacking subjective naturalism in exactly the form we have presented. So, we must make some very minor changes in his argument so as to make it apply to Westermarck's theory, as presented here. As modified, the argument goes as follows: Suppose two people, Smith and Jones, are debating the morality of a certain act of premarital sexual intercourse. Smith feels very strongly that it was bad. He says:

(S) That act of premarital sexual intercourse was bad.

Jones disagrees. She feels that the act in question was perfectly acceptable. She says:

(J) That act of premarital sexual intercourse was not bad.

Notice, next, that according to Westermarck's theory, statement (S) means exactly the same as:

(S') I, Smith, tend to feel disinterested hostile retributive emotion toward acts similar to that act of premarital sexual intercourse.

And statement (J) means the same as:

(J') I, Jones, do not tend to feel disinterested hostile retributive emotion toward acts similar to that act of premarital sexual intercourse.

It should be clear that there is no conflict between statements (S') and (J'). Each reports a psychological fact about its author, and there is no reason to doubt that each of them is correct. Thus, if Westermarck's theory is correct, and (S) and (J) mean the same, respectively, as (S') and (J'), then there is no conflict between (S) and (J) either. But isn't it pretty obvious that there in fact *is* a conflict between (S) and (J)? And, so, isn't it pretty obvious that (S) and (J) do not mean the same as (S') and (J')? If so, Westermarck's theory is false.

We can summarize the argument as follows:

No-Conflicts Argument

(1) If Westermarck's theory is true, (S) and (J) mean the same as (S') and (J').

(2) There is no conflict between (S') and (J').

(3) There is a conflict between (S) and (J).

(4) If there is no conflict between (S') and (J'), but there is a conflict between (S) and (J), then (S') and (J') do not mean the same as (S) and (J).

(5) Therefore, Westermarck's theory is not true.

In this form, the no-conflicts argument is valid. Many philosophers have decided that it is not only a valid but a sound refutation of Westermarck's view. In general, it may appear that if Westermarck's theory were true, there would be no such thing as moral conflict. Isn't this a bit too much to swallow? Shouldn't we conclude that any theory with such a consequence must be false?

In spite of its apparent strength, the no-conflicts argument has not convinced the naturalists. They steadfastly insist that their view is true. They may reply to the argument by claiming that there are really two sorts of conflict, which we may call *logical conflict* and *attitudinal conflict*. Two statements conflict logically provided that they cannot both be true; two statement conflict attitudinally provided that they express opposed attitudes. For example, if I say that I am hungry and you say that you are not hungry, our statements are logically consistent; nevertheless, they conflict attitudinally.

Making use of such a distinction, a subjective naturalist could claim that the no-conflicts argument suffers from the fallacy of equivocation. If we understand "conflict" in (2) and (3) as "logical conflict," then (2) is true but (3) is false. For there is no logical conflict between (S) and (J), according to the naturalist. On the other hand, if we understand "conflict" in (2) and (3) as "attitudinal conflict," then (2) is false. In either of these cases, the argument is alleged to have a fale premise. If we understand "conflict" in (2) as "logical conflict" and "conflict" in (3) as "attitudinal conflict," then both (2) and (3) are true, but the argument is equivocal and thus invalid. Hence, Westermarck's theory has not been refuted.

It appears, then, that the verdict turns on the question of whether (S) and (J) are in logical conflict. Moore would say that they are. They cannot both be true. Westermarck would say that they are not. They can both be true. It seems to be a matter that each reader must decide for himself.

In this chapter, we have seen a variety of naturalistic theories and a variety of objections to such views. In the next chapter, we will consider a single line of thought designed to show that any naturalistic theory, regardless of its details, must be false.

NOTES

1. Ralph Barton Perry, *Realms of Value* (Cambridge, Mass.: Harvard University Press, 1954), pp. 2-3.

2. *Ibid.*, p. 3

3. Roderick Firth, "Ethical Absolutism and the Ideal Observer," *Philosophy and Phenomenological Research*, 12 (1952),, pp. 317-345.

4. Edward Westermarck, *Ethical Relativity* (Paterson, N.J.: Littlefield, Adams, 1960).

5. *Ibid.*, p. 93.

6. A. C. Ewing, *The Definition of Good* (London: Routledge and Kegan Paul, 1947).

7. G. E. Moore, *Philosophical Studies* (London: Routledge and Kegan Paul, 1960), p. 333.

13

Moore and NonNaturalism

No single work of twentieth-century metaethics has been more influential than G. E. Moore's *Principia Ethica*.[1] The arguments and doctrines presented in that book have been debated, criticized, revised, and praised by succeeding moral philosophers. Those who share Moore's views consider him to be one of the great pioneers of modern moral philosophy. Even those who do not share his views must admit that Moore's work is of extraordinary importance, if only because so many philosophers have been persuaded by it.

One of Moore's main targets in *Principia Ethica* is naturalism. Moore apparently believes that each form of naturalism is false, and can be refuted independently. For each such form, there must be some argument, applicable to that form, that shows it to be false. But Moore does not hold merely that every form of naturalism that has been adopted is false. He also holds that naturalism in general, regardless of its specific form, has to be false. No matter what the details of its formulation, any theory that attempts to define "good" in purely naturalistic terms is unacceptable. The naturalistic approach in metaethics, Moore contends, is wrongheaded from the start.

We can divide Moore's attack on naturalism into two stages. In the first stage, Moore seems to be attempting to show that naturalists have not given us any good reason to accept their view. Somewhere in each naturalist's thinking, there is an error that leads him to accept naturalism. This mistake is called *the naturalistic fallacy*. However, even if naturalists were to admit that they have not proved their view to be true, they might still claim that it is true anyway. So in the second stage of his attack, Moore attempts to show that every form of naturalism is false.

193

This attempted refutation of naturalism has come to be known as *the open-question argument*.

One problem that we face in discussing the naturalistic fallacy and the open-question argument is that it is not clear how they ought to be formulated. After reading the first chapter of *Principia Ethica*, one knows that Moore thinks that naturalists have committed the naturalistic fallacy, but one probably finds that he is unable to say just what the naturalistic fallacy is supposed to be. That makes it very hard to decide whether Moore's claim is correct. Similarly, after reading *Principia Ethica*, one knows that Moore has presented a variety of closely related arguments against naturalism, but one may find it impossible to state these arguments in a clear, valid, and recognizably Moorean form. Until we can do this, we will not be able to decide whether Moore has refuted the naturalists.

Before we turn to Moore's attack on naturalism, let us review some of the main features of that position. In the first place, naturalists agree that "x is good" can be defined. Furthermore, they agree that it can be defined purely in naturalistic, or empirically verifiable, terms. Put metaphysically, these views seem to amount to the claim that goodness is a complex property that is analyzable into a set of constituent properties, every one of which is naturalistic. Naturalists hold that the naturalistic definition of "x is good" is not merely a stipulative definition, but is in fact an analytical definition. Hence, they are claiming to be revealing the true essence of goodness. Of course, in spite of this general agreement, naturalists disagree among themselves about which of the naturalistic definitions is the correct one.

The Naturalistic Fallacy

Moore begins his attack on naturalism by asking us to consider an analogous nonmoral case. He suggests that the property of being yellow is, like the property of being good, unanalyzable. He then points out that physicists may discover empirically that there is a "physical equivalent" to yellowness. Perhaps it will be found that all and only yellow things give off a certain kind of "light-vibration." Moore continues the argument as follows:

> But a moment's reflection is sufficient to show that those light-vibrations are not themselves what we mean by yellow. *They* are not what we perceive. . . . The most we can be entitled to say of those vibrations is that they are what corresponds in space to the yellow which we actually perceive. Yet a mistake of this simple kind has commonly been made about "good." It may be true that all things which are good are *also* something else, just as it is true that all things which are yellow produce a certain kind

of vibration in the light. And it is a fact, that Ethics aims at discovering what are those other properties belonging to all things which are good. But far too many philosophers have thought that when they named those other properties they were actually defining good; that these properties, in fact, were simply not "other," but absolutely and entirely the same with goodness. This view I propose to call the "naturalistic fallacy" . . . .[2]

A fallacy is an error in reasoning. One commits a fallacy when one's argument is of a defective form. In the passage just quoted, Moore seems to be alluding to a fallacious argument that a physicist might give. If a physicist, noting that all and only yellow things produce y-vibrations, were to conclude that "yellow" means the same as "produces y-vibrations," he would be committing an error of reasoning. For his argument would be of this form:

Argument A

(1) Something is yellow if and only if it produces y-vibrations.

(2) Therefore, x is yellow =df. x produces y-vibrations.

It should be obvious that argument A is not valid. For even if (2) is true, it is not entailed by (1). Suppose (1) is true "by accident," or merely as "a matter of fact." Then, although all and only yellow things produce y-vibrations, we can easily imagine something being yellow but not producing y-vibrations. This shows that "x is yellow" does not mean the same as "x produces y-vibrations," and thus that (1) does not entail (2).

Now let us apply this to the case of "x is good." Suppose a philosopher believes that he has discovered that all and only good things are things in which someone has a positive interest. That is, he thinks he has found that each good thing is a thing in which someone has a positive interest, and vice versa. He then argues as follows:

Argument B

(1) Something is good if and only if someone has a positive interest in it.

(2) Therefore, x is good =df. someone has a positive interest in x.

Notice that in this case, we begin with a relatively weak premise and then purport to deduce a form of naturalism. In other words, we infer an analytical definition from a mere generalization. Argument B is of the same form as argument A. In some cases, as we have seen, arguments of this form lead from a true premise to a false conclusion. Hence, argument B should not be trusted. It is not valid.

We can generalize this result. We can say that any argument of this form is suspect:

Argument C

(1) Something is good if and only if it is————.
(2) Therefore, x is good =df. x is————.

If naturalists use arguments of this form, in each case putting some naturalistic expression in the blank, then they argue fallaciously. For arguments of the illustrated form are not in general valid. We cannot infer a definition from the corresponding and perhaps accidental "if and only if" statement.

If this were the end of the matter, there would be no trouble in understanding the naturalistic fallacy. However, it isn't the end of the matter. In a passage following the one just quoted, Moore goes on to describe the error of the naturalists in greater detail. One puzzling aspect of the passage is that the error he goes on to describe is different from the error we have just discussed. Here is the passage in question.

> It is a very simple fallacy indeed. When we say that an orange is yellow, we do not think our statement binds us to hold that "orange" means nothing else than "yellow," or that nothing can be yellow but an orange.... We should not get any very clear notion about things, which are yellow—we should not get very far with our science, if we were bound to hold that everything which was yellow, *meant* exactly the same thing as yellow. We should find we had to hold that an orange was exactly the same thing as a stool, a piece of paper, a lemon, anything you like. We could prove any number of absurdities; but should we be nearer to the truth? Why, then, should it be different with "good"? Why, if good is good and indefinable, should I be held to deny that pleasure is good?[3]

In order to develop a clear interpretation of this rather dark passage, let us first introduce a new form of naturalism, so far not discussed. It is not a very plausible view, but it has been maintained by a few philosophers. It can be called *primitive hedonism*:

PH: x is good =df. x is pleasant.

Apparently, Moore thinks that a primitive hedonist might argue for this view from the premise that pleasure is good. In other words, a primitive hedonist might present this argument:

Argument D

(1) Pleasure is good.
(2) Therefore, x is good =df. x is pleasant.

Moore objects to argument D by presenting an argument of similar form, but one that has a true premise and an obviously false conclusion.

This argument is designed to show that argument D is of an invalid form. Moore's parody is this:

Argument E

    (1) Oranges are yellow.

    (2) Therefore, x is yellow =df. x is an orange.

It should be obvious that there is something profoundly wrong with Argument E, but it may not be entirely clear that the defects of E are the same as the defects of D. Let us concentrate on D.

    Premise (1) of argument D can be used to express either of two different thoughts. On the one hand, (1) might be used to express the idea that pleasure is a good thing, or that pleasure has goodness. This seems to be true, and can be expressed less ambiguously by:

    (1a) Pleasure is characterized by goodness.

On the other hand, if we assume that "good" in (1) functions as a name of goodness, then we might suppose that what (1) says is that pleasure and goodness are the same thing. In other words, (1) might be used to express obscurely what is expressed more clearly by:

    (1b) Pleasure is the same thing as goodness.

    The essence of Moore's objection to argument D can now be re-stated. If (1) means the same as (1a), then perhaps (1) is true. But in this case the argument as a whole is invalid. We cannot infer a definition of "good" from the mere fact that goodness characterizes a certain thing. The argument from (1a) to (2) is as silly as this argument:

Argument F

    (1) Life is short.

    (2) Therefore, x is short =df. x is alive.

    On the other hand, if (1) means the same as (1b), then the argument may be valid. For, given a certain theory of meaning, if "good" and "pleasant" expresses the same property, they have the same meaning. However, in this case the naturalist surely owes us an argument for his first premise, (1b). He must establish that pleasure and goodness are the same thing in order to use (1b) in the argument. But it certainly appears that (1b) is merely a metaphysically phrased variant of (2). Hence, (1b) is just as controversial as (2). The argument, then, seems to beg the question—it assumes as a premise the very thing it purports to establish. Naturalists surely cannot hope to convince anyone in this way.

    So here we seem to have a second interpretation of the naturalistic fallacy. We can state it in general terms:

Argument G

(1) ———is good.

(2) Therefore, x is good =df. x has———.

If a naturalist presents an argument of this form, putting a name of some natural property in the blanks, then he commits a fallacy. For arguments of this form are in general not valid. We cannot infer a naturalistic definition of "good" from the fact that goodness can be predicated of some naturalistic property.

If this were the end of the matter, our discussion of the naturalistic fallacy still would not be too complex. For we have two interpretations of the fallacy, and in each case it is pretty clear what the fallacy is, and that it is in fact a fallacy. But unfortunately, there is still more to be said. In another passage in Chapter 3 of *Principia Ethica*, Moore mentions the naturalistic fallacy again. What he says there is different from what he said previously: ". . . the naturalistic fallacy—the failure to distinguish clearly that unique and indefinable quality which we mean by good."[4] Moore seems to be suggesting here that the naturalistic fallacy is not a fallacy at all. That is, it is not an error in reasoning. Rather, the naturalistic fallacy is the failure to recognize that goodness is indefinable. This interpretation creates a puzzle.

The main problem with this interpretation of the naturalistic fallacy is that if naturalism is true, it is impossible for anyone to commit the naturalistic fallacy. For if goodness is a definable naturalistic property, as naturalists claim, then anyone who believes this believes the truth. Such a person cannot "fail to recognize that goodness is indefinable." In this case it would be Moore who fails to recognize that goodness *is* definable! So, according to this third interpretation, the naturalistic fallacy is not a fallacy at all, and may not even be a mistake. Thus, it is rather misleading to call it a fallacy.

Our conclusions concerning the naturalistic fallacy are somewhat "iffy." If the naturalistic fallacy is either of the errors involved in arguments of the forms illustrated by argument C and argument G, then the naturalistic fallacy is indeed a fallacy. It is an error in reasoning. Arguments of these forms are in general not valid, and so they do not serve to establish their conclusions. We would then have to consider whether in fact all naturalists make use of such arguments. In the unlikely event that they do, we may be confident that their arguments may be dismissed.

However, if the naturalistic fallacy is simply the error of believing in naturalism, or of identifying goodness with some natural or complex property, then our conclusion must be more guarded. We must say that if naturalism is false, then it is wrong to commit the naturalistic fallacy. If naturalism is true, then there is no such thing as the naturalistic fallacy. For if naturalism is true, it would not be an error to believe in naturalism.

The Open-Question Argument

Let us turn now to Moore's main argument against every form of naturalism. This is the famous open-question argument. One version of it appears in Chapter 1 of *Principia Ethica*:

> . . . it may easily be thought, at first sight, that to be good may mean to be that which we desire to desire. Thus if we apply this definition to a particular instance and say "when we think that A is good, we are thinking that A is one of the things which we desire to desire," our proposition may seem quite plausible. But, if we carry the investigation further, and ask ourselves, "Is it good to desire to desire A?" it is apparent, on a little reflection, that this question is itself as intelligible, as the original question "Is A good?"—that we are in fact, now asking for exactly the same information about the desire to desire A, for which we formerly asked with regard to A itself. But it is also apparent that the meaning of this second question cannot be correctly analysed into "Is the desire to desire A one of the things which we desire to desire?": we have not before our minds anything so complicated as the question "Do we desire to desire to desire to desire A?"[5]

This is a passage of remarkable complexity. It deserves very close attention.

We should note, first, that Moore is here attacking a form of naturalism that we have so far not discussed. It is the view that "to be good may mean to be that which we desire to desire." This view was once proposed by Moore's friend, Bertrand Russell. We can restate it in a somewhat more standard form as follows:

(DD) x is good =df. x is something we desire to desire.

(DD) is a form of naturalism, since it is the view that "good" can be defined in terms of some psychological expressions. (DD) makes goodness a complex psychological, or naturalistic, property. The theory may seem to have some merit. Some bad things, obviously, are desired, and some good things are not desired. But when we reflect on what we wish we would desire, it may seem that we wish to stop desiring bad things, if we desire them, and that we wish to start desiring good things, if we don't already desire them. Thus, it may be reasonable to suggest that good things are things we desire to desire.

Toward the end of the quoted passage, Moore mentions two questions. The open-question argument turns on some alleged facts about these questions. With some slight modifications, these questions are as follows:

Q_1:   Is the desire to desire A *something that is good*?

Q_2:   Is the desire to desire A *something that we desire to desire*?

Q_1 asks, with respect to the desire to desire A, whether it is good. Q_2 asks, with respect to the same thing, whether it is something that we desire to desire.

Next we must note that there is an intimate connection between (DD) and these two questions. The italicized phrase in Q_1 appears (roughly) as the definiendum of (DD), and the italicized phrase in Q_2 appears (roughly) as the definiens of (DD). If (DD) is true, then the italicized phrases have the very same meaning. This fact provides the basis for the open-question argument. For aside from the italicized phrases, the questions are alike. Hence, it would seem that if (DD) is true, Q_1 as a whole must mean exactly the same as Q_2.

Moore claims that if we think about it, we will realize that when we ask Q_1 we do not have anything so complicated "before our minds" as we have when we ask Q_2. This suggests that Q_1 does not mean the same as Q_2. If so, (DD) cannot be true. So, the argument as a whole looks like this:

Open-Question Argument

(1) Q_1 is not very complicated.

(2) Q_2 is very complicated.

(3) If Q_1 is not very complicated but Q_2 is very complicated, then Q_1 does not mean the same as Q_2.

(4) If Q_1 does not mean the same as Q_2, then (DD) is false.

(5) Therefore, (DD) is false.

When stated in this form, the open-question argument is valid. If the premises are true, then the conclusion must be true as well. Furthermore, it is easy to see how we could go on to construct similar arguments concerning other forms of naturalism. Indeed, it appears that for each form of naturalism there will be a suitable form of the open-question argument. Moore's view seems to be that in every case, the relevant open-question argument refutes the version of naturalism.

Concentrating for a moment on this version of the argument, let us reconsider each premise. Where did it come from? What reason is there to think it might be true?

The first premise comes from our observation of, and reflection about, Q_1. We look at that question, and we simply see that it is not a very complicated question. Similarly, when we look at Q_2, and reflect on it, we see that it, unlike Q_1, is rather complicated. Hence, premise (2) also comes from observation. Premise (3) is based on the principle that a given thing cannot both have and lack a given property. Q_1 has an uncomplicated meaning. Q_2 has a complicated meaning. Hence, they cannot have the same meaning.

The last premise, (4), is based on a principle of substitution. If two sentences are alike in all respects except that one contains a phrase, p, whereas the other contains a phrase, p', and p means the same as p', then the two sentences must have the same meaning. For example, if "brother" means the same as "male sibling," then "I have one brother" must mean the same as "I have one male sibling." Any difference in meaning between these two statements could not be ascribed to the parts they have in common—for these mean the same thing. Nor could such differences be ascribed to the parts with respect to which they differ —for these are synonymous. Hence, the sentences as a whole must be synonymous. The same holds true of questions Q_1 and Q_2. Thus, (4) seems to be unassailable, and the argument as a whole may be sound.

In this form, the open-question argument seems quite persuasive. Many philosophers have accepted it as a sound refutation of this form of naturalism. In spite of this, however, naturalism has continued to flourish. Obviously, not all naturalists have been convinced by the open-question argument that their view is false.

Some naturalists may feel that although the open-question argument is a sound refutation of many forms of naturalism, it does not refute all such forms. A given naturalist may feel that the argument is somehow defective when applied to his own preferred analysis of "good."

Others may take an even more skeptical position. They may claim that the argument is based on a confusion—that it in fact refutes no form of naturalism. To see their point, let us briefly consider an analogous argument. Suppose someone defines "x tells a lie" as "x utters a deliberate falsehood with the intention of deceiving someone." Can this definition be refuted by pointing out that whereas "Jones told a lie" is not complicated, "Jones uttered a deliberate falsehood with the intention of deceiving someone" is very complicated? It would seem not, for we already know that the definition is correct. Then why should we be any more convinced by the open-question argument?

A closer look at the argument reveals the source of the trouble. It may be admitted by all parties to the dispute that the *sentence* used to express Q_1 is less complicated than the *sentence* used to express Q_2. From this it follows that these are different sentences. But we all knew that from the start. The issue is whether they are synonymous, not whether they are identical. A naturalist may insist that the *meaning* of the sentence used to express Q_1 is exactly as complicated as the *meaning* of the sentence used to express Q_2. Thus, the naturalist may insist that there is no reason to suppose that we have two different meanings here at all.

We can put the point more formally as follows: If "Q_1" and "Q_2" refer to sentences, and not to their meanings, then (3) is false. A complicated sentence may have the same meaning as an uncomplicated one —the "tells a lie" example establishes this. On the other hand, if "Q_1" and "Q_2" refer to meanings, and not to sentences, then a version of (3) may be true. But then we have no reason to accept both (1) and (2). For it may be that Q_2 is just as complex a meaning as Q_1. The appearance of complexity arises solely from the words chosen to express that meaning.

In this form, then, it appears that the open-question argument is not entirely successful. It depends upon a pair of claims, (1) and (2), that the naturalist may reject. When Moore reflects on the meanings of the questions, he thinks he sees one to be more complex than the other. When the naturalist reflects on these meanings, he thinks he sees that there is really just one meaning here, and so he thinks that neither meaning is more complex than the other. It will be left to the reader to decide whether Moore or the naturalist is closer to the truth.

Someone might wonder why the open-question argument is so called. What does it have to do with "open questions"? Admittedly, in the form already discussed, it hasn't anything to do with open questions. But Moore presents several versions of the argument, and some of these versions do have to do with open questions. Let us briefly consider one such version of the argument.

In Chapter 1 of *Principia Ethica*, Moore says; "But whoever will attentively consider with himself what is actually before his mind when he asks the question 'Is pleasure (or whatever it may be) after all good?' can easily satisfy himself that he is not merely wondering whether pleasure is pleasant."[6] Let us say that a question is "open" provided that it is possible for a person to understand its meaning fully without knowing the correct answer. For example, the question "Are there any bananas in Iceland?" is open because it is possible to know what that question means but not know its answer. On the other hand, "Is every brother a sibling?" is not open. If you really know what this question means, you know that the answer must be yes.

Next, we introduce a form of naturalism:

(PH) x is good =df. x is pleasant.

(PH) is the theory we are going to try to refute. We attempt to refute it by considering two questions:

Q_3:   Is pleasure *pleasant*?

Q_4:   Is pleasure *good*?

The argument is formally quite like the one we just discussed. We start out by claiming that Q_3 is not an open question, but that Q_4 is an open question. From this it seems to follow that Q_3 does not mean the same as Q_4. However, Q_3 differs from Q_4 only in that Q_3 contains "pleasant" where Q_4 contains "good." Hence, "pleasant" must differ in meaning from "good." From this it follows that (PH) is false.

Second Open-Question Argument

(1) Q_3 is not open.

(2) Q_4 is open.

(3) If Q_3 is not open but Q_4 is open, then Q_3 does not mean the same as Q_4.

(4) If Q_3 does not mean the same as Q_4, then (PH) is false.

(5) Therefore, (PH) is false.

This is a valid argument, but primitive hedonists may refuse to be moved by it. They may claim that (2) is false. If their view is correct, the statement that pleasure is good is analytic—that is, it is true in virtue of its meaning alone. Hence, Q_4 is not an open question. Anyone fully understanding its meaning would know the answer to be yes. Moore, and others following him, would not accept this response.

Moore's Nonnaturalism

In the first two sections of this chapter, we have considered Moore's criticism of naturalism. We found that his criticism is persuasive, but not entirely conclusive. Now let us turn briefly to Moore's own positive contribution to metaethics.

Moore's main thesis in *Principia Ethica* is that goodness is an unanalyzable, nonnatural property. Put linguistically, this thesis is the view that "good" cannot be defined, and is not synonymous with any naturalistic expression. This thesis has two main parts:

(A) "Good" is indefinable.

(B) "Good" is not synonymous with any naturalistic expression.

We have already given some attention to the topic of definition. In light of that discussion, it should be fairly easy to understand what Moore means by thesis (A).

In our discussion of naturalism, however, we did not make a very great effort to explain what is meant by "naturalistic expression." Thus, thesis (B) may not be entirely clear. Let us now consider what Moore says on this topic.

In one important passage in *Principia Ethica*, Moore explains that a naturalistic property is a property of natural object; a natural object is an object of a kind that is studied in the natural sciences. The class of natural objects "may be said to include all that has existed, does exist, or will exist in time."[7] If we discover that some object did, does, or will exist, then "we may know that that object is a natural object, and that nothing, of which this is not true, is a natural object."[8] This suggests the following definitions:

D_1: x is a natural object =df. x did, does, or will exist.

D_2: F is a natural property =df. F is a property of some natural object.

D_3: φ is a naturalistic expression =df. φ expresses a natural property.

It is easy to see that according to this set of definitions, such expressions as "x is red," "x is angry," and "x approves of pleasure" are naturalistic. For in each case, the expression expresses a property of things that exist in time. But unfortunately, these definitions make "x is good" a naturalistic expression too. For there are some good things. Since such things exist, they are natural objects, according to D_1. By D_2, all of the properties of these natural objects, including goodness, are natural properties. Since "x is good" expresses goodness, a naturalistic property, it is a naturalistic expression, according to D_3. Hence, given these definitions, Moore's thesis (B) turns out to be false.

Moore recognizes this problem, and attempts to draw the distinction between natural and nonnatural properties in a different way. He proposes a test that, he hopes, will serve to make the distinction:

> . . . my test for [natural properties] also concerns their existence in time. Can we imagine "good" as existing *by itself* in time, and not merely as a property of some natural object? For myself, I cannot so imagine it, whereas with the greater number of properties of objects—those which I call the natural properties—their existence does seem to me to be independent of the existence of those objects.[9]

In this passage, Moore seems to be proposing that his test for natural properties is this: A property is natural provided that it can exist by itself in time. Moore suggests that properties such as redness and anger can exist by themselves in time, whereas goodness cannot exist by itself in time. If goodness exists, then there must be some good object that exists, too.

This suggestion is baffling. Does Moore really mean to say that redness can exist in time without there being any red object? If so, why can't goodness exist in time without there being any good object? It is very hard to understand what Moore could have been thinking of.

Perhaps it would be better to tie down the concept of naturalness to the concept of observability. We can say that a natural property is one whose presence can be observed. For example, redness is a natural property because there are some things that we can see to be red. Approval is a natural property because when we approve of something we can feel, or introspect, our approval. Such properties can be observed. But goodness cannot be seen, or smelled, or tasted. We may judge a thing to be good on the basis of what we observe, but we do not observe its goodness directly. So, the proposal, not developed by Moore,[10] is this:

D_4: F is a natural property =df. it is possible to observe that something has F.

D_5: φ is a naturalistic expression =df. φ expresses a natural property.

Even this proposal has some serious drawbacks. For one, it seems to imply that properties such as being magnetic, being radioactive, and being forty-five years old are not natural properties. For we do not directly observe the presence of any of these. We infer them on the basis of evidence. Another difficulty is that some will say that we have a faculty of "intuition," which enables us to "see" that something is good. If we do have such a faculty, then goodness is, in a sense, observable, and so "good" becomes a naturalistic expression under these definitions.

The upshot of this discussion is that we really do not know exactly what Moore means by "naturalistic expression" or "natural property." Perhaps we have some vague idea of the meaning of these terms. Perhaps we can tell a natural property when we see one. But Moore did not give, and we cannot give, a clear account of what these terms mean. Hence, it may be fair to conclude that we really do not have a firm grasp on one of the main doctrines of Moore's nonnaturalism.

In order to understand some of Moore's other important doctrines about goodness, we must recognize that when Moore speaks about goodness, he is for the most part talking about intrinsic goodness, not extrinsic goodness. Intrinsic goodness, or goodness as an end, is the allegedly unanalyzable property. We can analyze extrinsic goodness. To say that something is extrinsically good is just to say that it is a means to something that is intrinsically good.

Moore adopts a test for intrinsic goodness. If we apply this test to any good thing, we may be able to determine whether it is intrinsically good or whether it is good merely as a means. The test is called the "test of isolation." We ask ourselves whether the good thing would still be good even if it existed in utter isolation—without any causes, effects, or any other kind of connection with any other thing. If a thing would still be good even in this extreme isolation, then it is intrinsically good.

Consider food, clothing, and shelter. These are obviously good things. But are they intrinsically good? Moore would say they are not. Let us apply the test of isolation, to see what it implies. Suppose a very good cheeseburger exists all by itself. Suppose that there is no chef who enjoyed cooking it, no person to enjoy eating it, not even a fly to enjoy walking on it. Suppose, if possible, that the cheeseburger exists utterly by itself. Would it have any value under these circumstances? Moore would say not. Similarly, food, clothing, shelter—in fact, just about every good thing—ultimately flunks the test of isolation.

One thing that allegedly passes the test is "the love of beauty." This is a rather complex state. We can conceive of it as being the state of affairs of someone loving some beautiful object for its beauty. Try to imagine a universe in which there is just one person and one beautiful object, and assume that the person loves the object for its beauty. Would that universe be better or worse than an empty universe? Would it be better than a universe in which the one person does not love the one beautiful object? Moore would say that the universe in which there is "love of beauty" is better than either of the others. This apparently suggests that the love of beauty is intrinsically good as an end.

Moore maintains an interesting thesis about intrinsically good states of affairs. It is a thesis of *universality*. That is, if a certain state of affairs is intrinsically good, then each time that state of affairs occurs, it has exactly the same amount of intrinsic goodness. For example, if the state of affairs of someone feeling pleasure is intrinsically good, then every time someone feels pleasure, that state of affairs is equally intrinsically good. Even if one occurrence of pleasure has terrible effects and deplorable causes and another occurrence has good causes and effects, their intrinsic values must be exactly the same. This seems to follow from the fact that if we were to consider each occurrence in isolation, apart from all of its causes and effects, the two occurrences would be of equal value.

The principle of universality provides the background for a principle Moore felt to be of great importance—the principle of *organic unities*. You might think that if something is composed of two parts, and if each part is intrinsically bad, then the whole thing must be intrinsically bad. Indeed, if one part is intrinsically bad to degree 10, and if the other part is intrinsically bad to degree 5, then the whole should be bad to degree 15. You might hold the same notion about intrinsically good things. You might think that a complex thing composed of intrinsically good parts would have as its intrinsic value the sum of the intrinsic values of the parts. This is precisely what Moore denies. He says, "The value of such a whole bears no regular proportion to the sum of the values of its parts."[11]

One of the most puzzling features of the principle of organic unities is the concept of part and whole that seems to be employed. What kind of "whole" and "part" does Moore have in mind? Does he mean to suggest that, for example, a piece of jewelry composed of a diamond and a ruby might be worth more than the diamond and ruby considered separately? Apparently not, for here is Moore's example: "The consciousness of a beautiful object is certainly a whole of some sort in which we can distinguish as parts the object on the one hand and the being conscious on the other."[12]

We can interpret Moore's example as follows: First, let us suppose that the things with intrinsic value are all states of affairs. Let us symbolize three states of affairs as follows:

p = there being someone conscious of a beautiful object

q = there being someone conscious

r = there being a beautiful object

Moore's point in his example seems to be that the intrinsic value of p is very great, the intrinsic value of q is negligible, and r may have no intrinsic value at all. Hence, the value of p greatly exceeds the sum of the value of q and the value of r. Hence, this is an example of an organic unity whose value does not "bear a regular proportion to" the sum of the values of its parts.

Other states of affairs are "mere sums": their value is just the sum of the values of their parts. Here is an example:

s = Smith being happy and Jones being happy and Brown being happy

t = Smith being happy

u = Jones being happy

v = Brown being happy

Assuming, for the sake of the example, that t, u, and v are of equal intrinsic value, it would seem that the value of s is just the sum of the values of t, u, and v. So, s is a mere sum, unlike p in the previous example.

We may propose, then, that the principle of organic unity is the doctrine that there are some states of affairs whose values are different from the sums of the values of their parts.

In spite of its apparent simplicity and its plausibility, the principle of organic unities is really a very obscure doctrine. The main puzzle with it emerges upon reconsideration of our second example. Have we added together the values of *all* the parts of *s*? It seems clear, intuitively, that *t*, *u*, and *v* are parts of *s*. But what about (*t* and *u*)? What about (*u* and *v*)? If each of these is also a part of *s*, then we must take the sum of all of these values and compare it with the value of *s* alone. If the two values are unequal, as they surely are, then *s* is an organic unity.

So, the main problem with the principle of organic unities is that it makes use of a very obscure concept of "part." How can we understand "part of" so that the only parts of *p* are *q* and *r*, and the only parts of *s* are *t*, *u*, and *v*? This is a very difficult problem, perhaps too difficult to be pursued further here.

In the last chapter of *Principia Ethica*, Moore presents his view about which things are in fact intrinsically good and which things are in fact intrinsically bad. According to Moore, the method of isolation reveals that "the most valuable things, which we know of or can imagine, are certain states of consciousness, which may be roughly described as the pleasures of human intercourse and the enjoyments of beautiful objects."[13] More precisely, Moore's view seems to be that the great intrinsic goods fall into two main categories. In one group we have great goods that are "unmixed"—that do not contain any bad parts. These consist of the love of beautiful objects and the love of good objects. The "mixed" great goods are the hatred of ugliness and the hatred of evil. Some well-recognized virtues, such as courage and pity, fall into the category of mixed goods.

The great intrinsic evils fall into the same two categories. The great unmixed evils are evils that do not contain any good parts. According to Moore, there are three main great unmixed intrinsic evils: the love of ugly objects, the love of evil objects, and the consciousness of pain. The great mixed intrinsic evils are the hatred of beautiful objects and the hatred of good objects. In this category we find the vices of cruelty, lasciviousness, envy, and contempt. So, Moore's categorization as a whole seems to be as follows:

A. Great Intrinsic Goods
 1. Unmixed
   a. the love of beauty
   b. the love of goodness
 2. Mixed
   a. the hatred of ugliness
   b. the hatred of evil
B. Great Intrinsic Evils
 1. Unmixed
   a. the love of ugliness
   b. the love of evil

   c. the consciousness of pain
2. Mixed
   a. the hatred of beauty
   b. the hatred of goodness

A number of features of Moore's categorization may seem surprising. For one, Moore ranks the consciousness of pain as a great evil but fails to rank the consciousness of pleasure as a great good. Apparently, when Moore reflected on the state of affairs of someone being in pain, and considered how valuable that state of affairs would be if it existed in an otherwise empty universe, he "saw" that it would be very bad. On the other hand, when he performed the same thought experiment on the state of affairs of someone feeling pleasure, he "saw" that it would not be very good. Perhaps others performing the same experiments would derive different results. Surely, a hedonist such as Mill would disagree.

The consciousness of pain is unusual for another reason. Of all the items mentioned in Moore's list, it appears to be the only one that is not an organic unity.

Many readers may be shocked to find that Moore does not include knowledge, freedom, beauty, health, and peace in his list of great goods. Nor does he mention their opposites in his list of great evils. But the explanation of this is simple. These things may be great goods, but they are not great *intrinsic* goods. Consider knowledge, for example. Knowledge is extremely useful, and often it is quite pleasant. But in itself, apart from the pleasure or other good results it may have, knowledge is not terribly good. Imagine two persons, each existing in total isolation. One knows that two and two are four, and the other does not. In every other respect, they are exactly alike. The one with knowledge gains absolutely nothing from his knowledge. Is he any better off than the other person? Is the state of affairs in which someone knows something, when considered in total isolation, better than the state of affairs in which someone has a false belief, or no belief at all? Moore would say that there is very little difference in value here, if any.

Moore's metaethical position has been subjected to a wide variety of criticism. One of the most persistent objections is that if Moore's theory were true, it would be very hard to understand how we determine that things are good and bad. For if goodness is an invisible, undetectable property, what possible reason can anyone have for supposing it to be present in something? If one person claims that a certain thing is good and another person denies this, how can the two attempt to settle their difference? No empirical evidence seems to have any bearing on the question. This objection, if correct, is surely serious. For if Moore's theory implies that we cannot know what's good and what's bad, then Moore's theory is incorrect.

This line of objection may take a number of different forms. One form is as follows:

Knowledge Objection

(1) If Moore's theory were true, nothing would ever be known to be good.

(2) Some things are known to be good.

(3) Therefore, Moore's theory is not true.

The first premise is based on the view that according to Moore, goodness is a nonnatural property. Whatever else this may mean, it apparently implies that goodness is not observable. It is not an empirically detectable property, nor is it analyzable in terms of empirically detectable properties. Many philosophers in the empiricist tradition would insist that if a property is nonempirical, and if it is not analyzable in terms of empirically detectable properties, then there is no way for human beings to come to know that it is present in anything. Hence, these philosophers would insist that if Moore's theory were true, we could never know anything to be good. So, premise (1) has some plausibility, at least for those who accept the main tenets of empiricism.

The second premise seems uncontroversial. Moore himself suggests that he knows that the pleasures of human intercourse are good. Hence, even he would have to accept (2). Obviously, given (1) and (2), (3) must be admitted.

A defender of Moore might respond to this criticism by claiming that (1) is false. Moore's theory does not imply that we have no knowledge of good and evil, he could maintain. This defense would be based on the idea that in addition to our ordinary faculties of sense—sight, smell, taste, touch, and hearing—we have another faculty for gaining knowledge. By thinking very carefully about certain possible states of affairs, we can simply "intuit" that some of them are good and others are evil. Thus, a defender of Moore would appeal to a special sort of knowledge, one that is not explainable in purely empirical terms. Since this faculty is often called *intuition*, Moore's position concerning knowledge of good and evil is sometimes called *intuitionism*.

The question of whether there is any such faculty as intuition is a vexing question in epistemology, or theory of knowledge. We cannot pursue it here without entering into a hopelessly complex digression. So we must leave it to the reader to reflect on whether or not we have a special faculty, not explainable in empirical terms, by means of which we can intuit that some possible states of affairs are good and others bad. If you think that all knowledge ultimately "comes in through the senses," then it would appear that you will have to say that there simply is no such thing as intuition.

Many other objections have been raised against the nonnaturalism of Moore. Some philosophers have attempted to prove that there simply cannot be any such property as goodness. Others have attempted to show that we use moral language in ways that are incompatible with goodness being merely a property—even a nonnatural one. These philosophers would claim that evaluative language is used to tell people how to behave, to provoke them to take up certain attitudes, and to guide them to make their choices in certain ways rather than in others. All this, it has been maintained, would not be possible if goodness were merely some invisible property. These philosophers, the emotivists and the prescriptivists, would deny that evaluative language is used primarily for the stating of facts. Rather, such language is used for expressing emotions, issuing commands, and telling others how to behave and feel.

In order to gain a more adequate understanding of these criticisms, we must look more closely into the views of the emotivists and the prescriptivists. Their views are the subjects of the next two chapters.

NOTES

1. G. E. Moore, *Principia Ethica* (Cambridge: Cambridge University Press, 1962). First published in 1903.

2. *Ibid.*, p. 10.

3. *Ibid.*, p. 14.

4. *Ibid.*, p. 59.

5. *Ibid.*, pp. 15–16.

6. *Ibid.*, p. 16.

7. *Ibid.*, p. 40.

8. *Ibid.*

9. *Ibid.*, p. 41.

10. *Ibid.*, pp. 38–39.

11. *Ibid.*, p. 27.

12. *Ibid.*, p. 28.

13. *Ibid.*, p. 188.

14

Emotivism

The first half of the twentieth century witnessed a revival of philosophical interest in the workings of language. Philosophers began to reflect upon the various ways in which language can be used. Surely, language is not merely an instrument for the making of statements. Language can be used to issue commands, make requests, give expression to emotions, and perform rituals. These and other non-statement-making uses of language became the subject of serious philosophical thought.

This new emphasis on language had a profound effect in the field of metaethics. Philosophers were freed of the presupposition that moral sentences must be used simply to state moral facts. As soon as they began to think seriously about the variety of uses moral sentences may serve, they began to formulate new and exciting hypotheses. Perhaps moral sentences serve primarily to express emotions, or to issue commands. Perhaps they are not used to state facts at all! One of the most important metaethical positions to develop in this period is called *emotivism*.

The emotivists recognized, and wanted to account for, some important facts about moral language. For one, the emotivists wanted to emphasize that moral language, in its typical uses, is often accompanied by strong emotions. When a moral conservative says that communal living is evil, he usually speaks with some feeling. He isn't stating simply and coldly what he takes to be a fact. Similarly, when a rabid organic gardener denounces the use of persistent insecticides, he is likely to have strong negative feelings toward the use of such chemicals. Equally, those who pass favorable moral judgments on certain things often have warm, positive feelings toward the things they praise.

Thus, moral judgments are closely associated with positive and negative feelings, or emotions. Some forms of naturalism attempt to account for this association by claiming that a moral judgment is nothing more than the assertion that such an emotion is being felt. "Communal living is evil," according to this view, simply means the same as "I have negative feelings toward communal living." However, if Moore's open-question argument is accepted and every form of naturalism is judged to be false, then this naturalistic view cannot provide the correct account of the connection between emotions and moral judgments.

The emotivists recognized another important fact about moral language. They saw that such language is often intimately associated with action. Quite often, when the organic gardener denounces the use of insecticides, he is trying to persuade other gardeners to stop using such chemicals. In fact, it sometimes appears that the point of such a judgment could be expressed just as well by a request, or a command. "Please stop using those chemicals" or "Stop using DDT" might serve the gardener's purposes just as well. Equally, it may seem that positive moral judgments have a "requesting" aspect. "It is your duty to tell the police what you know" seems to suggest, at any rate, a command. The speaker might almost have said, "Tell the police what you know!" Thus, moral judgments seem to be connected with action in something like the way that requests and commands are connected with action.

In general, emotivists felt that moral judgments are used to "give vent to," or express, emotions, and to command, or issue imperatives. These two uses of language can be called the *expressive* and the *imperatival*. Insofar as an utterance merely "gives vent" to an emotion, or commands, it has no truth value. It is neither true nor false. Some emotivists, of a rather radical sort, believed that the *only* uses of moral expressions are the expressive and the imperatival. They accepted the conclusion that moral judgments are neither true nor false. Other emotivists, of a more moderate sort, insisted merely that no account of the meaning of moral expressions would be complete if it left out the expressive and imperatival aspects. Let us first consider the more radical position.

Radical Emotivism

There are many reasons why a philosopher might become a radical emotivist. Historically, two reasons seem to be the most important. The first reason is that it has seemed to some philosophers that there is simply no viable alternative to radical emotivism. To see how this view could come about, consider a philosopher who finds himself in the following perplexity. On the one hand, he has been convinced that every form of naturalism is false. Moore's open-question argument or some similar argument seems to him to show that "good" cannot be defined in terms of any combination of naturalistic expressions. On the other hand, he is also convinced that nonnaturalism is untenable, perhaps because it makes goodness so mysterious and so remote from emotions and actions. If goodness were a nonnatural property, he feels, no one would have noticed it or attempted to make statements about it.

Thus, our philosopher seems to be in quite a fix. "Good" does not express any natural property, nor does it express any nonnatural property. If every property is either natural or nonnatural, the consequence is clear: "good" does not express any property at all. According to some standard theories of meaning, this implies that "good" must be meaningless. Our philosopher is driven to the conclusion that moral sentences are, strictly speaking, not statements at all! The only metaethical theory compatible with this view would appear to be radical emotivism.

The second main reason for adopting radical emotivism is that it seems to be a consequence of a very enticing theory of meaningfulness. The *verification theory*, or the *verifiability criterion of meaningfulness*, is the view that a sentence is meaningful, strictly speaking, only if it expresses something that can in principle be shown to be true (verified) or shown to be false (falsified) on the basis of empirical observations. If we cannot even imagine some observations that would verify or falsify some alleged statement, then there is no statement. There is only a meaningless sentence that misleadingly appears to express some statement.

Let us consider some examples to see how the verification principle is supposed to work. Some sentences are verifiable and meaningful. For example:

(1) There are bananas in Iceland.

We can easily imagine someone going to Iceland, checking every grocery store and kitchen cupboard, and eventually discovering a banana. In this case, this person's observation of the banana in Iceland would verify (1). Similarly, a team of observers might determine after long and hard work that there are no bananas in Iceland. In this case, their observations would falsify (1). Since such observations are in principle possible, (1) is meaningful according to the verification principle. Statement (1) is judged to express something that is either true or false.

Now consider this statement:

(2) Tootie frootie, a rootie.

It should be obvious that there are no empirical observations that would even tend to verify or falsify (2). Where would we look? What would we look for? Thus, the verification principle implies that (2) is meaningless. It does not express anything that is either true or false.

It is very important to realize that the verification principle is not a principle about *importance*. The conclusion that (1) is meaningful should not be confused with the conclusion that (1) is an important, or weighty, statement. Indeed, (1) may be utterly trivial, silly, and ridiculous. Nevertheless, the verification principle implies that it is, strictly speaking, meaningful. Perhaps it would be better to say "cognitively meaningful." Statement (1) expresses something that is either true or false, something that can be believed or disbelieved, perhaps something that is known to be true. According to the verification principle, (2) is unlike (1) in every one of these respects.

Now let us apply the verification principle to a moral judgment. Consider, for example, this sentence:

(3) Pain is evil.

What sort of observations would verify or falsify (3)? We certainly cannot verify (3) by undergoing some pain and finding that we do not like it. Such a procedure might tend to verify the proposition that we do not like pain, but it would not show that pain is evil. Nor would it be useful to attach meters, wires, or machines of any kind to our bodies while we undergo some pain. All that would be verified by this procedure would be that pain causes increased blood pressure, or raises the pulse rate, or whatever. It would not verify or falsify (3). In general, then, it may seem that moral sentences cannot be verified or falsified empirically.

Many emotivists find in this feature of moral sentences a second main argument for their view. They might argue as follows: Moral sentences cannot be verified or falsified empirically. A sentence is cognitively meaningful only if it can be verified or falsified. Hence, moral sentences are not cognitively meaningful. Therefore, the only use of moral sentences must be to express emotions, issue commands, or function in some other such nonassertive way. This may seem to be a persuasive argument for anyone who accepts the verification principle. One such philosopher is A. J. Ayer, who was once a leading proponent of a radical form of emotivism.[1] At one point in his career, he seems to have come to believe in emotivism largely as a result of reflecting on an argument like the one just mentioned.

Obviously, the radical emotivist cannot simply affirm that moral sentences are cognitively meaningless. Such a view would be quite empty. He has to go on to explain why we utter them so often; why they seem so important; how they are related to the emotions that frequently accompany them; and how they are related to action. The answers to these questions constitute the positive side of emotivism.

Emotive Meaning

Some emotivists have attempted to draw a broad distinction between two kinds of meaning. On the one hand there is *cognitive meaningfulness*. The verification principle is alleged to be the criterion for this. A cognitively meaningful sentence expresses something true or false—something that can be believed, known, or doubted. We can say that only a cognitively meaningful sentence can be used to make a statement, or assertion. On the other hand, there is *emotive meaning*. An expression such as "Ugh!" or "Bah!" or "Oh wow, far out!" does not have any cognitive meaning, but it can be used to give vent to, or express, certain emotions. If you observe something sufficiently disgusting, the feeling of disgust may well up in you and cause you to exclaim, "Ugh!" When this happens, your utterance has emotive meaning, but no cognitive meaning. This sort of emotive meaning is *expressive*.

Another sort of emotive meaning is *imperatival*. When you order someone to do something, you may utter a sentence that is neither true nor false. For example:

(4) Watch your step!

There is no way to verify or falsify (4). According to the verification principle, it is cognitively meaningless. However, (4) does have imperatival emotive meaning. It can be used to issue a command.

We can categorize these distinctions as follows:

A. Cognitively meaningful sentences: these state something that is either true or false, something that can be verified or falsified. Example: "The door is shut."
B. Emotively meaningful sentences:
1. Expressive: these give vent to an emotion, are neither true nor false, and cannot be verified or falsified. Example: "Ugh!"
2. Imperatival: these are used to command, are neither true nor false, and cannot be verified or falsified. Example: "Shut the door!"
C. Meaningless: these have neither emotive nor cognitive meaning, are neither true nor false, and cannot be verified or falsified. Example: "Tootie frootie, a rootie."

It should be clear that in some cases a sentence will function in a variety of ways. For example, a sentence may be expressive as well as assertive:

(5) Holy cow! The barn is on fire!

Or a sentence may combine the expressive and the imperatival. This might occur when a person raging with anger issues a threatening command:

(6) You get out of here and keep out!

A sentence such as (6) serves not only to command, it serves to give vent to, or express, anger.

It is also important to recognize, in the case of two or more utterances involving the same emotion, the difference between the assertive and the expressive utterances. For example, suppose a person is in great pain and says rather cooly:

(7) I am in pain.

This sentence asserts that the person is in pain. It does not express the pain. On the other hand, if the person had said:

(8) OUCH!

his utterance would have expressed, or given vent to, his feeling of pain, but it would not have asserted that he was in pain. The differences between (7) and (8) are important. Statement (7) is cognitively meaningful, either true or false, and assertive. Statement (8) is cognitively meaningless, neither true nor false, and emotive.

Radical Emotivist Accounts of "Good" and "Bad"

Radical emotivists maintain that moral sentences such as:

(9) Pain is intrinsically bad.

are cognitively meaningless. They are to be categorized with sentences such as (6) and (8) rather than with assertive sentences such as (7). This view about normative sentences supposedly follows from the fact that they cannot be verified or falsified. Emotivists also maintain, however, that such sentences are emotively meaningful. Indeed, they are alleged to have both expressive and imperatival emotive meaning. Thus, it might be said that when a person utters (9), he gives vent to some negative emotion that he feels for pain, and he commands his listeners to share his emotion. Thus, we might try to rewrite (9) as:

(9′) Pain! Ugh! Please hate pain.

It should be clear that radical emotivism is quite different from subjective naturalism. A standard subjective naturalist account of the meaning of (9) might be:

(9″) I hate pain.

The differences between (9′) and (9′′) are important. Statement (9′′) is cognitively meaningful, it can be verified or falsified, and it is either true or false, depending upon whether or not I hate pain. In every one of these respects, (9′) is different from (9′′). We can say that whereas (9′′) is used to *assert* that I hate pain, (9′) is used to *express*, evince, or give vent to that hatred without asserting anything. Similarly, it should be noted that the final part of (9′) does not mean the same as "I want you to hate pain." "Please hate pain" is a command, it is neither true nor false, and it cannot be verified or falsified. Nor can it be believed, known, or even doubted. "I want you to hate pain," on the other hand, differs in every one of these respects.

So, according to the radical emotivist, sentences of the form "*x* is bad" are not used to make assertions. Rather, they are used primarily to give vent to, or express, negative emotions, and to command others to have similar emotions. This constitutes an account of the connection between moral sentences, on the one hand, and emotions and actions, on the other. Moral sentences are not used to assert the occurrence of emotions. Rather, they serve to give vent to those emotions. Hence, it is only reasonable that people feel strongly when they make moral judgments. If they did not feel strongly, there would be nothing for them to express, or to give vent to. A steam whistle won't blow if there's no pressure. The connection between moral sentences and action is also quite clear. According to the emotivists, part of what is meant by a moral sentence is a command to action.

It should be obvious that we cannot present an emotivist definition of "*x* is good" and "*x* is bad." We can give an analytical definition of an expression only if it expresses some concept. Since sentences of the form "*x* is good" allegedly have no cognitive meaning, we cannot hope to provide a precise account of their cognitive meaning! So instead of attempting to define "*x* is good," radical emotivists must be content to formulate an account of its emotive meaning. To do this, they simply specify its main functions. Thus, the central thesis of the radical emotivists may be formulated as follows:

> *RE*: Sentences of the form "*x* is good (bad)" have no cognitive meaning. They are used (i) to express positive (negative) emotions, and, (ii) to command others to feel similar emotions.

If radical emotivism is true, then moral sentences do not serve any assertive function. They are not used to make statements. Nor are such sentences either true or false. Thus, for example, the sentence "Pain is bad" could not be used to assert anything. It could only be used expressively or imperatively. Consequently, it would seem that no one could know, or even believe, that pain is bad. For there simply is no such thing as the "fact" that pain is bad, according to radical emotivism. Thus, emotivism entails that there can be no "moral knowledge." For this reason, emotivism is sometimes classified as a form of *noncognitivism*.

Objections to Radical Emotivism

Let us now turn to some criticisms of radical emotivism. In one respect, emotivism is like subjective naturalism. For each of these views entails that there are, strictly speaking, no moral conflicts. If I say that thrift is good and you say that it is bad, then according to radical emotivism, each of us has given vent to an emotion and issued a command. Neither of us has said anything true or false, and there is no belief about which we are debating. But it has appeared to many philosophers that in such a case the radical emotivist is wrong. They have felt that in such cases there is a conflict. So, the argument, a revised version of the no-conflicts argument, is this:

No-Conflicts Argument (revised)

    (1) If radical emotivism is true, then there are no moral conflicts.

    (2) There are moral conflicts.

    (3) Therefore, radical emotivism is not true.

Ayer responds to this argument in an astonishing way. He rejects (2). He says, "We hold that one really never does dispute about questions of value." He goes on to attempt to explain this rather odd claim:

> This may seem, at first sight, to be a very paradoxical assertion. For we certainly do engage in disputes which are ordinarily regarded as disputes about questions of value. But, in all such cases, we find, if we consider the matter closely, that the dispute is not really about a question of value, but about a question of fact.[2]

Ayer's response to this objection reveals that he takes the notion of "conflict" very seriously. Apparently, he would say that a conflict occurs only if there is some belief that one person affirms and another denies. In moral cases, then, there can be no conflicts, since, according to Ayer, there are no moral beliefs. Ayer attempts to explain why it so often appears that moral conflict is occurring. In such cases, what is really happening is that the disputants are arguing about some factual matter. For example, suppose I say "Thrift is good" and you say "Thrift is bad." The sentence "Thrift is good" has no truth value; it does not formulate any belief. Hence, we are not debating about it. Rather, we are probably debating such factual issues as whether thrift brings happiness, or whether thrifty people tend to be stingy and cold. Our conflict, if there is one, will be about some such factual question.

Ayer might just as well have responded to this objection in another way. He could have drawn a distinction between two kinds of conflict. He could have said that there are *disagreements in belief* and *disagreements in attitude*. A disagreement in belief occurs when one person affirms a proposition, another denies it, and each tries to convince the other to change his belief. A disagreement in attitude occurs when one person has a positive attitude toward something, another person has a negative attitude toward that same thing, and each tries to make the other change his attitude. In disagreements in belief, we aim at altering each other's beliefs. In disagreements in attitude, we aim at changing each other's feelings.

Ayer could have said that radical emotivism implies that there are no moral disagreements in belief. He could have claimed that the no-conflicts argument gains its plausibility by glossing over this important distinction. As we will see later, Charles Stevenson, a more moderate emotivist, did respond to this objection in this way.

A second objection to radical emotivism is based upon the fact that we sometimes make moral judgments when we feel no emotion at all. Several amusing variations of this argument were developed by Brand Blanshard.[3] We will discuss two. Suppose that a person observes a rabbit in a trap. Feeling very great horror at the thought of the rabbit's pain, the person says:

(10) It was a bad thing that the little animal should suffer so.

Suppose that in time the person calms down, and in fact no longer has any strong feelings about the rabbit trap. Perhaps he has been given a tranquilizer, and as a result his emotional state is quite unlike what it was previously. Now we ask him what he thinks of the pain the rabbit endured, and he says:

(11) It was a bad thing that the little animal should suffer so.

According to radical emotivism, neither sentence expresses anything true or false. They have no cognitive meaning. The only kind of meaning they might have is emotive meaning. It is fairly plausible to say that (10) was used to give vent to a negative emotion the person felt toward the suffering of the rabbit. At any rate, that is what a radical emotivist would say. But since (11) was uttered at a time when no emotion was being felt, it could not have been used to give vent to any emotions. It would appear, then, that (11) has no emotive meaning. On this basis, we can formulate an argument against radical emotivism.

First Rabbit Argument

(1) If radical emotivism is true, then (11) has neither cognitive nor emotive meaning.

(2) If (11) has neither cognitive nor emotive meaning, then (11) has no meaning at all.

(3) But (11) obviously has some meaning.

(4) Therefore, radical emotivism is not true.

It is not clear how a radical emotivist would respond to this argument. Perhaps he would say that (11) has emotive meaning since it is used to give vent to an emotion that was felt previously. Perhaps he would insist that tranquilizer or no, if the person actually uttered (11), he must have felt some emotion. Otherwise, he would have said that he didn't care about the suffering of the rabbit. A final approach would be to bite the bullet and deny (3). The radical emotivist could say that in the imagined circumstances, (11) is utterly without meaning. It is not clear that any of these responses is adequate.

We can make use of the rabbit example to develop another argument against radical emotivism. First, we should recall that neither (10) nor (11) has any cognitive meaning, according to radical emotivism. Second, we should notice that the emotive meaning of (10) seems to be the strong feelings of revulsion felt at the time of the utterance of (10). In other words, the emotions then expressed seem to be the emotive meaning of the sentence. Clearly, when (11) was uttered, no such intense emotions were being felt. So the emotive meaning of (11) is different from the emotive meaning of (10). From this it seems to follow that the meaning as a whole of (11) is different from the meaning as a whole of (10). So here we have the basis of our second argument:

Second Rabbit Argument

(1) If radical emotivism is true, (10) does not mean the same as (11).

(2) (10) does mean the same as (11).

(3) Therefore, radical emotivism is not true.

Evaluation of this argument is left to the reader.

Another sort of objection to radical emotivism is based on some facts about moral reasoning. Consider the following argument:

Argument A

(1) Every act of charity is good.

(2) This is an act of charity.

(3) Therefore, this act is good.

It seems pretty obvious that argument A is valid. The conclusion, (3), follows from the premises. This is not to say that the premises are true; it is only to say that they logically entail the conclusion. This seemingly uncontroversial fact is incompatible with radical emotivism. For according to radical emotivism, lines (1) and (3) lack cognitive meaning. They have no truth value. Thus, argument A as a whole is no more valid than this preposterous pseudoargument:

Argument B

(1) Tootie frootie.

(2) This is an act of charity.

(3) Therefore, a rootie.

On the face of it, this seems to be a devastating objection. Can we accept a theory that implies that argument A is as illogical as argument B? Surely, it must be admitted that from the point of view of logic, argument A is better than argument B.

Some emotivists have attempted to deal with this argument by expanding the concept of validity. They have suggested that in a broader sense, an argument may be considered to be "emotively valid" if it succeeds in producing the desired emotion in the person addressed. Thus, if I can get you to feel positively about my act of charity by presenting argument A, then argument A is valid. In this respect, argument A is better than argument B. For it is doubtful that I will produce any changes either in your beliefs or in your emotions by presenting argument B.

This position has been widely criticized. Some commentators have claimed that the emotivists are committed to the absurd view that any brainwashing technique, propaganda, threat, or rhetoric that succeeds in changing the emotions of the "victim" is *valid*. This strikes some as being an immoral doctrine, since it seems to justify any persuasive technique, as long as it works. It strikes others as being incorrect, since we have always distinguished between logical validity and rhetorical persuasiveness. According to this emotivist position, it might be said, the grossest fallacy is valid if you can use it to convince your listeners.

In light of these and other objections, it has seemed to many philosophers that radical emotivism is quite untenable. Its insights into the importance of emotions and actions in the analysis of moral sentences have been carried too far. A more moderate view, one that incorporates these valuable insights, is to be preferred. Such a view has been developed in very great detail by Charles Stevenson. Let us now turn to a consideration of that view.

Moderate Emotivism

In his classic work *Ethics and Language*,[4] Stevenson defends two general patterns of analysis of "*x* is good." Before he presents his first pattern of analysis, however, Stevenson presents some allegedly inadequate analyses. He tries to show that these analyses are incorrect, and that they need modifications of certain kinds. The modifications result in the first pattern of analysis. So it may be best to begin where Stevenson begins, and to try to understand why he wants to reject these earlier attempts.

We may start with a version of subjective naturalism. Stevenson agrees that attitudes are of great importance in the analysis of moral sentences. But he denies that they play the role suggested by this theory:

> SN: "This is good" means "*I approve of this and I want you to do so as well.*"

According to this theory, moral sentences are used to express our beliefs about our own attitudes. If I say that thrift is good, I am merely saying something about how I feel. That is, I am saying that I approve of thrift and that I want you to approve of thrift too. Stevenson calls this a "bare introspective report of the speaker's state of mind."[5]

Stevenson objects to SN on the ground that it fails to bring out the fact that moral sentences are used "not only in expressing beliefs about attitudes, but in strengthening, altering, and guiding the attitudes themselves."[6] The "bare introspective report" that I have certain feelings is unlikely to move you to share these feelings. But the statement that thrift is good does have some such "dynamic aspect." Hence, SN is inadequate.

A related problem with SN is that it fails to account for conflict. If I say "Thrift is good" and you say "Thrift is not good," we seem to be in conflict. Yet according to SN, we may both be speaking the truth. If I do approve of thrift and do want you to approve of it as well, and you do not approve of thrift or do not want me to approve of it, we have each spoken the truth. Then where is the conflict? Hence, Stevenson accepts a version of Moore's no-conflicts argument.

Stevenson considers another proposal.[7] This view differs from the preceding one only in one relatively minor detail. According to this view, when we say that something is good, we assert that we have a favorable attitude toward that thing. In this respect, this view is just like SN. But according to this view, when we make such a statement, we also issue an imperative, or command. We command our listeners to have the same sort of attitude. In this respect, this second theory is reminiscent of Ayer's radical emotivism. This second theory, which Stevenson calls a "working model," may be formulated as follows:

WM: "This is good" means "I approve of this; do so as well."

There is a crucial difference between SN and WM. According to SN, moral sentences have truth values. According to WM, they do not. This follows from the fact that according to WM, each moral sentence has two meaning components. One component is factual. It is the assertion that the speaker has a certain attitude. This part has a truth value. But the other component is a command. Commands are neither true nor false. So if a moral sentence is based upon a combination of two such components, one with and one without truth value, then the sentence must lack truth value as a whole. Thus, we can see that WM is a noncognitivist metaethical theory. According to WM, moral sentences do not have truth values. In this respect, WM is unlike SN.

Stevenson rejects WM. He claims that it misrepresents the emotive aspect of the moral sentence. The problem is that the emotive aspect of the moral sentence is more subtle than the command aspect. We can illustrate the difference by comparing two sentences:

(12) Diligent study is good.

(13) I approve of diligent study; do so as well.

Notice, first, that according to WM, these two sentences should have the same meaning. But Stevenson tries to show that they do not. He points out that (13) is a "blunt instrument" with a "stultifying effect." He goes on to say:

> If a person is explicitly commanded to have a certain attitude, he becomes so self-conscious that he cannot obey. Command a man's approval and you will elicit only superficial symptoms of it. But the judgment, "this is good," has no trace of this stultifying effect.[8]

The idea is that if we *command* a person to have a certain attitude, he is unlikely to obey. However, according to Stevenson, (12) does not have any such stultifying effect. We can use (12) to elicit a favorable response from our hearer. Hence, Stevenson concludes that (12) does not mean the same as (13), and so WM is false.

Stevenson's argument is apparently based on a rather broad concept of meaning. He seems to assume that expressions are synonymous only if they produce the same sort of psychological response in those who hear them. This is a somewhat extreme view. Don't we often say, for example, that although two words are synonymous, one of them is vulgar and insulting whereas the other is polite and acceptable? If Stevenson's assumption were correct, this would be impossible. Nevertheless, Stevenson rejects WM on the grounds that it misrepresents the way in which emotions are elicited by moral sentences.

In place of WM, Stevenson proposes what he calls "the first pattern of analysis." He holds that no other English expression has exactly the same meaning as "good." He infers that it is impossible to give a definition of "good." So the first pattern of analysis is not supposed to be a definition. Rather, it is Stevenson's attempt to characterize the meaning of "good," when used as a' term of moral evaluation.

According to Stevenson's first pattern of analysis, the meaning of "good" has two main components. The first is the "descriptive meaning," or the "factual component." Stevenson holds that the descriptive meaning of "good" is adequately captured by WM. That is, when a person says that something is good, he means that he feels approval for that thing. Stevenson amplifies this account by stating that there is a special sort of approval that is specifically moral. He claims that this sort of approval is "marked by a special seriousness or urgency."[9] He also suggests that when a person feels this sort of approval, he may feel a "heightened sense of security."[10] Although it may be difficult to isolate this kind of approval, let us assume that we know what Stevenson means, and let us call this approval "moral approval." Thus, if someone says, for example, "Altruism is good," then his statement is supposed to have the same descriptive meaning as the statement, "I feel moral approval for altruism."

The emotive component of the meaning of "good" is rather hard to pin down. It can vary widely. But no matter what else may be said of it, the emotive meaning of "good," according to the first pattern of analysis, must be such as to "evoke the favor of the hearer."[11] In other words, when someone says "Altruism is good," his sentence is designed to evoke in the hearer a favorable attitude toward altruism. In one extreme sort of case, the speaker may intend his utterance to have an immediate and decisive effect on his hearer. He may wish to provoke instant admiration for altruism. In this sort of case, the attempt at evocation may be almost as obvious and blunt as that in the imperative, "I demand that you approve of altruism!" In the opposite extreme, a speaker may hardly care whether his hearer approves or not. His statement may be barely more than the purely factual statement, "I approve of altruism."

Thus, in different cases the relative importance of the two meaning components may vary. Nevertheless, they both must be present. So, we can state the main thesis of the first pattern of analysis as follows:

FPA: For any person, S, if S says "*x* is good," then S means what S would mean if S were to say, in such a way as to evoke a favorable response in his hearer, "I feel moral approval for x."

In order to gain a clearer understanding of Stevenson's first pattern of analysis, let us briefly compare it with Ayer's radical emotivism and with a standard form of subjective naturalism. According to Ayer's view, as we have seen, a sentence such as "Altruism is good" has only emotive meaning. It serves to express (not assert) a positive attitude toward altruism, and it commands the having of a similar attitude on the part of the hearer. It has no descriptive meaning. Stevenson would disagree with Ayer on every one of these points. First, Stevenson would say that on the basis of the first pattern of analysis, Ayer has not described the emotive component in the sentence correctly. The emotive component is not like a command, for a command is "too blunt an instrument." Rather, the emotive component is better described by saying that the sentence serves to evoke in the hearer a favorable response toward altruism. Second, according to the first pattern of analysis, the expression of a favorable attitude is not part of the meaning of "Altruism is good." Third, according to the first pattern, the sentence does have a descriptive, or factual, component. It means the same as "I feel moral approval for altruism." Thus, according to Stevenson, the sentence is used to assert (not express) the presence of an emotion.

Stevenson's moderate emotivism is therefore significantly different from Ayer's radical emotivism. The main difference seems to be this: Whereas in Ayer's view moral sentences are said to lack truth value, under Stevenson's first pattern of analysis each such sentence is either true or false. In this respect, Stevenson's view seems to be much closer to a form of subjective naturalism. For, like the subjective naturalist, Stevenson wants to say that a moral sentence is used to assert the presence of a certain attitude in the speaker. The sentence is true if the speaker has the attitude; otherwise it is false.

The main difference between the first pattern of analysis and subjective naturalism is that Stevenson insists that there is more to the meaning of a moral sentence than simply the fact that it is used to assert the presence of an attitude. The sentence also has emotive meaning, which is not mentioned by the subjective naturalist. To describe the meaning of such sentences fully, one would also have to say that they are used emotively to evoke a favorable attitude on the part of the hearer.

Objections to the First Pattern of Analysis

Although much more could be said about Stevenson's first pattern of analysis, perhaps we can gain some deeper insight into this theory by reflecting on some objections that may be leveled against it.

It should be clear that the first pattern of analysis will have to face up to a version of the no-conflicts argument. For, like subjective naturalism, the first pattern entails that there is no logical conflict between two persons when one says that something is good and the other says that it is bad. To see this more clearly, we can consider an example. Suppose Smith says:

(14) Idleness is bad.

and Jones says:

(15) Idleness is good.

According to the first pattern of analysis, Smith's statement means the same as:

(14′) I, Smith, feel moral disapproval for idleness (said in such a way as to evoke an unfavorable response).

Jones's statement means the same as:

(15′) I, Jones, feel moral approval for idleness (said in such a way as to evoke a favorable response).

Clearly, (14′) and (15′) may both be true. If (14) and (15) mean the same, respectively, as (14′) and (15′), then (14) and (15) may both be true. Hence, there is no logical conflict between (14) and (15), according to the first pattern of analysis.

Stevenson grants that sentences such as (14) and (15) are logically compatible. They may both be true. But he claims that the fact that they have been uttered reveals the presence of a deeper form of conflict, which he calls "disagreement in attitude." Roughly, two persons are said to disagree in attitude when they have opposed attitudes toward the same object and at least one of them tries to alter the attitude of the other. Thus, Stevenson can account for our intuitive feeling that there is a conflict in this sort of case, without giving up his first pattern of analysis. All he has to say is that the conflict is purely attitudinal. It shows up only in the emotive components of the meanings of the sentences. Logically speaking, the sentences do not conflict. Stevenson's account of disagreement in attitude is clearly useful, but some philosophers would feel uneasy about the claim that (14) and (15) may both be true. They certainly appear to be logically incompatible! The reader must decide for himself whether he can accept Stevenson's claim.

Stevenson discusses another, rather curious sort of objection that might be raised.[12] It has to do with truth. Suppose Smith is an industrious person who hates idleness. He observes Jones loafing on the job. Smith says:

(14) Idleness is bad.

According to the first pattern of analysis, Smith's statement means the same, descriptively, as:

(14′) I, Smith, feel moral disapproval for idleness.

Let us imagine that Jones, the loafer, realizes that (14) means the same as (14′). Let us also imagine that Jones knows full well that Smith disapproves of idleness. Recognizing all of this, Jones might say:

(16) Yes, Smith, what you say is true. Nevertheless, idleness is not bad.

If the first pattern of analysis were correct, Jones's statement (16) would make perfectly good sense. For it would simply be Jones's way of saying:

(16′) Yes, Smith, you *do* disapprove of idleness. Nevertheless, I, Jones, do not disapprove of idleness.

However, many people would feel that Jones's statement (16) verges on self-contradiction. Thus, there may seem to be something wrong with the first pattern of analysis.

Stevenson replies to this objection by drawing a distinction between two senses of "true." Sometimes, we use the word "true" to endorse, or show our assent to, another person's statement. For example, if you say that grass is green and I say "That's true," I am in effect saying that grass is green. But Stevenson says that there is another use of "true"—as a sort of "ditto mark," roughly meaning "me too." Thus, if you say "I'm hungry" and I say "That's true," my remark serves to indicate that *I* am hungry also.

Making use of "ditto truth," we can develop a reply to the objection. Stevenson suggests that in ordinary circumstances, when a person says "That's true" after a moral sentence, he's using "true" in the "ditto truth" sense. So if Smith says that idleness is bad and Jones says "That's true," then their conversation really amounts to this:

(14′) I, Smith, feel moral disapproval for idleness.

(17) I, Jones, feel the same way.

Going back to the original objection, we can see how Stevenson would reply. He would say that the word "true" in (16) is interpreted most naturally in the "ditto truth" sense, since it appears in a response to a moral sentence. But if "true" in (16) expresses "ditto truth," then (16) really means the same as:

(16″) I, Jones, feel the same way about idleness, Nevertheless, I Jones, do not disapprove of idleness.

It is obvious that, given what Smith has said, (16″) verges on inconsistency. So, Stevenson can account for the apparent inconsistency of (16). All he must say is that it is correct to paraphrase (16) as (16″). His theory about "ditto truth" allows him to do so.

The most striking question to be raised about this reply is this: Is there really any such thing as the "ditto truth" sense of "true"?

Stevenson's Second Pattern of Analysis

Let us now turn briefly to Stevenson's second pattern of analysis. Perhaps the best way to begin is by reflecting on Stevenson's important insight about *persuasive definition*.

Many terms may be said to have fairly constant, and fairly strong, emotive meaning. That is, these terms may be relied upon to evoke a certain sort of emotional response in the hearer. Examples of such terms might be "democracy," "freedom," "happiness," "squalor," "bigot," and "unnatural." In some cases, the descriptive meaning is less firmly fixed than the emotive meaning. Thus, although we're all quite certain that democracy is a good thing, there is very little agreement about precisely what democracy *is*. Words that have fixed and strong emotive meaning but vague and variable descriptive meaning are prime targets for persuasive definition. To see what a persuasive definition is, let us consider an example. The word "free" has fairly strong and constant favorable emotive meaning. It tends to arouse a positive emotional reaction. A speaker might try to "cash in" on this emotive meaning, and at the same time specify a somewhat novel descriptive meaning for "free." In this way, the favorable attitudes might be redirected toward the object of the speaker's choice. He might say:

(18) A person is truly free only when he has no desires at all.

The point behind uttering (18) might be to attempt to persuade others to feel more favorable toward the state of desirelessness. Persuasive definitions of this sort are common rhetorical devices in advertising, politics, and religion.

In the case of "good," we have a rather strange and extreme situation. "Good" obviously has strong, constant, and favorable emotive meaning. It just about always tends to evoke a favorable response on the part of the hearer. Stevenson suggests that there are very many possible descriptive meanings for "good." A speaker may use this word to draw favorable attention to just about anything, within very wide boundaries.

If I like pleasure, I may use the word "good" in such a way that it has the same descriptive meaning as "pleasant." Thus, when I say "that was a good show," the descriptive meaning of my sentence is the same as the

descriptive meaning of the sentence "That was a pleasant show."
Equally, if you like virtue, you may use the word "good" in such a way
that it has the same descriptive meaning as the word "virtuous." In this
case, when you say "He is a good person," what you mean, descriptively,
is that he is a virtuous person. In any case in which it is used, however,
the word "good" has the same emotive meaning. It expresses and evokes
approval.

In general, we may say that "good" cannot be defined, since, according to the second pattern of analysis, it may be used to mean so many
different things. But we can give an account of its meaning, in fairly
abstract terms:

> SPA: "This is good" has the meaning of "This has qualities or
> relations $x, y, z, . . .$" except that "good" has as well a lauda-
> tory emotive meaning that permits it to express the speaker's
> approval, and tends to evoke the approval of the hearer.

This is Stevenson's second pattern of analysis.[13]

The second pattern of analysis differs from the first pattern in a few
respects. For one, the second pattern allows that the descriptive meaning
of "good" may vary rather widely. In the first pattern, the descriptive
meaning was restricted to an assertion of the presence of approval in the
speaker. Another respect in which the two patterns differ is this: In the
first pattern, it is not claimed, in regard to the emotive component of
"good," that "good" is used to express approval; "good" only evokes
approval in the hearer. But in the second pattern, "good" is alleged to do
two main emotive jobs; it both expresses and evokes approval.

As a whole, Stevenson's view seems to be that "good" is used in
accordance both with the first pattern of analysis and with the second.
On some occasions one will be more appropriate, and on others the
other will be more appropriate. So, the word "good" turns out to have a
very wide variety of possible meanings. Descriptively, it may mean the
same as any of these: "pleasant," "virtuous," "approved by me," "productive of social harmony," and "industrious." Stevenson does not try to
draw any boundaries. "Good" may be used with any of a very great many
different descriptive meanings. Emotively "good" may be used either
simply to evoke approval, or both to express and to evoke approval. The
amount and kind of approval involved may vary widely.

We can now see the main problem with Stevenson's theory. It is
difficult to see how Stevenson could explain the simple fact that we often
seem to understand each other when we use the word "good." If you tell
me that your neighbor is a good person, I seem to understand what you
mean—although I might not yet know your reason for believing this of
him. Yet if Stevenson's theory were correct, it would be hard for me to

tell what you mean. For in his view, you might mean that your neighbor is pleasant, or that he is virtuous, or that he is someone you approve of, or just about anything else.

So it appears that Stevenson has been overgenerous. He has allowed the word "good" to have far too many meanings. If it had all these meanings, it would be a word of such monumental ambiguity as to be utterly useless. We would rarely be able to figure out what another person has in mind when he says that something is good. Perhaps Stevenson adopted this view as a result of confusing the reason for which something is said to be good, on the one hand, with the meaning of the word "good," on the other.

Be this as it may, we must conclude that Stevenson's view, as a whole, seems to be open to serious question. He is surely right to emphasize the enormous range of emotions that may be associated with utterances of the word "good." And he is also surely right to insist that different individuals have widely different reasons for saying that things are good. But it is doubtful that all of these combinations of possible emotions and reasons constitute different senses of the word "good." Thus, we still don't know precisely what this word means.

NOTES

1. See Ayer's *Language, Truth and Logic* (London: Gollancz, 1936)

2. *Ibid.,* p. 110.

3. Paul Taylor, ed., *The Moral Judgment* (Englewood Cliffs, N.J.: Prentice-Hall, 1963), pp. 143–152.

4. Charles L. Stevenson, *Ethics and Language* (New Haven: Yale University Press, 1972). First published in 1944.

5. *Ibid.,* p. 24.

6. *Ibid.,* p. 25.

7. *Ibid.,* p. 21.

8. *Ibid.,* p. 32.

9. *Ibid.,* p. 90.

10. *Ibid.*

11. *Ibid.*

12. *Ibid.,* pp. 169-173.

13. *Ibid.,* pp. 206–26.

15

Prescriptivism

In recent years, moral philosophers have tended to concentrate their attention in one or the other of two main areas of research. Some have attempted to develop formal systems that display the logical features of such concepts as preferability, obligation, permission, and forbiddenness. Recent developments in deontic logic illustrate the results of this approach. Others have attempted to deal more directly with concrete moral problems. Studies on abortion, suicide, civil rights, and sexual morality illustrate this approach. Thus, modern moral philosophy may be said to be split into two camps—those pursuing rather abstract logical enquiries into the moral concepts, and those pursuing rather concrete normative enquiries into specific moral problems. Of course, many philosophers have attempted to work in both fields.

Thus, it sometimes seems that the last few years have not seen any major new metaethical theories that would constitute alternatives to the classic doctrines of naturalism, nonnaturalism, and emotivism. Some might even say that there simply are not any such alternatives, and so it is no wonder that none have been produced!

However, one fairly important metaethical view has emerged, and has been the subject of considerable debate. This view has come to be known as *prescriptivism*, and its main proponent is R. M. Hare. Hare developed and defended his view in two important books (*The Language of Morals* and *Freedom and Reason*)[1] and a variety of journal articles, some of which have been collected in Hare's *Essays on the Moral Concepts*.[2] Hare's views have changed and grown over the years, and so it would be difficult to formulate any single adequate account of his overall prescriptivist position. So in this chapter, I will attempt to formulate a relatively simple, coherent form of prescriptivism, one based largely on the view Hare presented in his earlier book, *The Language of Morals*. It should be understood, however, that the position presented in this chapter is not intended to be identical at all points either with Hare's position in *The Language of Morals* or to his present position.

Prescriptivism in General

The most fundamental thesis of prescriptivism is the thesis that evaluative language is used "to guide choices." Roughly speaking, when we use language in such a way as to guide someone's choices, we use it in such a way as to tell him how to choose. Hare argues for this point in a number of places. In one interesting passage, he discusses some typical uses of the evaluative word "good," and tries to show how this word is used prescriptively, to guide choices:

> We should not speak of good sunsets, unless sometimes the decision had to be made, whether to go to the window to look at the sunset; we should not speak of good billiard-cues, unless sometimes we had to choose one billard-cue in preference to another; we should not speak of good men unless we had the choice, what sort of men to try to become. Leibniz, when he spoke of "the best of all possible worlds," had in mind a creator choosing between the possibilities. The choice that is envisaged need not ever occur, nor even be expected to occur; it is enough for it to be envisaged as occurring, in order that we should be able to make a value-judgment with reference to it.[3]

Associated with this doctrine is the view that the most natural and appropriate way to guide choices is by the use of imperatives, either explicit or merely implied. Thus, if I want to guide you to choose to tell the truth, I may do this quite naturally by using the imperative, or command, "Tell the truth!" In this case, I have used a sentence in the imperative mood to prescribe a course of action, or to guide you to choose that course of action. According to Hare, "the language of morals is one sort of prescriptive language."[4] Prescriptivists hold that when we say that something is right, or that something ought to be the case, or that something is good, our statement either is a sort of imperative, or entails an imperative (or at least entails that there is a suitably related imperative). This imperatival element insures that such evaluative language is genuinely prescriptive. Such language can be used to guide choices because it involves an imperative. An imperative can be used to tell someone how to choose.

A second main tenet of prescriptivism is that moral language is *reasonable*. When we say that something is good, for example, we must have in mind some feature of that thing in virtue of which we hold it to be good. Furthermore, our judgment must be universalizable. That is, whatever our reason may be for holding that x is good, it must be such that we would agree that anything else like x with respect to that reason would also be good. So if I say that my new chair is a good one, I must have a reason for saying this. Perhaps I hold it to be a good chair because it is a pristine example of eighteenth-century Connecticut Valley Chippendale. If this is my reason for holding that chair is a good one, then according to Hare and the prescriptivists, I am committed to the view that *any* chair that is a pristine example of eighteenth-century Connecticut Valley Chippendale would also be a good chair.

This gives rise to some important terminological points. First, when someone says that something is good, he must have in mind some *class of comparison*. This is a general category of things such that a thing is judged to be good within that category. In the example above, the class of comparison was the class of chairs.

A good way to apply this point is as follows: If a person says, "That's a good one," it always makes sense to ask, "Good what?" If you point to an automobile and say, "That's a good one," it makes sense for us to ask, "Good what?" For you might mean to say that it is a good family car, or you might mean that it is a good sports car, or you might mean that it is a good economy car. You might even mean that it is a good example of Detroit styling. When you answer this question, you have specified the class of comparison. Clearly, something might be good relative to one class of comparison (for example, economy cars) but not very good relative to another class of comparison (for example, cars to be used for towing large trailers).

A second terminological point has to do with *good-making characteristics*, or *virtues*. When you say that something is good relative to some class of comparison, you must have in mind some feature of that thing in virtue of which you hold it to be good. This feature is its virtue, or good-making characteristic, relative to that class of comparison. So if you say that your car is good relative to the class of family cars, then you must have in mind some feature of it in virtue of which you hold it to be a good one. Let us suppose that the feature in question is this complex feature—being comfortable, reliable, economical, and safe. If so, you hold that this feature—being comfortable, reliable, economical, and safe—is a good-making characteristic, or virtue, of family cars. In this case, you are committed to the view that any family car that has this complex feature would also be a good family car.

This leads to a third terminological point. As we have seen, if you say that some car, c, is a good family car, then you are committed to the view that there are some virtues, V, of c that make c be a good family car.

You are also committed to the view that any other family car having these virtues, V, would also be a good one. This fact about evaluative judgments is called *universalizability*. In general, we can say that a judgment, "*x* is a good A," is universalizable because the person who makes that judgment must have in mind some virtues, V, such that he holds that any A that has V would also be a good A. Another way to put this is as follows: When you say that something is good of its kind, then you are committed to the view that anything else of that kind that is like it in the relevant respects would also be good relative to that kind.

Hare held that although both kinds are universalizable, there is a subtle but important difference between purely factual judgments and evaluative ones. A factual judgment such as

(1) My car is red.

is universalizable in virtue of a *meaning rule*. If I say (1), I am committed to holding that there is some feature of my car such that any car having it would also be red. Obviously, the feature in question is redness itself. On the other hand, if I say

(2) My car is good.

then I am committed to a substantive evaluative principle, such as the principle that all comfortable, reliable, economical, and safe cars are good. This is not a meaning rule. Its truth, if it is true, does not depend upon any alleged synonymy between "comfortable, reliable, economical, and safe car" and "good car." Perhaps some naturalist or *descriptivist* would say that these terms are equivalent in meaning. Hare, on the other hand, denies this. He says that the evaluative principle behind a judgment such as (2) must be *synthetic*. That is, it is a substantive evaluative principle giving an alleged criterion of goodness for cars.

Thus we have a brief summary of some of the main doctrines of prescriptivism. Perhaps the general outlines of this view will be clearer if we consider how it differs from some views we have already discussed. So let us turn to the question of how prescriptivism compares with naturalism, nonnaturalism, and emotivism.

In the first place, the prescriptivist would want to reject any form of naturalism. According to the prescriptivist, moral language is used to commend things, and to guide people's choices. According to prescriptivism, when we tell someone that something is good, we are commending that thing. Roughly, we are telling that person that given the opportunity, he should choose that thing over any worse alternative. Naturalism, however, seems to be unable to account for this feature of moral language. For if an evaluative judgment is just a disguised factual one, then when we tell someone that something is good, we are merely describing that thing, and not telling that person how to behave with respect to it. We are not guiding his choices, or prescribing any sort of choice. Hence, prescriptivists reject naturalism on the grounds that it fails to account for the commendatory, or prescriptive, aspect of evaluative language.

To see how this objection to naturalism might proceed, let us consider a possible naturalistic theory that Hare would want to reject. Suppose, for example, that some naturalist holds that "good" means the same as "approved by the leaders of my culture circle." Let us call this doctrine "C." Next, suppose that someone wants to commend the taste of the leaders of his culture circle. That is, he wants to say that they approve of the right things. He might say:

(3) Whatever is approved by the leaders of my culture circle is in fact good.

It is pretty clear that (3) can be used to commend the taste of the leaders of the culture circle. It might be said that (3) guides people to choose as the leaders of the culture circle choose. However, if the naturalistic doctrine, C, were true, then (3) would mean the same as:

(4) Whatever is approved by the leaders of my culture circle is in fact approved by the leaders of my culture circle.

Clearly, however, (4) cannot be used to commend the taste of the leaders of the culture circle, since (4) is a trivial tautology. Statement (4) does not guide anyone to choose anything at all! Hence, the naturalistic doctrine, C, must be false. It fails to account for one of the most important features of evaluative language. Evaluative language, unlike purely descriptive language, can be used to commend, to prescribe, or to guide choices.[5]

It is clear that this line of argument against naturalism is a refined version of Moore's open-question argument. Its strengths and weaknesses, presumably, are similar to those of its predecessor.[6]

Prescriptivists object to nonnaturalism too. And their objections here are similar to their objections to naturalism. According to nonnaturalists, such as Moore, goodness is a nonempirical property. When we say that something is good, we are saying merely that it has this rather unusual property. The prescriptivist rejects this account partly because it fails to make any sense of the commendatory function of evaluative language, and partly because it makes moral "facts" rather mysterious. What sort of property is this alleged goodness supposed to be? How do we get to know that something has it? The prescriptivist feels that nonnaturalism gives rise to such questions as these but cannot provide satisfactory answers to them.

Superficially, it may appear that prescriptivism is quite similar to emotivism. Indeed, many commentators would classify prescriptivism as a refined version of the emotivist doctrine. However, Hare would surely want to stress the important differences between his own view and that of the classic emotivists, such as Ayer and Stevenson. There are several respects in which emotivism and prescriptivism differ. For one, Hare would insist that "emotivity" is a very common characteristic of language, one that is not restricted to evaluative judgments. Second, he would insist that the imperatival element in evaluative judgments is not adequately explained by the emotivists. The imperative in an evaluative judgment must be universalizable, according to Hare. The emotivists have never specified any such requirement. Finally, Hare would claim that the emotivists fail to give an adequate account of the logic of imperatives. Imperatives do not serve merely to *cause* people to act in certain ways, as Stevenson seems to suggest. Rather, they are used *to tell people* to act in those ways. Furthermore, there are relations of entailment among imperatives that the emotivists have never adequately recognized.

So much, then, for the rough outlines of prescriptivism. Let us turn now to a more detailed account of some prescriptivist analyses of some important evaluative concepts.

Prescriptivist Analyses of Evaluative Concepts

Prescriptivism is based on the idea that evaluative judgments involve imperatives.[7] However, the imperatives involved are somewhat unlike ordinary ones. So, before we can discuss the proposed analyses, we must consider how an "enriched imperative mood" might be developed.

An imperative, or command, such as:

(5) Shut the door!

obviously has much in common with an ordinary indicative, or factual, judgment, such as:

(6) You are going to shut the door.

In a rough-and-ready sense, we may say that (5) and (6) have the same *propositional content*. That is, they both involve the same possible state of affairs—your shutting of the door in the immediate future. Hare calls this propositional content the *phrastic*. He would say that (5) and (6) have the same phrastic.

Equally obviously, there is a difference between (5) and (6). Statement (5) is used to command, whereas (6) is used to state. Statement (5) is neither true nor false, but (6) must be either true or false, depending upon whether you are going to shut the door or not. This difference in linguistic role may be illuminated by rewriting (5) and (6) as:

(5′) Your shutting of the door in the immediate future, please.
(6′) Your shutting of the door in the immediate future, yes.

The "please" in (5′) indicates that (5′) is a command, or imperative. The "yes" in (6′) indicates that it is an assertion, or judgment of fact. These elements express what Hare calls the *neustics* of the two sentences. Hence, we may say that (5′) and (6′) have the same phrastic but different neustics.

This way of looking at imperatives may be useful, for it allows us to distinguish the essentially imperatival element, the neustic, from the propositional element, the phrastic. Thus, we can consider what is special about imperatives while keeping our eye on the respects in which imperatives are like ordinary assertive judgments.

Typical ordinary-language imperatives are usually directed toward specific individuals. For example, (5) is directed toward some anonymous "you." Also, they are usually directed toward the future, as (5) seems to be. But once we have separated the imperative neustic from the sort of phrastic to which it is typically connected, we can see that it can, in principle, be connected to any sort of phrastic. So, if we like, we can add the imperative neustic "please" to any phrastic we like. The resulting imperatives will in some cases be rather odd, and may not have any ordinary language equivalent. Nevertheless, they apparently can be understood.

Let us consider phrastics with three main features. First, they all are *fully general*. That is, they are of the form "all As being Bs," and they are assumed to refer to all times, past, present, and future. Second, they are *logically contingent*, that is, they are neither necessarily true nor necessarily false. Third, they contain no reference to specific individuals. Thus, no proper names occur in them.[8] Some phrastics of this sort might be:

(7) All promises being kept.
(8) All applicants being given equal treatment.
(9) All thieves being electrocuted.

In principle, there is no reason why we should not attach the imperative neustic "please" to each of these. The results, of course, would be:

(7′) All promises being kept, please.
(8′) All applicants being given equal treatment, please.
(9′) All thieves being electrocuted, please.

Imperatives of this odd form play a major role in Hare's metaethical theory. But before we turn to that theory, it may be worthwhile to point out a crucial feature of such imperatival sentences. This feature is that these sentences have logical implications. This may seem odd, since they also seem to be lacking in truth value. After all, no clear sense can be attached to the claim that a command, such as "Shut the door!" is true. Nevertheless, this "inference" seems valid:

(7′) All promises being kept, please.
(10) This is a promise.
(11) This being kept, please.

In ordinary language, this inference might be expressed as follows: "Let it be the case that all promises are kept. But this is a promise. So let it be the case that this promise is kept." The idea that imperatives have these entailments is rather novel, and, as we will see shortly, is fairly important to Hare's position.

It is also important to see that two imperatives may be *logically inconsistent*. For example:

(7′) All promises being kept, please.
(12) All promises being broken, please.

To issue both of these commands would be as inconsistent as to issue the command, "Stop where you are, but keep moving!"

With all this as background, we are finally in a position to consider the first example of a prescriptivist analysis of an evaluative concept, the concept of "*ought*." Hare does not claim that this is an analysis of the concept of "ought" in ordinary use, but he does suggest that he intends it to be an analysis of a concept that closely approximates our familiar "ought." He emphasizes the difference by italicizing the term for his new concept. His claim, roughly, is that the concept expressed by "*ought*" does many of the most characteristic evaluative jobs done by our old concept, expressed by "ought." Here, at last, is the analysis of the concept of "*ought*" with respect to universal statements:

P_1: All As *ought* to be Bs =df. all As being Bs, please.

So, according to prescriptivism, the statement "All promises ought to be kept" means pretty much the same as "All promises *ought* to be kept," and this in turn is defined by P_1 as meaning the same as "All promises being kept, please." Thus, universal ought statements turn out to be little more than suitably enriched imperatives, or commands. A rough-and-ready prescriptivist might hold, then, that when we say that all promises ought to be kept, what we mean is just what we would mean if we were to say, "Let it be the case that all promises are kept!"

There is much to be said in favor of this analysis. A fully general, unrestricted imperative such as:

(7′) All promises being kept, please.

is addressed to no one in particular. It serves merely to express the speaker's view that it would somehow be to his liking for all promises to be kept. Couldn't he express this same view just as well by saying "All promises ought to be kept"? If not, what's the difference?

Emotivists, of course, had claimed that there is an imperatival element in some evaluative language. But the emotivists never went so far as to introduce enriched imperatives, nor did they bring out the logical aspects of such talk. Hence, P₁ goes pretty far beyond anything to be found in Ayer or Stevenson. Nevertheless, P₁ is hardly all of prescriptivism. It is just the basis.

In *The Language of Morals*, Hare attempts to define a sense of *"ought"* suitable for particular *ought*-judgments, such as "You ought to shut the door." It is important to recognize that these judgments are not equivalent to simple imperatives, such as "Shut the door!" Roughly, Hare said that such particular *ought*-judgments are equivalent to judgments of the form, "If you don't shut the door, you will be violating a universal *ought*-judgment to which I hereby subscribe." A more precise version of this prescriptivist view might be:

> P₂: You *ought* to do *a* =df. there are terms, A and B, such that (i) all As *ought* to be Bs, and (ii) if you fail to do *a*, that will be a case of an A that is not a B.

This analysis is fairly complex, so let's stop for a moment to see how it is supposed to work. Suppose you are wondering whether to keep a promise you have made, and you come to me for advice. I might tell you that you ought to keep your promise. Analysis P₂ suggests that my statement might be based on my view that all promises ought to be kept, and on my view that your failure to keep your promise would be a case of a promise not being kept.

In general, then, to say that someone *ought* to do an action, *a*, is to imply that you subscribe to a general *ought*-principle, of the form "all As *ought* to be Bs," and that if the person fails to do *a*, he will be violating your principle. Once again, this view has some plausibility. For if you tell someone that he ought to do something, you undoubtedly have some general principle in mind that would explain why, in your view, he ought to do it. For example, if you tell me that I ought to respect my parents, and I ask why, you may say, "Because all children ought to respect their parents." If I proceed to show disrespect for my parents, I will have violated your principle.

It is essential to recognize that the *"ought"* on the right side of P₂ can be eliminated in favor of an enriched imperative. This is so because that *"ought"* appears in a general *ought*-principle (or at least in a "variable general *ought*-principle") and such *"oughts"* have been defined for us by P₁. Analysis P₂ can be rewritten so as to reveal this, as follows:

> P₂′: You *ought* to do *a* =df. there are terms, A and B, such that (i) all As being Bs, please, and (ii) if you fail to do *a*, that will be a case of an A that is not a B.

Thus, particular *"ought"*-judgments can be seen to involve enriched imperatives too. Hence, they are prescriptive, and can be used to guide choices. The manner in which they do so, however, is slightly different from the manner in which the general *ought*-judgments guide choices.

One of the most interesting aspects of Hare's moral view emerges at this point. It is a consequence of what has come before, but it is in some ways rather striking, and is even reminiscent of some ideas we encountered in our consideration of Kant's first categorical imperative.[9]

Notice, first, that if Smith says that someone *ought* to do something, then P₂ implies that Smith has implicitly appealed to some general *ought*-principle. So, for example, if Smith says:

(13) You *ought* to keep your promise.

then Smith must have made a covert appeal to some general principle. Perhaps the general principle is:

(14)   All promises *ought* to be kept.

In accordance with P₁, (14) may be rewritten as:

(14′) All promises being kept, please.

As we have seen earlier, Hare thinks that imperatives such as (14′) have logical consequences, and can enter into logical arguments. Suppose Smith has made a promise himself and knows that he has done so. Then, to be logically consistent, he must admit that he should keep that promise, for he accepts both premises of this logically valid argument:

(14′) All promises being kept, please.

(15) My promise is a promise.

(16) Therefore, my promise being kept, please.

In effect, then, Smith has to issue a command to himself to keep his own promise.

Thus, if Smith is to be consistent, he has to admit that the moral principles he adopts for others are also applicable to himself. He cannot require others to abide by some principle while he excuses himself from its requirements. Thus, in Hare's view the logic of the moral concepts yields something like the golden rule. The relevant principle for Hare might be:

(H) If a person requires that others abide by a certain moral principle, then, to be logically consistent, he must abide by that principle too.

Hare emphasizes his conviction that this principle reflects merely a "logical" or conceptual truth, and is not a substantive moral doctrine.

Let us turn to the next stage in the prescriptivist analysis of the evaluative concepts. It should be clear that once we have a suitable concept of "*ought*," it won't be too hard to define a concept of "*right*." This can be done as follows:[10]

P_3: It is *right* for you to do a =df. it is not the case that you *ought* to refrain from doing a.

We may also introduce a concept of "*wrong*":

P_4: It is wrong for you to do a =df. you *ought* to refrain from doing a.

These terms, obviously, are designed to do much the same work as our ordinary terms, "right" and "wrong," in corresponding applications.

The most exciting prospect for prescriptivism, however, is the prospect of offering an analysis of the meaning of "good," or at least of some artificial concept, "*good*," that would do the same work. It is here that we face the most interesting, as well as the most difficult, challenge. We must approach this concept via the concept of *betterness*. That is, following Hare, we must first consider what it means to say that x is a *better* A than y. Then, making use of this concept of *betterness*, we will attempt to deal with the main target, the concept of *goodness*.

Prescriptivism, as we have seen, is based on the idea that evaluative language is used to guide choices. This emerges most clearly in the prescriptivist analysis of *betterness*. For, according to this view, to say that something, x, is a *better* A than y, is to say, roughly, that if you have to choose an A, and you must choose between x and y, then you ought to choose x. Hence, to say that x is a *better* A than y is to guide your hearer to a choice of x over y, if he should be forced to choose an A. So, for example, if I tell you that Introduction to Ethics is a *better* course than Introduction to Astrology, my statement may be taken to mean, roughly, that if you have to choose a course, and you have to choose between the ethics course and the astrology course, then you *ought* to choose the ethics. This last phrase, again, is to be analyzed according to P_1 and P_2, and so it all comes down to an enriched imperative in the end. Our prescriptivist analysis of "*better*" is as follows:[11]

P_5: x is a *better* A than y =df. if one is choosing an A, and one must choose either x or y, then one *ought* to choose x.

We should notice that we have not given an analysis of "x is *better* than y" Rather, we have analyzed "x is a *better* A than y." This reflects the view that whenever we make a comparative evaluation, we have some class of comparison in mind. So if someone says, in some context, that something is better than something else, he must have some class of comparison in mind. Otherwise, his statement is not fully intelligible. So we might say, following Hare, that sentences of the form "x is better than y" are always short for sentences of the form "x is a better A than y," where "A" represents the relevant class of comparison.

We should also notice that this concept of *betterness* is not supposed to be equivalent to our traditional concept of betterness, but is only supposed to be a model for it. It is supposed to display the essential prescriptivist elements in a rather simplified form.

Now let us turn to "*good*." Hare says, "We define a *good* man as follows: he is a man who is better than men usually are."[12] Although Hare never gives a general definition of "*good*," this remark surely suggests the following:

P_6: x is a *good* A =df. x is a *better* A than most As are.

Once again, three points need to be made. First, this is a prescriptivist analysis of *goodness*, since "*good*" has been defined by reference to "*better*," and "*better*" has been defined by reference to "*ought*," and "*ought*" has been defined by reference to enriched imperatives. Second, we have here a definition of "*good* A" rather than simply of "*good*." This reflects the need for a class of comparison. Third, we have defined an artificial concept, *goodness*, rather than our old familiar concept of goodness. This is so because Hare would hold that the meanings of such terms of ordinary language as "good" are too complex to be captured in so simple a formula as P_6. In one interesting passage, Hare says; "It would be absurd, however, to claim that any artificial word could ever do exactly all the jobs, and no others, that are done by a natural word; our ordinary language is much too subtle, flexible, and complicated to be imitated in this offhand way."[13]

Let us reflect, for a moment, on this analysis of *goodness*. According to prescriptivism, when I say that, for example, my new chair is a *good* example of eighteenth-century Connecticut Valley Chippendale, my statement implies that my chair is a *better* than average example of eighteenth-century Connecticut Valley Chippendale. This, in turn, implies that most such chairs are such that if you have to choose between my chair and one of them, then you *ought* to choose mine. And to say this, finally, is to acknowledge that I subscribe to some sort of general principle about chair choices. Perhaps it is this: "All choices of eighteenth-century Connecticut Valley Chippendale chairs being choices of chairs that have excellent design, finish, and craftsmanship, please." Thus, to say that my chair is a good one, in the long run, implies that I accept some universal imperative. It implies that I accept some prescription about how chairs should be chosen. Hence, it serves, in an indirect way to guide choices.

Evaluation of Prescriptivism

Many aspects of the prescriptivist doctrine presented here may be challenged. One that seems pretty clearly wrong is an aspect of P₆. Analysis P₆ implies that a *good* A is an A that is *better* than most As. This seems wrong. Some people would surely hold that when the general quality of a given class of comparison is sufficiently low, then even the best members of that class are not good ones. For example, it might be said that although some ways of being tortured are much better than most, no way of being tortured is a good way of being tortured. This would cast some doubt on the suitability of P₆, since P₆ implies that any way of being tortured that is *better* than most, is a *good* way of being tortured. This criticism, even if it holds, is obviously not terribly important.

The example about the chair may be used to illustrate what appears to be a much more serious difficulty with the prescriptivist approach. Let us suppose I am at an antiques auction and I see a particularly beautiful eighteenth-century Connecticut Valley Chippendale chair. Let's call this chair "*c*." Suppose I say to myself:

(17) *c* is a good chair.

Suppose I hope to be able to buy this chair and keep it for myself. According to P₆, my statement (17) means pretty much the same as:

(18) *c* is better than most chairs.

According to P₅, (18) means pretty much the same as:

(19) Most chairs are such that if one is choosing a chair, and one must choose either one of them or *c*, then one ought to choose *c*.

In other words, to say that *c* is a good chair is to guide people to choose *c* over most other chairs. Statement (19) is supposed to imply that I subscribe to some general principle about chair choices. Suppose the principle is this: All chair choices being choices of chairs that have excellent design, finish, and craftsmanship, please.

And here the problem becomes apparent. For I most certainly do *not* subscribe to any such universal imperative. In fact, if I had the opportunity to command how others would choose with respect to chairs, I would command them to choose ugly, rickety old chairs rather than to choose beautiful ones like c. Obviously, if everyone else is motivated to choose the good chairs, then the bidding on c will be very intense, the price will be driven up, and I won't be able to buy it! Surely, I would prefer that others choose bad chairs, so as to leave the good ones for me. This attitude of mine may be selfish, but it is clearly not inconsistent. Hare's prescriptivist approach, however, seems to imply that it would be self-contradictory of me to hold that c is a good chair while not being willing to command others to choose chairs relevantly like c.

This criticism, if it can be sustained, goes to the heart of prescriptivism. For the criticism purports to show that one may recognize a certain sort of choice to be a good one, without in the least wishing to encourage others to make that sort of choice. Thus, one may see that it is good to choose beautiful chairs, but may not want to guide others to so choose. If this is correct, evaluative language apparently does not always serve to guide choices, and so is not always prescriptive.

There are a number of ways in which a prescriptivist might try to answer this objection. For one, he might claim that my statement (17) is not genuinely evaluative. That is, even though I said that c is a good chair, I was not really evaluating c. Perhaps he would insist that if I do not endorse the relevant command concerning chair choices, then when I utter (17) all I mean is:

(17′) c is the sort of chair most people would call "good."

Clearly, if (17) means the same as (17′), then (17) is not genuinely evaluative. And if (17) is not genuinely evaluative, then there is no problem about the fact that (17) does not entail the relevant command. Hare can simply assert that he has attempted to provide a model for full-blooded evaluative uses of "good," and not for degenerate ones such as the one in (17).

This response is weak. For it certainly does seem that I can make a full-blooded evaluation of a chair, express it by means of (17), and yet not wish to encourage others to choose chairs of that sort. I, for one, would be inclined to say that there is a big difference between evaluating something and telling others how to behave with respect to it. So I don't see any inconsistency in saying, for example, "This is a good one, but I don't care whether you choose it or not." Our prescriptivist theory would apparently find this statement to be practically self-contradictory. In any case, we seem to have here the makings of a serious objection to prescriptivism, in the form in which we have presented it.

Some commentators seem to feel that prescriptivism also has to face up to what may be called "the problem of the fanatic." This objection may be formulated as follows: Suppose that someone, Smith, is a racist, and is willing to assert:

(20) All minority-group members ought to be deported.

If prescriptivism is true, Smith's statement is an enriched imperative. It is not a statement of fact—not even of "moral fact." It means the same as:

(21) All minority-group members being deported, please.

If we don't like Smith's racist attitude, we may point out to him that in saying what he has said, he implies that if he were a member of a minority group then he should be deported too. More precisely, (21) allegedly implies:

(22) If Smith is a minority-group member, then Smith's being deported, please.

So we can say to Smith, "How would you like it if your principle were used against you?" Some racists might be moved to reflect on their racist views in this way and some might realize that they cannot accept the implication of what they have said. Thus, they might realize that they formerly held inconsistent views. For it is inconsistent to accept a general principle but reject one of its implications.

However, if Smith's racism runs deep, he may be willing to accept (22). He may be willing to agree that if he had been a minority-group member, then he should have been deported too. Thus, Smith reveals himself to be a consistent racist.

Some critics see in this a major defect of prescriptivism. The problem is that if Smith is willing to accept (22), and so shows himself to be logically consistent, there seems to be *nothing* wrong with his statement (20). Nonracists may say that they would never assert (20). They may shout at Smith, or try to make him feel bad. But, if prescriptivism is true, they cannot reasonably claim that Smith's view is *false*. For, if prescriptivism is true, Smith's "view" is not a belief at all. When he utters (20), he is merely issuing an enriched imperative. Imperatives are neither true nor false. When I say "Shut the door!" I use language in a non-statement-making way. I issue a command that is not subject to evaluation from the point of view of truth and falsity. The same holds for the richer imperative in (20), as is revealed by the fact that according to prescriptivism, (20) means the same as (21).

So if Smith's remark cannot be faulted on grounds of inconsistency, and cannot be faulted on grounds of falsehood, how can it be faulted? It seems that it cannot be faulted at all. If Hare's view has this consequence, then it surely seems to make evaluative language significantly poorer in one important respect. I, for one, want to say that there is something seriously wrong with the racist's statement. The problem as I see it is that what he has said is false.

So it turns out that prescriptivism, like the theories it is supposed to supplant, is not entirely satisfactory either. The main problem seems to be that prescriptivism is too one-sided. Moral language can surely be used to guide choices, as Hare has emphasized. However, it is implausible to maintain that the whole meaning of moral language is tied up with choice guidance. Perhaps we should say that choice guidance is an important part of the *pragmatics* of evaluative language. That is, it is an important function that such language can be used to serve. However, it is not strictly a part of the meaning, or *semantics*, of such language.

Some may feel that it would be worthwhile, at this point, to reconsider the views of Moore, Ayer, and perhaps even some of the naturalists. It may turn out that Hare's insights into the commendatory function of evaluative language can be combined in some way with the more strictly semantic views of these other philosophers. In any case, the consideration of such views will not be undertaken here. It will have to wait for another time.

NOTES

1. R. M. Hare, *The Language of Morals* (New York: Oxford University Press, 1964), and *Freedom and Reason* (New York: Oxford University Press, 1965).

2. R. M. Hare, *Essays on the Moral Concepts* (Berkeley and Los Angeles: University of California Press, 1972).

3. Hare, *The Language of Morals*, p. 128.

4. *Ibid.*, p. 1.

5. *Ibid.*, see Chapter 5 for an elaboration of this discussion.

6. For a discussion of Moore's open-question argument, see pp. 199–203.

7. The remainder of this chapter is based largely upon material in Chapter 12 of *The Language of Morals*, but is not supposed to be identical at all points with the views expressed there. I have made alterations in an attempt to achieve greater simplicity and intuitiveness.

8. Hare's views on this point seem to have changed over the years. Nothing I say in criticism will turn on it.

9. For a discussion of Kant's first categorical imperative, see pp. 103–106.

10. This definition of "*right*" is substantially different from Hare's.

11. This definition of "*better*" is slightly different from Hare's.

12. Hare, *The Language of Morals*, p. 186.

13. *Ibid.*, p. 183.

16

Conclusions

Now that we have concluded our consideration of some of the main views in moral philosophy, perhaps the time has come for us to attempt to deal with some possible complaints.

One complaint that may arise is that we have failed to discover the truth about any of the main issues we have discussed. In normative ethics, we have found serious difficulties with act utilitarianism, several forms of rule utilitarianism, Kantianism, Ross's theory, and egoism. Thus, we have not found the answer to the question "What makes right acts right?" In metaethics, we have found reasons to reject several varieties of naturalism, nonnaturalism, and emotivism. Thus, we haven't answered the question about the meaning of "good." In light of these rather large-scale failures, doesn't it seem that the whole project has been a waste of time?

There are a number of comments that can be made in response to this sort of complaint. In the first place, some might say that it is a good thing that these questions have not yet been answered satisfactorily. For as things now stand, each of us still has the chance to make a major contribution to philosophy. Each of us, that is, has the chance to discover the truth about what makes right acts right, and about what "good" means. The value of our study of these defective theories, it might be said, is that it shows us some views that won't work, and thus helps us in our attempt to discover one that will.

From a somewhat less romantic point of view, it is also important to recognize that even these failures may be quite instructive. The failure of act utilitarianism, for example, teaches us a lot about the moral value of justice and the importance of promises. The failure of egoism may show us something interesting about moral motivation. The weaknesses of Kantianism may reveal some truths about the golden rule, and about what's involved in the notion that it's never right to act in a way in which you would not want others to act. The apparent failures of naturalism and emotivism seem to show that there really is such a thing as goodness, however difficult it may be to say just what it is.

In general, therefore, we can say that we have found a lot of truths about normative ethics and metaethics, even though we have not found the answers to our main questions in these fields. Admittedly, many of the truths we have found are truths to the effect that something or other is false. But, in matters as complex and important as these, perhaps we should be grateful for small successes.

Finally, it might be maintained that we *have* discovered the correct answers to our main questions—but we didn't recognize them when we found them. Surely, Mill would insist that we found the truth in normative ethics, and Moore would say the same about metaethics. Of course, many other philosophers would claim that although we did find the truth, it is not where Mill and Moore think it to be. They would disagree about precisely which of the theories we have seen is the true one.

Another complaint that might be raised is that we have failed to come to grips with any of the serious problems of morals. We have spent a lot of time thinking about dozens of rather arid moral theories, it might be argued, but we have not yet even considered the more pressing moral problems of racism, sexism, abortion, sexual morality, and poverty. Many would say that this shows a sort of perversion of priorities. Shouldn't we direct our attention at first to the more pressing problems, and then, when these are solved, turn to the rather abstract issues of moral philosophy?

This sort of complaint deserves serious consideration. Two main points seem to be in order. In the first place, the complaint seems to be based on the idea that there is some sort of conflict between the study of ethical theory, on the one hand, and the study of moral problems, on the other. But this is surely false. We can engage in both of these enquiries. There is no conflict between them. It simply is not a matter of "either/or."

Second, we should reflect on the question of priorities. Is it really the case that we should work on the pressing practical problems first, before we attempt to formulate a general moral principle? It could be argued that it is impossible to come to a rational, considered decision on a practical moral problem unless we have accepted, at least implicitly, some general criterion of right action. Let us see why this may be so.

Suppose two individuals, Smith and Jones, are discussing the question of what ought to be done about seriously defective babies. Smith holds that such babies should be given the chance to live, no matter what the expense, whereas Jones feels that all such babies should be allowed to die peacefully as soon as their defects are recognized. Unless Smith and Jones are just idly expressing their irrational prejudices on this question, they must have reasons for holding the views they hold. Perhaps Smith believes that the babies should live because he believes, with Kant, that people are intrinsically good, and are never to be treated merely as means. Suppose, on the other hand, that Jones believes, with Mill, that an act is morally right only if it maximizes utility, and that the utility of letting the babies die exceeds the utility of trying to keep them alive.

Smith and Jones can proceed in a variety of ways. For one, each of them can attempt to defend his position *without* appeal to any general moral principle. For example, Smith can cite examples of defective babies who grew up to be intelligent, healthy, and worthy adults, and Jones can describe a tragic instance in which a defective baby lingered on for a long time, draining its parents emotional and financial resources.

Although such argumentation undoubtedly occurs frequently, it is not clear what it is supposed to accomplish. Smith may grant that in some cases saving the babies is a very unhappy business. Similarly, Jones may grant that in some cases the defective babies might grow up successfully. This would surely be a happy outcome. But these emotional appeals should not have any moral weight with either party. Each should grant the other's point and then demand to know its relevance. As it stands, it looks like a case of sheer rhetorical persuasion without any reason to back it up. In general, then, if we debate a moral issue but refuse to examine our general principles, we are likely to reach a stalemate. No progress will be made.

Smith and Jones can proceed in another way. Each can attempt to show that his own opinion in fact accords with his own basic moral principle. In other words, Smith can insist that killing the babies really does violate the Kantian principle about treating people as ends. Jones can pile up evidence about the pain that would be produced by letting the babies live. But what would be the point of such an exercise? Since they disagree about basic principles, nothing is to be gained by showing that their views about the babies accord with their principles.

Thus, it seems that the most reasonable way to proceed here is to move away from a consideration of the immediate moral problem and toward a consideration of the general moral principles themselves. Smith should ask Jones to state his utilitarian principle clearly and precisely. Once this is done, the principle can be evaluated on its own merits. They can attempt to determine whether it generates correct results in less difficult cases. If it proves acceptable (which is rather unlikely), Smith and Jones can then turn to a consideration of its impact on the much harder case concerning the defective babies. Similarly, Jones should ask Smith to state his Kantian principle clearly and precisely. If it proves acceptable (which is even more unlikely), they can proceed from there. If neither can formulate his principle in an acceptable way, then each must admit that his view on the morality of letting the babies die is based not on reasoned principles, but on unsupported intuition, or prejudice. Here, of course, there is little place for argument.

Thus, if someone should complain that in this book we have considered rather abstract moral theories but have not dealt with pressing moral questions, we have an answer. The answer is that if we want to investigate a serious moral issue rationally, we must first understand our general principles. Once we have reached agreement on these, we can consider their application. So we have started at the beginning. Admittedly, we have not gotten very far even in this first step. This, of course, is to be regretted. However, we do have an answer to the claim that our priorities are perverted.

A third complaint that might be raised is that even though moral philosophy is studied carefully, it does not make its students morally better persons. Two points should be made about this complaint. In the first place, some philosophers have held that this objection is based on a misunderstanding of the purpose of moral philosophy. G. E. Moore, for example, says that "the direct object of Ethics is knowledge and not practice. . . ."[1] When we engage in moral philosophy, our aim is to discover the truth about morality. If someone discovers the truth but chooses to ignore it, then so much the worse for him. He surely has a problem. But it is not a problem in moral philosophy. It is a problem in human development. It is a problem for his friends, his family, and his conscience, if he has one.

In the second place, it might be argued that the study of moral philosophy may, in an indirect way, help to make us better persons. After studying moral philosophy, we may be less inclined to accept crackpot moral theories, or to be moved by faddish moral arguments. We may be more inclined to look upon such aberrations with a skeptical eye. For after we have studied moral philosophy, we begin to sense the enormous difficulty of the subject. It becomes clear to us that even the most careful and intelligent person can easily go wrong. Thus, we may develop a more cautious, reflective attitude toward the latest popular moral slogans. We know how to test such slogans, and we are less likely to be swept up by such irrational faddism. If it is better to be thus insulated against moral extremism, then perhaps the study of moral philosophy can help in some small way to make us better persons.

NOTES

1. G. E. Moore, *Principia Ethica* (Cambridge: Cambridge University Press, 1962), p. 20.

Index

253